Crew AI in Action, 2nd Edition

A Practical Guide to Building and Managing Multi-agent AI Systems for
Advanced Automation

©

Written By

Charles Sprinter

Copyright Page

Disclaimer:
The information provided in this book is for general informational purposes only. The author and publisher make no representations or warranties with respect to the accuracy or completeness of the contents of this book and specifically disclaim any implied warranties of merchantability or fitness for a particular purpose. In no event shall the author or publisher be liable for any loss or damage, including but not limited to, special, incidental, or consequential damages, arising from the use of this book or the information contained herein.

Trademarks:

All trademarks, service marks, and other proprietary identifiers are the property of their respective owners.

Table of Content

Foreword

Welcome to the second edition of **"Crew AI in Action."** As the field of artificial intelligence (AI) evolves, so does the necessity for resources that accurately reflect the current state of technology and anticipate future developments. This book is such a resource. Aimed at professionals in the tech industry—from software developers to project managers—it provides a comprehensive overview of multi-agent AI systems, emphasizing practical application and strategic insight.

Since the publication of the first edition, we have seen significant advancements in AI technologies and methodologies. Multi-agent systems, in particular, have become increasingly crucial in complex AI solutions due to their ability to solve problems more efficiently and with greater flexibility. Recognizing these developments, the second edition of this book not only updates all previous topics but also introduces new content on emerging technologies and approaches.

This book will guide you through understanding the foundational concepts of multi-agent AI, implementing these systems in real-world scenarios, and optimizing their performance. Whether you are looking to enhance your current systems or develop new AI solutions from scratch, this guide will serve as an indispensable tool in your professional toolkit.

I commend the author for his thorough revision and for their commitment to providing a resource that is both instructive and accessible. I am confident that this second edition will empower you to take full advantage of the potential that multi-agent AI systems have to offer.

By

Dr. Kai Akira

Preface

About This Edition

This second edition of **"Crew AI in Action"** represents a significant update and expansion of the first edition, which has served as a valuable resource in the AI community. Our goal with this edition is to provide an authoritative guide to multi-agent AI systems, reflecting the latest advancements in the field and incorporating feedback from readers and industry experts.

Key Updates and Additions:

- **Technological Advances:** Introduction of new chapters on blockchain technology, quantum computing, and their applications in multi-agent systems.
- **Updated Case Studies:** Inclusion of recent case studies that highlight the practical applications of multi-agent AI across different industries such as healthcare, finance, and logistics.
- **Enhanced Practical Guides:** Detailed tutorials and step-by-step guides for designing, implementing, and managing multi-agent AI systems.
- **Expanded Content on Ethics and Governance:** A new section dedicated to the ethical implications and governance of AI, addressing the growing importance of responsible AI practices.

How to Use This Book

"Crew AI in Action, 2nd Edition" is structured to accommodate a variety of learning preferences and professional needs:

- **Sequential Study:** For readers new to multi-agent AI, we recommend progressing through the book from start to finish.
- **Focused Learning:** Experienced professionals may prefer to focus on specific chapters or sections that are most relevant to their needs.
- **Supplementary Material:** Each chapter includes tables, code snippets, and practical examples to enhance understanding and provide tools for real-world application.

Navigational Tips:

- **Tables and Code Snippets:** Detailed explanations accompany all tables and code examples to ensure clarity and utility.
- **Glossary:** A comprehensive glossary of terms is included to help readers understand technical language used throughout the book.

Acknowledgments

Producing this edition was a collaborative effort that involved numerous people whose contributions were invaluable. Special thanks to:

- **Technical Reviewers and Contributors:** Who provided critical insights and expert knowledge that greatly enhanced the quality of this book.
- **The Editorial and Production Teams:** Whose dedication and attention to detail made this publication possible.
- **Our Readers:** Whose feedback on the first edition helped shape the content and focus of this updated version.

I am are grateful for the support and commitment of everyone involved and hope this book serves as a useful and insightful resource for all readers.

Part I: Foundations of Multi-agent AI Systems

Chapter 1: Introduction to Multi-agent AI Systems

1.1 What is Multi-agent AI?

Multi-agent AI systems refer to systems where multiple intelligent agents interact with each other within an environment to achieve individual or collective goals. Each agent in the system is an autonomous entity capable of perceiving its surroundings, reasoning, making decisions, and acting upon the environment based on the information it receives. These agents communicate, coordinate, or even compete with each other to perform tasks or solve complex problems.

In simple terms, a **multi-agent system (MAS)** consists of several agents that work together (or sometimes in opposition) to perform tasks that might be too complex for a single agent to handle alone.

Key Features of Multi-agent AI:

1. **Autonomy:** Each agent operates independently without direct human control.
2. **Decentralization:** No single agent has control over the entire system; decisions are made by the agents themselves.
3. **Interaction:** Agents communicate and interact with each other to solve problems or achieve goals.
4. **Adaptability:** Agents can adapt to changing environments or tasks based on feedback from the environment or other agents.
5. **Cooperation and Coordination:** Agents may collaborate to achieve shared objectives or compete to optimize individual goals.

Example: In a multi-agent system for traffic management, each traffic light can be viewed as an independent agent. These agents can communicate with each other to optimize traffic flow at intersections, adjusting signal timings based on real-time traffic data from their environment and neighboring signals.

Real-world Example:

- **Autonomous Vehicles**: Multiple autonomous cars, acting as agents, communicate with each other to avoid collisions, optimize traffic flow, and navigate in complex environments.

1.2 Key Characteristics of Multi-agent Systems

Multi-agent systems are distinguished by several key characteristics that make them unique and effective for certain types of problems. Below are some of the most prominent features:

1.2.1 Interaction and Communication

Agents in a multi-agent system often communicate with each other to share information, coordinate tasks, or negotiate. Communication can take many forms, such as:

- **Direct Communication:** One agent sends a message directly to another agent.
- **Indirect Communication (or "stigmergy"):** Agents leave signals or markers in the environment, which other agents interpret and react to (e.g., ant colonies).

1.2.2 Autonomy

Each agent in the system has the capability to make its own decisions and execute actions based on its environment or internal logic. This autonomy is crucial in enabling the system to operate without constant human intervention.

1.2.3 Cooperation vs. Competition

Agents can cooperate with one another to achieve common goals (collaborative multi-agent systems), or they may compete to maximize individual outcomes (competitive multi-agent systems). Both types of behavior are important in different scenarios.

- **Cooperative MAS:** Agents work together to achieve a shared goal. For instance, in a supply chain, agents representing different companies might work together to optimize the delivery of products.
- **Competitive MAS:** Agents act based on their own goals, such as in economic or game-theory applications, where different agents might strive to achieve the highest benefit at the expense of others.

1.2.4 Adaptation and Learning

Agents can adapt to changes in the environment or the system itself. Learning can occur both individually (through experience) and collectively (through shared information or joint strategies). Reinforcement learning (RL) is often used in multi-agent systems, where agents learn through trial and error to improve their performance.

1.3 Real-World Applications of Multi-agent AI

Multi-agent AI systems have a wide range of applications across various domains. Below are a few examples of how multi-agent systems are being used to solve real-world problems:

1.3.1 Autonomous Vehicles

In the context of **autonomous vehicles**, each car acts as an agent that senses its surroundings, makes decisions about speed, and communicates with other cars to prevent accidents and optimize traffic flow. These agents work together to form a **cooperative multi-agent system**, ensuring safer and more efficient roadways.

1.3.2 Robotics

Multi-agent systems in robotics can coordinate the actions of multiple robots to accomplish tasks that would be difficult or impossible for a single robot. For example, **robotic swarm systems** are used in agriculture to monitor crops, clean solar panels, or assist in large-scale construction projects. In these systems, robots cooperate by sharing tasks and information in real-time.

1.3.3 Supply Chain Management

In **supply chain management**, multi-agent systems can simulate and optimize the movement of goods, track inventory, and manage the delivery process. Each agent could represent a different component of the supply chain, such as a warehouse, shipping company, or distributor. These agents work together to minimize costs and improve efficiency.

1.3.4 Healthcare

In the **healthcare industry**, multi-agent systems are used for patient monitoring, scheduling, and coordination among doctors, nurses, and medical devices. For instance, different agents can collaborate to ensure that a patient's records are updated, treatments are administered on time, and medical equipment is functioning properly.

1.3.5 Financial Markets

In **financial markets**, agents represent traders or automated trading bots that interact with each other to buy and sell stocks, bonds, or other assets. These agents may be programmed to react to market conditions, creating a dynamic and constantly evolving environment that requires careful coordination and decision-making.

1.3.6 Energy Management

In **smart grids**, multi-agent systems manage the distribution of energy across different sources (e.g., solar, wind, traditional power plants) and consumers. Agents communicate with each other to balance supply and demand, minimize energy waste, and ensure the most efficient use of resources.

1.4 Challenges and Opportunities in Multi-agent AI

While multi-agent AI systems offer significant potential, they also come with their own set of challenges and opportunities:

1.4.1 Challenges

- **Complexity of Coordination:** As the number of agents increases, ensuring that all agents are effectively coordinated becomes more complex. Communication delays, conflicting goals, and computational bottlenecks can make coordination difficult.
- **Scalability:** Large-scale systems with many agents may face issues with scaling. Ensuring that a multi-agent system remains efficient as the number of agents grows is a significant challenge.
- **Distributed Decision-Making:** In decentralized systems, decisions must be made by individual agents without a central authority. This can lead to issues such as inconsistent decision-making and the "free-rider" problem, where some agents may not contribute as much to the system's goals.
- **Ethical Concerns:** As multi-agent systems become more autonomous, ethical considerations around decision-making, privacy, and fairness become more pressing. For instance, how do we ensure that agents make ethical choices when interacting with people or other systems?
- **Security:** The interaction between multiple agents can introduce vulnerabilities in terms of data privacy, hacking, and unauthorized access. Securing these systems against malicious agents is crucial.

1.4.2 Opportunities

- **Efficiency and Optimization:** Multi-agent systems can greatly improve the efficiency of processes by enabling decentralized decision-making and allowing agents to work in parallel toward shared goals. For example, in supply chain management, agents can collaborate to ensure that goods are delivered in the most cost-effective manner.
- **Flexibility and Adaptability:** Multi-agent systems are highly adaptable, allowing for the integration of new agents or the modification of existing ones without disrupting the overall system. This makes them suitable for applications in dynamic environments like autonomous driving or robotics.
- **Improved Decision-Making:** By distributing tasks and responsibilities among different agents, multi-agent systems can make more informed and timely decisions. For instance, in financial markets, agents can continuously analyze data and make buy/sell decisions faster than human traders.

- **Collaborative Problem Solving:** Multi-agent systems can tackle complex problems by allowing different agents to work together, each contributing their own expertise and perspective. This is particularly useful in applications like healthcare, where different agents (doctors, nurses, medical devices) must collaborate to provide effective care.

1.5 Reflection Questions

At this point in the chapter, it's important to reflect on what you've learned so far about multi-agent AI systems. Consider the following questions to test your understanding and think critically about how these concepts apply to real-world scenarios:

1. **What distinguishes a multi-agent system from a single-agent system?**
   Reflect on the differences in behavior, decision-making, and interaction between the two.
2. **How do agents in a multi-agent system communicate, and why is communication important?**
   Consider different communication methods like direct communication versus stigmergy and their relevance in solving problems.
3. **In what types of industries would multi-agent systems be most beneficial, and why?**
   Think about industries you are familiar with and how multi-agent AI could improve efficiency, decision-making, or innovation in those sectors.
4. **What challenges might arise when scaling a multi-agent system to handle thousands or millions of agents?**
   Reflect on scalability challenges and potential solutions for managing large-scale systems.
5. **How can ethical issues be addressed in multi-agent AI systems, and why is this important?**
   Consider the ethical implications of autonomous agents and how these systems can be designed to make responsible decisions.

In this chapter, we've introduced multi-agent AI systems, emphasizing their defining characteristics, applications, challenges, and opportunities. Understanding these concepts provides the foundation for deeper exploration into how multi-agent systems can be designed, developed, and deployed in real-world environments. As we progress through the book, we will explore how to build and manage these systems, address their challenges, and leverage their full potential for advanced automation and problem-solving.

Tables and Code Examples

Throughout this chapter and the rest of the book, we will use **tables** and **code examples** to clarify key concepts. Here is an example of a simple table summarizing the differences between **single-agent** and **multi-agent** systems:

Feature	Single-agent System	Multi-agent System
Number of Agents	One	Multiple (autonomous agents)
Decision-making	Centralized (one decision-maker)	Decentralized (agents make individual decisions)
Communication	None (agents don't communicate)	Communication between agents is key
Complexity	Lower (single decision-maker)	Higher (interaction, coordination, conflicts)
Applications	Simple tasks (e.g., navigation)	Complex tasks (e.g., swarm robotics, traffic control)

Code Example (Multi-agent Communication):

```python
# Simple Python code for agent-to-agent communication
class Agent:
    def __init__(self, name):
        self.name = name

    def communicate(self, message, other_agent):
        print(f"{self.name} sends message: {message} to {other_agent.name}")

# Creating two agents
agent1 = Agent("Agent 1")
agent2 = Agent("Agent 2")
```

```
# Communication between agents
agent1.communicate("Hello, Agent 2!", agent2)
```

In this simple Python example, two agents communicate with each other by sending messages. This highlights how agents in a multi-agent system interact and exchange information, an essential characteristic of MAS.

Chapter 2: Understanding Crew AI

2.1 Overview of Crew AI

Crew AI is a specialized multi-agent AI framework designed to facilitate the development and management of systems where multiple autonomous agents interact to achieve shared or individual goals. Unlike traditional AI systems that focus on a single decision-making unit, Crew AI allows for decentralized, autonomous decision-making among a collection of agents. Each agent operates independently, but they communicate and cooperate (or compete) to solve complex problems, optimize tasks, or simulate real-world systems.

Key Features of Crew AI:

1. **Decentralization:** There is no central controller. Each agent makes its own decisions based on the information it receives from its environment and other agents.
2. **Autonomy:** Agents operate independently without direct human intervention.
3. **Collaboration and Coordination:** Crew AI systems enable agents to work together, sharing information and coordinating efforts toward common objectives.
4. **Scalability:** Crew AI can scale up or down depending on the number of agents needed in the system, making it adaptable to a wide range of applications.
5. **Flexibility:** Agents in Crew AI can be designed to handle a variety of tasks, from simple operations to complex, real-time decision-making processes.

Why Crew AI is Important:

- **Distributed Decision Making:** Crew AI is suitable for tasks that require distributed decision-making, where no single agent can perform the task independently.
- **Automation at Scale:** It enables the automation of large-scale systems, such as smart cities, traffic control, autonomous vehicles, and even complex manufacturing systems.

- **Real-time Adaptability:** Agents can adapt to changing environments and new information, making Crew AI ideal for dynamic systems that require continuous optimization.

2.2 Core Components of Crew AI

Crew AI is structured around several key components that work together to form a functioning multi-agent system. Each component plays a crucial role in ensuring that the agents can interact effectively, learn from their environment, and work toward achieving their goals. Below are the core components of Crew AI:

2.2.1 Agents

At the heart of Crew AI are the **agents**, each of which has its own set of behaviors, goals, and decision-making processes. These agents can vary in complexity, from simple reactive agents to sophisticated agents capable of advanced learning and reasoning.

- **Reactive Agents:** These agents respond to stimuli from their environment with predefined behaviors.
- **Deliberative Agents:** These agents can plan, reason, and make decisions based on available data and expected outcomes.

2.2.2 Environment

The **environment** is the external context in which the agents operate. The environment can provide agents with data or feedback, influencing their actions and decisions.

- The environment can be static (unchanging) or dynamic (constantly changing).
- In Crew AI, the environment is often modeled as a shared space where agents interact and influence each other's behavior.

2.2.3 Communication

Communication is essential for cooperation between agents. Crew AI enables agents to share information, negotiate, or collaborate to achieve a goal.

- **Direct Communication:** One agent sends a message to another to exchange information.
- **Indirect Communication (stigmergy):** Agents leave markers or signals in the environment that other agents interpret.

2.2.4 Coordination and Negotiation

In multi-agent systems, coordination ensures that agents work together toward common goals. **Negotiation** enables agents to resolve conflicts or agree on resource distribution.

- **Coordination Mechanisms:** Ensure that agents' actions do not conflict and that they complement one another.
- **Negotiation:** Allows agents to reach agreements or compromise on how to allocate resources or tasks.

2.2.5 Learning and Adaptation

Crew AI systems support **machine learning** techniques, which allow agents to improve their performance over time based on their experiences.

- **Reinforcement Learning (RL):** Agents learn by receiving rewards or penalties based on their actions, allowing them to adapt to their environment.
- **Supervised Learning:** Agents can be trained with labeled data to predict outcomes or behaviors.

2.3 Benefits of Using Crew AI

Crew AI offers a wide range of benefits, particularly in environments that require flexibility, scalability, and the ability to perform tasks autonomously. Below are some of the key advantages:

2.3.1 Scalability and Flexibility

- **Scalability:** Crew AI systems can scale from small systems with a few agents to large systems with thousands of agents. Each agent in the system can operate independently, ensuring that the system can grow efficiently.
- **Flexibility:** Crew AI is adaptable to a wide variety of applications, including robotics, autonomous vehicles, smart cities, and supply chain management. New agents can be added easily to address new tasks or goals.

2.3.2 Efficiency in Complex Systems

- **Distributed Problem-Solving:** By distributing tasks among multiple agents, Crew AI enables the system to tackle complex problems more efficiently. This is especially useful for real-time optimization problems, where different agents can specialize in specific aspects of the task.
- **Parallel Processing:** Agents work in parallel to complete tasks faster, reducing bottlenecks that might occur in centralized systems.

2.3.3 Robustness and Resilience

- **Fault Tolerance:** Since Crew AI systems are decentralized, the failure of one or more agents does not necessarily cause the entire system to fail. Other agents can continue operating, ensuring the system remains functional.
- **Adaptability:** Agents in Crew AI systems can adapt to changes in their environment, making the system resilient to disruptions and capable of handling dynamic conditions.

2.3.4 Cost-Effectiveness

- **Resource Efficiency:** Multi-agent systems can optimize resource usage by allowing agents to specialize in specific tasks. This minimizes redundancy and reduces costs.
- **Automated Decision Making:** By automating decision-making processes, Crew AI systems reduce the need for human intervention, allowing organizations to save on labor costs and improve operational efficiency.

2.3.5 Enhanced Decision Making

- **Decentralized Decision Making:** In Crew AI, each agent makes decisions autonomously based on its observations, leading to faster decision-making in complex scenarios.
- **Collaborative Decision Making:** Agents can share information and work together to make more informed, accurate decisions, particularly in situations that require collective intelligence.

2.4 Comparison with Other Multi-agent AI Frameworks

While Crew AI offers unique capabilities, it's important to compare it with other popular multi-agent frameworks to understand its strengths and potential limitations. Below, we compare **Crew AI** with two widely-used multi-agent frameworks: **JADE** (Java Agent Development Framework) and **OpenAI's Gym** (used for reinforcement learning).

Feature	Crew AI	JADE	OpenAI Gym
Primary Use	Autonomous agents in complex systems	Agent-based simulation and development	Reinforcement learning environments
Communication Model	Direct and indirect communication	Agent-based direct communication	Not primarily for multi-agent communication
Scalability	Highly scalable, adaptable for large systems	Moderate scalability, focused on simulation	Limited scalability for multi-agent systems
Learning Capabilities	Supports machine learning (e.g., RL, supervised learning)	Limited learning capabilities, focuses on agent behaviors	Primarily reinforcement learning-based
Platform	Open-source, supports various languages	Java-based, focused on distributed systems	Python-based, specifically for RL

Feature	Crew AI	JADE	OpenAI Gym
Ease of Use	User-friendly API, flexible for different tasks	Requires knowledge of Java and agent systems	Requires knowledge of RL and Python
Applications	Robotics, autonomous vehicles, smart cities, supply chain management	Research, educational tools, agent simulation	Primarily for reinforcement learning research

Key Takeaways from the Comparison:

- **Crew AI** stands out for its **scalability**, **flexibility**, and its ability to integrate machine learning capabilities, making it a powerful tool for building complex, autonomous systems that adapt to real-time conditions.
- **JADE** is a robust framework for simulating and developing multi-agent systems, but it's more focused on Java-based applications and lacks the built-in machine learning capabilities that Crew AI offers.
- **OpenAI Gym**, while a great platform for reinforcement learning, is not as focused on multi-agent systems and lacks features for real-time communication and coordination between agents, which Crew AI excels at.

2.5 Quiz

Now that we have discussed the core components, benefits, and comparisons of **Crew AI**, let's test your understanding with the following quiz:

1. What is the primary feature that distinguishes Crew AI from other multi-agent AI systems?

- a) Centralized decision-making
- b) Machine learning integration
- c) Single-agent operation
- d) Direct communication between agents

2. Which of the following is a benefit of using Crew AI for large-scale systems?

- a) Limited adaptability
- b) Scalability and fault tolerance
- c) Centralized management
- d) Lack of agent communication

3. What is the role of communication in Crew AI?

- a) To ensure agents do not interact
- b) To allow agents to share information and coordinate actions
- c) To limit the autonomy of agents
- d) To centralize control over decision-making

4. Which of the following is NOT a core component of Crew AI?

- a) Agents
- b) Environment
- c) Centralized server
- d) Learning and adaptation

5. How does Crew AI improve decision-making in complex systems?

- a) By relying on a single decision-maker
- b) Through decentralized, autonomous decision-making by agents
- c) By centralizing all decisions to a human supervisor
- d) By eliminating agent communication

Answers:

1. **b)** Machine learning integration
2. **b)** Scalability and fault tolerance
3. **b)** To allow agents to share information and coordinate actions
4. **c)** Centralized server
5. **b)** Through decentralized, autonomous decision-making by agents

Chapter 3: Setting Up a Crew AI Development Environment

In this chapter, we will walk through the process of setting up your development environment for **Crew AI**. This includes understanding the system requirements, installing Crew AI, creating a new project, and performing basic configuration. Additionally, we will provide an exercise to help you set up your first Crew AI project.

3.1 System Requirements

Before you can begin developing with **Crew AI**, it's important to ensure that your system meets the necessary requirements. Crew AI is a flexible framework that can be run on various platforms, but the following specifications will ensure smooth performance and compatibility:

Minimum System Requirements:

Component	Specification
Operating System	Windows 10, macOS, or Linux (latest stable versions)
CPU	Dual-core processor (Intel i5 or equivalent)
RAM	8 GB or higher
Storage	10 GB of free disk space
Java	Java 8 or newer
Python	Python 3.6 or newer
Network	Internet connection for installation and updates
IDE	IntelliJ IDEA, Visual Studio Code, or PyCharm

Recommended System Requirements:

Component	Specification
Operating System	Windows 10 Pro, macOS 10.15, or Linux (Ubuntu 20.04)
CPU	Quad-core processor (Intel i7 or equivalent)
RAM	16 GB or higher
Storage	SSD with 20 GB of free space
Java	Java 11 or newer
Python	Python 3.8 or newer
Network	Stable internet connection (for updates and dependencies)
IDE	IntelliJ IDEA, Visual Studio Code, PyCharm with Python or Java plugin

Additional Tools:

- **Docker** (for containerized environments)
- **Git** (for version control)
- **JDK (Java Development Kit)**: Required for building and running Crew AI if Java is used in your project.

3.2 Installing Crew AI

Once your system meets the requirements, you can proceed with installing **Crew AI**. The installation process will vary depending on the platform you are using, but the steps below outline the general process.

Installation Steps for Windows:

1. **Download Java Development Kit (JDK):**
   - Visit the Oracle JDK download page.
   - Download and install **JDK 11** or a newer version, ensuring that the JAVA_HOME environment variable is correctly set up.
2. **Download Python:**
   - Visit the Python Downloads Page.

- o Download and install Python 3.6 or higher. Make sure to check the box that says "Add Python to PATH" during installation.
3. **Clone Crew AI Repository (using Git):**
   - o Open **Command Prompt** or **Git Bash** and run the following command to clone the Crew AI repository from GitHub:
4. `git clone https://github.com/crew-ai/crew-ai.git`
   - o Navigate into the directory:
5. `cd crew-ai`
6. **Install Dependencies:**
   - o Crew AI may require specific dependencies (e.g., external libraries or packages). To install them, run:
7. `pip install -r requirements.txt`

This will install the necessary Python libraries.

8. **Verify Installation:**
   - o Once installed, verify that **Crew AI** is properly set up by running the following command in your terminal:
9. `python -m crew_ai --version`

This should return the current version of Crew AI if the installation was successful.

Installation Steps for macOS/Linux:

1. **Install Java:** Follow the same steps for downloading and installing **JDK** as mentioned for Windows.
2. **Install Python:** Similarly, download and install **Python 3.6+** from the official site or using a package manager (e.g., `brew install python` for macOS).
3. **Clone the Repository:** Run the same `git clone` command as above in your terminal.
4. **Install Dependencies:** Run `pip install -r requirements.txt` to install the required Python libraries.
5. **Verify Installation:** Use the same command to check if Crew AI is installed correctly.

3.3 Creating a New Project

Now that you have **Crew AI** installed, let's walk through the process of creating a new project. A project in **Crew AI** consists of a collection of agents and their associated behaviors, environments, and communication mechanisms.

Steps to Create a New Crew AI Project:

Create a Project Directory:

Start by creating a new directory for your project:

```
mkdir my_crew_ai_project
cd my_crew_ai_project
```

Initialize the Project:

Inside the directory, initialize a new Python project by creating a `requirements.txt` file, where you'll specify the dependencies:

```
crew-ai==<latest_version>
```

Create the First Agent Class:

In your project directory, create a new Python file, e.g., `my_agent.py`, and define the basic structure for your agent:

```python
from crew_ai import Agent

class MyAgent(Agent):
    def __init__(self, name):
        super().__init__(name)
        self.state = "idle"

    def act(self):
        if self.state == "idle":
            print(f"{self.name} is idling.")
        else:
            print(f"{self.name} is active.")

    def communicate(self, message):
        print(f"{self.name} communicates: {message}")
```

This code snippet defines an agent class that inherits from **Agent** in Crew AI. It has basic state management and a communication function.

1. **Set Up the Environment:**
   o Create a basic environment where your agent will operate. In `environment.py`, set up a simple environment for your agent to interact with:

```python
from crew_ai import Environment

class MyEnvironment(Environment):
    def __init__(self):
        self.agents = []

    def add_agent(self, agent):
        self.agents.append(agent)

    def update(self):
        for agent in self.agents:
            agent.act()
```

Run the Project:

Finally, create a script to run the project, e.g., `main.py`, where you instantiate the agent and environment:

```python
from my_agent import MyAgent
from environment import MyEnvironment

# Initialize environment
env = MyEnvironment()

# Create and add agent
agent1 = MyAgent("Agent1")
env.add_agent(agent1)

# Run the environment
env.update()
```

This script will start the environment and let the agent perform actions based on its state.

3.4 Basic Configuration

Once the basic project structure is set up, you may need to configure several parameters and settings to optimize the behavior of agents and the system.

Configuration File:

It is often helpful to keep the configuration of your system in a separate file. This allows you to easily change parameters without modifying the main codebase. Here's an example of a basic `config.json` file:

```json
{
  "agent_speed": 5,
  "agent_communication_range": 10,
  "environment_size": 100
}
```

In your Python code, you can load and use these configurations:

```python
import json

# Load configuration
with open('config.json', 'r') as f:
    config = json.load(f)

agent_speed = config["agent_speed"]
communication_range = config["agent_communication_range"]
```

This allows you to modify the configuration settings easily, without diving into the code itself.

3.5 Exercise: Setting Up Your First Crew AI Project

Objective:

Create a basic Crew AI project with one agent that interacts within an environment.

Steps:

1. **Set up your development environment** by following the installation steps mentioned in **3.2**.
2. **Create a new directory** for your project (`my_first_crew_ai_project`).
3. **Create a new agent class** (`my_agent.py`) that has:
   - A state (idle or active).
   - A `communicate` method to print messages.
4. **Create an environment** (`environment.py`) that holds agents and updates them.
5. **Run your project** with a script (`main.py`) that initializes the environment, adds an agent, and calls `env.update()` to simulate the agent's behavior.
6. **Test the system** by running `python main.py` and verifying that your agent prints out its actions correctly.

This exercise will give you hands-on experience setting up and running a basic Crew AI system and provide a foundation to build more complex multi-agent systems.

In **Chapter 3**, we've walked through the process of setting up a **Crew AI development environment**, including system requirements, installation, creating a project, and configuring agents and environments. By following the steps outlined in this chapter, you can easily start building your own multi-agent AI systems, and the exercise will help you consolidate your understanding by creating your first basic Crew AI project.

Chapter 4: Designing Multi-agent Systems with Crew AI

Designing an effective multi-agent system (MAS) with **Crew AI** involves careful consideration of several factors, including defining the roles and responsibilities of agents, enabling communication and coordination, supporting decision-making and planning processes, and determining the right agent architecture. This chapter will guide you through the essential steps in designing a robust and efficient multi-agent system, providing you with the tools and concepts necessary to create and manage such systems in real-world scenarios.

4.1 Defining Agent Roles and Responsibilities

In a multi-agent system, agents are designed to perform specific tasks that contribute to the system's overall objectives. Defining **agent roles and responsibilities** is essential for ensuring that each agent operates within the bounds of its purpose while also cooperating effectively with other agents.

Key Considerations for Defining Agent Roles:

1. **Task Specialization:**
   - Each agent should be designed to handle a particular task or set of tasks within the system. This division of labor allows for a more organized and efficient system, as each agent can focus on a specific responsibility.
2. **Collaboration Needs:**
   - Agents must interact with each other to complete tasks that require joint efforts. For example, in a supply chain management system, different agents might be responsible for inventory management, order processing, and delivery, but they must all collaborate to ensure smooth operations.
3. **Autonomy:**
   - While agents should cooperate, they must also have sufficient autonomy to make decisions and execute tasks independently, without requiring constant human intervention.
4. **Scalability:**

o Roles should be scalable to accommodate additional agents as the system grows. New agents should be able to take on new roles or extend the capabilities of existing ones without disrupting the overall system.

Example: Defining Roles in a Multi-agent Robotics System

Consider a multi-agent robotics system used for warehouse management:

- **Robot A (Picker Agent):** This agent's role is to pick items from shelves.
- **Robot B (Mover Agent):** This agent is responsible for transporting items from the picker to the packing station.
- **Robot C (Packager Agent):** This agent packs the items into boxes.

Each robot has a specialized role, and they coordinate to complete the task of fulfilling customer orders. The agents must communicate with each other to pass information about item availability, the need for more supplies, and other dynamic factors.

4.2 Agent Communication and Coordination

Effective communication and coordination are at the core of any successful multi-agent system. Agents must share information and align their actions to achieve the system's goals.

Types of Agent Communication:

1. **Direct Communication:**
   o Agents communicate with each other by sending messages directly. This type of communication is synchronous (where agents wait for a response) or asynchronous (where agents do not wait for a response).

   Example:

   o **Direct Messaging:** Agent A sends a request to Agent B: "Please pick up the item from shelf 5."
2. **Indirect Communication (stigmergy):**

o   In this form of communication, agents leave markers in the environment that other agents can detect and act upon. For example, agents might leave flags in a shared space to indicate a task has been completed or needs attention.

Example:

o   **Stigmergy in Robotics:** Robot A leaves a marker on the floor where an item needs to be picked up. Robot B detects this marker and picks up the item.

Coordination Mechanisms:

Coordination ensures that agents work together without conflicts or redundancies. There are two primary types of coordination:

1. **Centralized Coordination:**
   o   A central controller or system coordinates all agents. This method is simpler but can become a bottleneck and a single point of failure.
2. **Decentralized Coordination:**
   o   Each agent has the freedom to coordinate with others based on local information. This approach is more scalable and fault-tolerant but requires sophisticated algorithms for conflict resolution and collaboration.

Example: Agent Coordination in a Traffic System

In a traffic management system, each traffic light (agent) must coordinate with neighboring traffic lights to avoid congestion. Decentralized coordination ensures that each light operates based on real-time traffic data, adjusting its timing to optimize flow without a central controller.

4.3 Agent Decision-Making and Planning

In any multi-agent system, agents need to make decisions based on the available information and their goals. The complexity of these decisions depends on the agent's role, the environment, and the level of autonomy required.

Types of Decision-Making Approaches:

1. **Reactive Decision-Making:**
   - Agents respond directly to stimuli from the environment. This approach is fast and efficient but limited in complexity.

   Example: A robot in a factory that avoids obstacles by reacting to sensors detecting objects in its path.

2. **Deliberative Decision-Making:**
   - Agents plan their actions based on reasoning, often using models or simulations of the environment. This allows for more complex behaviors and longer-term strategies but requires more processing power.

   Example: A delivery robot that plans its route using a map of the environment, avoiding obstacles and selecting the shortest path.

3. **Hybrid Decision-Making:**
   - A combination of reactive and deliberative decision-making. This approach allows agents to quickly respond to immediate situations while also planning for long-term goals.

Planning Algorithms:

Planning algorithms help agents decide the best course of action to achieve their goals. Some commonly used algorithms are:

- *A Algorithm:** Used for pathfinding and graph traversal. It finds the shortest path between two points in a grid or map.
- **Markov Decision Processes (MDPs):** A mathematical framework for modeling decision-making in environments with stochastic (random) elements.

*Example: Using A for Pathfinding**

Below is an example of using the A* algorithm to help an agent navigate a grid from a starting point to a destination:

```
import heapq

# A* algorithm implementation
```

```python
class AStar:
    def __init__(self, grid):
        self.grid = grid
        self.rows = len(grid)
        self.cols = len(grid[0])

    def heuristic(self, a, b):
        return abs(a[0] - b[0]) + abs(a[1] - b[1])

    def a_star(self, start, goal):
        open_list = []
        heapq.heappush(open_list, (0 + self.heuristic(start,
goal), 0, start))
        came_from = {}
        g_score = {start: 0}
        f_score = {start: self.heuristic(start, goal)}

        while open_list:
            _, current_cost, current =
heapq.heappop(open_list)

            if current == goal:
                path = []
                while current in came_from:
                    path.append(current)
                    current = came_from[current]
                path.append(start)
                return path[::-1]  # Return reversed path

            for neighbor in self.get_neighbors(current):
                tentative_g_score = current_cost + 1  #
Assume all edges have weight 1
                if tentative_g_score < g_score.get(neighbor,
float('inf')):
                    came_from[neighbor] = current
                    g_score[neighbor] = tentative_g_score
                    f_score[neighbor] = tentative_g_score +
self.heuristic(neighbor, goal)
                    heapq.heappush(open_list,
(f_score[neighbor], tentative_g_score, neighbor))

        return None  # No path found

    def get_neighbors(self, node):
        # Return the 4 neighbors (up, down, left, right)
        x, y = node
        neighbors = []
        for dx, dy in [(-1, 0), (1, 0), (0, -1), (0, 1)]:
            if 0 <= x + dx < self.rows and 0 <= y + dy <
self.cols:
                neighbors.append((x + dx, y + dy))
```

```
    return neighbors
```

In this example, an agent navigates a grid using the A* algorithm to find the shortest path between a start and goal point. The algorithm considers both the distance traveled (g-score) and a heuristic estimate (f-score) of the remaining path.

4.4 Designing Agent Architectures

The **architecture** of an agent defines its internal structure and how it processes information, makes decisions, and interacts with the environment. A well-designed architecture is crucial for ensuring that an agent behaves efficiently and effectively within the multi-agent system.

Common Agent Architectures:

1. **Reactive Architecture:**
   o Agents using reactive architecture respond directly to their environment without maintaining any internal state. This architecture is suitable for tasks that require quick, simple actions.
2. **Deliberative Architecture:**
   o In this architecture, agents maintain internal representations of the environment and plan their actions. These agents perform reasoning to determine the best course of action.
3. **Hybrid Architecture:**
   o Hybrid architectures combine the benefits of reactive and deliberative architectures. Agents can react to immediate changes while also planning for long-term goals.

Example: Hybrid Agent Architecture

Below is an example of a hybrid agent architecture in which the agent can both react to immediate environmental changes and plan for future tasks:

```
class HybridAgent:
    def __init__(self, name):
        self.name = name
        self.state = "idle"
```

```
def react(self, environment):
    # Respond to immediate environmental changes
    if environment.detect_obstacle():
        self.state = "avoiding_obstacle"
        print(f"{self.name} is avoiding obstacle!")
    else:
        self.state = "idle"
        print(f"{self.name} is idle.")

def plan(self, task):
    # Plan long-term goals based on the task
    if task == "deliver_package":
        print(f"{self.name} is planning delivery route.")
    else:
        print(f"{self.name} has no task assigned.")
```

In this hybrid model, the agent first reacts to obstacles in its path and can also plan for a long-term task, like delivering a package.

4.5 Reflection Questions

To deepen your understanding of the material, consider the following reflection questions:

1. **Why is it important to define clear roles and responsibilities for each agent in a multi-agent system?**
   - Reflect on how this approach improves efficiency and reduces potential conflicts in a system with many agents.
2. **What are the key differences between reactive and deliberative decision-making in agents?**
   - Think about how each approach might be used in different types of applications and how they contribute to overall system performance.
3. **How can communication mechanisms impact the effectiveness of agent coordination in a multi-agent system?**
   - Consider how direct communication and stigmergy could affect collaboration and task allocation in a system.
4. **What advantages does a hybrid agent architecture offer over purely reactive or deliberative systems?**
   - Reflect on the strengths and limitations of each architecture, and why a combination of both might be beneficial in certain applications.

5. **How can agent learning capabilities enhance decision-making and planning in complex environments?**
    - o   Think about the role of machine learning in improving an agent's ability to adapt and optimize its behavior over time.

Part II: Building Multi-agent AI Systems

Chapter 5: Implementing Agents with Crew AI

In this chapter, we will explore the process of implementing agents within a multi-agent AI system using **Crew AI**. This chapter focuses on the practical aspects of creating agents, defining their behaviors, implementing their decision-making logic, and interacting with the Crew AI framework to facilitate coordination and execution. By the end of this chapter, you will have a solid understanding of how to build functional agents that can operate autonomously and interact with each other within a shared environment.

5.1 Creating Agent Classes

The first step in implementing agents in **Crew AI** is to create an **Agent class**. In object-oriented programming, an agent is represented as a class, where each instance of the class represents an individual agent with its own properties and behaviors.

Steps to Create an Agent Class:

1. **Define the Class:**
   - Every agent class should inherit from the **Agent** base class provided by **Crew AI**. This allows the agent to take advantage of Crew AI's built-in functionality, such as communication and interaction with other agents.
2. **Initialize Agent Properties:**
   - An agent may have various properties, such as its name, state, goals, and available resources. These properties define the agent's characteristics and can be initialized in the class constructor.
3. **Agent Behavior:**
   - Define the agent's behavior by implementing methods that determine how the agent will act in the system. This might include moving, interacting with the environment, or communicating with other agents.

Example: Basic Agent Class

```python
from crew_ai import Agent

class MyAgent(Agent):
    def __init__(self, name, initial_state="idle"):
        super().__init__(name)  # Initialize the agent with a name
        self.state = initial_state  # Define the initial state of the agent

    def act(self):
        if self.state == "idle":
            print(f"{self.name} is idling.")
        elif self.state == "active":
            print(f"{self.name} is performing tasks.")
        else:
            print(f"{self.name} is in an unknown state.")

    def change_state(self, new_state):
        self.state = new_state
        print(f"{self.name} state changed to {self.state}.")
```

Key Points:

- The **MyAgent** class inherits from **Agent**.
- The constructor initializes the **name** and **state** of the agent.
- The **act** method defines the agent's behavior based on its current state.
- The **change_state** method allows the agent's state to be updated.

In this example, the agent performs different actions based on its state, such as idling or performing tasks.

5.2 Defining Agent Behaviors

Once the agent class is set up, the next step is to define the **agent's behavior**. An agent's behavior is typically determined by its internal state and the environment around it. These behaviors are implemented as methods or functions within the agent class and are triggered based on certain conditions or stimuli.

Types of Agent Behaviors:

1. **Reactive Behaviors:**
   - In **reactive agents**, the agent's actions are directly driven by the environment. For example, an agent might avoid obstacles as soon as it detects them in its environment.
2. **Deliberative Behaviors:**
   - **Deliberative agents** engage in more thoughtful behavior, often using a reasoning or decision-making process to determine their actions. This might involve setting long-term goals and considering multiple actions to achieve those goals.
3. **Hybrid Behaviors:**
   - **Hybrid agents** combine both reactive and deliberative behaviors. This allows them to react to immediate stimuli while also planning for long-term objectives.

Example: Implementing Behaviors

```python
class ReactiveAgent(Agent):
    def __init__(self, name):
        super().__init__(name)
        self.state = "idle"

    def act(self, environment):
        # React to obstacles or other environmental stimuli
        if environment.is_obstacle_detected(self):
            self.state = "avoiding_obstacle"
            print(f"{self.name} is avoiding an obstacle.")
        else:
            self.state = "idle"
            print(f"{self.name} is idling.")

class DeliberativeAgent(Agent):
    def __init__(self, name, goal):
        super().__init__(name)
        self.state = "idle"
        self.goal = goal  # Set long-term goal

    def act(self):
        if self.state == "idle":
            print(f"{self.name} is planning actions to
achieve the goal.")
            self.plan()
        elif self.state == "performing_task":
            print(f"{self.name} is executing the task.")

    def plan(self):
```

```
        print(f"{self.name} is planning to reach the goal:
{self.goal}")
        # Plan the steps to achieve the goal here
```

In this example:

- **ReactiveAgent** reacts to obstacles in its environment.
- **DeliberativeAgent** plans actions based on a long-term goal and shifts between different states based on its progress.

5.3 Implementing Agent Logic

The next step in building your agent is defining its **logic**. Agent logic dictates how an agent makes decisions, plans actions, and responds to changes in the environment or other agents. The logic can be simple (reactive) or more complex (deliberative), depending on the task.

Key Considerations for Implementing Agent Logic:

1. **Input Processing:**
   o The agent receives information from its environment or other agents. This could be sensory data, status updates, or direct messages.
2. **Decision Making:**
   o The agent uses algorithms or decision rules to determine the next action. This can be as simple as a set of if/else conditions or as complex as a reinforcement learning algorithm.
3. **Execution:**
   o The agent executes the chosen action. In a physical system, this might involve sending commands to a robot or device; in a simulated environment, this might involve updating the agent's state or the environment.

Example: Implementing Decision Logic Using if/else

```
class TaskAgent(Agent):
    def __init__(self, name):
        super().__init__(name)
        self.state = "idle"

    def act(self, task):
```

```
if task == "deliver_package":
    self.state = "delivering_package"
    print(f"{self.name} is delivering the package.")
elif task == "charge_battery":
    self.state = "charging"
    print(f"{self.name} is charging.")
else:
    self.state = "idle"
    print(f"{self.name} is idle.")
```

In this example, **TaskAgent** decides what action to take based on the task it is given. The agent performs different actions based on simple decision logic.

5.4 Interacting with the Crew AI Framework

In **Crew AI**, agents interact with the environment and with each other to achieve their goals. The **Crew AI framework** provides built-in functions and methods to facilitate communication, coordination, and collaboration among agents.

Key Interactions with Crew AI:

1. **Agent Communication:**
   o Agents can send and receive messages to/from other agents using Crew AI's messaging system. This allows agents to share information, request help, or coordinate actions.
2. **Environment Interaction:**
   o Agents interact with the environment to receive sensory input (e.g., location, obstacles, resources) and to act upon it (e.g., moving, collecting items).
3. **Task Coordination:**
   o Crew AI provides methods for agents to coordinate tasks, share responsibilities, and prevent conflicts when multiple agents are trying to perform the same task.

Example: Agent Communication and Coordination

```
class CoordinatingAgent(Agent):
    def __init__(self, name):
        super().__init__(name)
```

```
        self.state = "idle"

    def communicate(self, message, recipient_agent):
        print(f"{self.name} sends message: {message} to
{recipient_agent.name}")
        recipient_agent.receive_message(message)

    def receive_message(self, message):
        print(f"{self.name} received message: {message}")

    def act(self):
        print(f"{self.name} is performing its tasks.")
```

In this example:

- **CoordinatingAgent** can send and receive messages from other agents, facilitating communication and task coordination.
- The **communicate** method sends a message to another agent, while the **receive_message** method processes the received message.

5.5 Exercise: Developing Your First Agent

Objective:

Create and implement a basic **Crew AI agent** that can interact with its environment, perform tasks, and communicate with other agents.

Steps:

1. **Set up your development environment** by following the setup instructions from previous chapters.
2. **Create an agent class** (e.g., MyAgent) that:
   o Has an initial state (idle, working, or resting).
   o Can change its state based on interactions with the environment.
3. **Add behaviors** to your agent:
   o Make it reactive to certain conditions in the environment (e.g., detect obstacles or signals).
4. **Enable communication** between agents:
   o Implement basic messaging functionality where one agent can send a message to another.

5. **Run the agent in an environment** that changes over time and observe how the agent reacts and interacts with other agents.
6. **Extend your agent's capabilities**:
   - Add more advanced behaviors (e.g., decision-making, task planning).

Example: MyAgent Implementation

```python
from crew_ai import Agent

class MyAgent(Agent):
    def __init__(self, name):
        super().__init__(name)
        self.state = "idle"

    def act(self):
        if self.state == "idle":
            print(f"{self.name} is waiting.")
        elif self.state == "working":
            print(f"{self.name} is working hard!")

    def change_state(self, new_state):
        self.state = new_state
        print(f"{self.name} changed state to: {self.state}")
```

Run the agent with different states to simulate its behavior and see how it interacts with the environment.

Chapter 6: Building Agent Teams

In a multi-agent system, agents often need to work together to achieve complex objectives. Building and managing **agent teams** is a fundamental aspect of developing efficient, scalable, and adaptable systems. A well-structured agent team can help distribute workloads, leverage specialized skills, and collaborate to solve problems more efficiently. In this chapter, we will explore the process of forming agent teams, assigning tasks, coordinating actions, and managing team dynamics and conflicts.

6.1 Forming Agent Teams

The first step in creating an effective agent team is forming the team itself. This involves selecting the right agents for the team, determining the structure of the team, and defining how agents will collaborate.

Key Considerations for Forming Agent Teams:

1. **Task Requirements:**
   - Identify the tasks that the team needs to perform. For example, in a delivery system, tasks could include picking up, transporting, and delivering goods. Each agent's role should align with these tasks.
2. **Agent Skills and Specialization:**
   - Agents should be selected based on their skills and capabilities. A diverse team may consist of agents with complementary abilities, such as one agent specialized in navigation and another in picking up items.
3. **Team Size:**
   - The team size should be appropriate for the complexity of the task. A small team may suffice for simple tasks, but more complex problems may require larger teams with specialized agents.
4. **Autonomy and Cooperation:**
   - Agents must be able to act autonomously but also cooperate with other agents. This requires clear roles and efficient communication within the team.

Example: Forming an Agent Team in a Warehouse System

Consider a warehouse where the task is to pick and deliver items to specific locations. You could form a team of agents as follows:

- **Agent A (Picker Agent):** Specializes in picking up items.
- **Agent B (Transporter Agent):** Transports items to designated areas.
- **Agent C (Delivery Agent):** Delivers the items to the customer or destination.

Each agent has a specialized role, and they need to communicate and collaborate to achieve the overall goal of the system.

6.2 Task Assignment and Distribution

Once the team is formed, the next step is to assign and distribute tasks among the agents. Effective task assignment ensures that each agent's skills are used appropriately, and workloads are balanced across the team.

Types of Task Assignment:

1. **Centralized Task Assignment:**
   - A central authority (such as a team leader or controller) assigns tasks to individual agents. This approach is straightforward but can become a bottleneck as the team size grows.
2. **Decentralized Task Assignment:**
   - In this approach, agents make decisions independently based on local information. Agents may negotiate or communicate with one another to allocate tasks, making it more scalable but potentially more complex.
3. **Dynamic Task Assignment:**
   - Tasks may change over time based on environmental factors or agent performance. This requires agents to be flexible and able to adapt to changing conditions.

Task Assignment Example Using Centralized Approach

Consider a task assignment system where a **Coordinator Agent** assigns tasks to a team of **worker agents**:

```python
class CoordinatorAgent(Agent):
    def __init__(self, name):
        super().__init__(name)
        self.tasks = ["pick_item", "transport_item",
"deliver_item"]

    def assign_task(self, agent):
        if self.tasks:
            task = self.tasks.pop(0)
            print(f"{self.name} assigns {task} to
{agent.name}")
            agent.receive_task(task)

class WorkerAgent(Agent):
    def __init__(self, name):
        super().__init__(name)
        self.current_task = None

    def receive_task(self, task):
        self.current_task = task
        print(f"{self.name} received task:
{self.current_task}")

    def perform_task(self):
        if self.current_task:
            print(f"{self.name} is performing:
{self.current_task}")
            self.current_task = None
```

In this example:

- **CoordinatorAgent** assigns tasks to **WorkerAgent** instances.
- Each worker agent receives a task and performs it accordingly.

6.3 Team Coordination and Collaboration

Effective coordination is essential for ensuring that all agents work together efficiently toward a shared goal. Coordination mechanisms help agents avoid conflicts, share information, and collaborate on tasks.

Coordination Strategies:

1. **Shared Goals:**
   - Agents must understand the overall objective of the team. In a cooperative environment, agents work together to achieve this common goal.
2. **Communication:**
   - Continuous communication between agents allows them to share important information such as task status, environmental conditions, and available resources.
3. **Conflict Resolution:**
   - Conflicts may arise when multiple agents attempt to perform the same task or when their actions interfere with one another. Effective coordination involves resolving these conflicts promptly to ensure smooth operation.
4. **Synchronization:**
   - In some cases, agents need to synchronize their actions. For instance, in a robotic assembly line, agents may need to work in sync to assemble a product.

Example: Coordinating Agents in a Delivery System

Let's implement a simple coordination system where agents send updates about the progress of their tasks:

```
class Agent:
    def __init__(self, name):
        self.name = name
        self.current_task = None

    def communicate(self, message):
        print(f"{self.name} sends message: {message}")

class Coordinator(Agent):
    def __init__(self, name):
        super().__init__(name)

    def coordinate(self, agents):
        for agent in agents:
            agent.communicate(f"Update from {self.name}: Task
in progress.")

# Example usage
agent1 = Agent("Agent1")
agent2 = Agent("Agent2")
```

```
coordinator = Coordinator("Coordinator")

coordinator.coordinate([agent1, agent2])
```

In this example, the **Coordinator** sends out updates to all agents to keep them informed about the status of their tasks.

6.4 Managing Team Dynamics and Conflict

In multi-agent teams, agents must work together harmoniously to achieve their goals. However, agents may encounter conflicts, misunderstandings, or inefficiencies in their interactions. Managing **team dynamics** and resolving conflicts are critical for maintaining the system's performance.

Strategies for Managing Team Dynamics:

1. **Role Clarity:**
   o Ensure that each agent has a clear understanding of its role and responsibilities. This helps to avoid overlapping efforts and confusion within the team.
2. **Conflict Resolution Mechanisms:**
   o Agents must have predefined protocols for resolving conflicts, such as negotiating, reassigning tasks, or deferring to a leader. Mediation strategies can also be implemented in the system.
3. **Performance Monitoring:**
   o Regularly monitor agent performance to ensure that agents are contributing effectively. Agents who are underperforming or causing disruptions may need to be reassigned or retrained.

Example: Conflict Resolution Between Two Agents

In this example, two agents must negotiate to resolve a conflict where both want to pick up the same item:

```
class NegotiationAgent(Agent):
    def __init__(self, name):
        super().__init__(name)

    def negotiate(self, other_agent):
```

```
        print(f"{self.name} is negotiating with
{other_agent.name}.")
        # Assume a simple strategy where both agents take
turns
        print(f"{self.name} agrees to let {other_agent.name}
pick up the item first.")

# Example usage
agent1 = NegotiationAgent("Agent1")
agent2 = NegotiationAgent("Agent2")

agent1.negotiate(agent2)
```

In this case, **Agent1** negotiates with **Agent2** to resolve the conflict over the item. After negotiation, **Agent1** agrees to let **Agent2** pick up the item first, demonstrating a basic conflict resolution strategy.

6.5 Quiz

Now that you have learned about building agent teams, task assignment, coordination, and managing team dynamics, let's test your understanding with the following quiz:

1. What is the main goal of forming agent teams in a multi-agent system?

- a) To reduce the number of agents in the system.
- b) To divide tasks and optimize the performance of the system.
- c) To allow each agent to work independently.
- d) To eliminate communication between agents.

2. What is decentralized task assignment?

- a) A single controller assigns tasks to all agents.
- b) Agents decide independently which tasks to perform based on local information.
- c) Tasks are assigned based on agent's physical location.
- d) Agents work without performing any tasks.

3. Which of the following is a key challenge in team coordination?

- a) Ensuring that only one agent can act at a time.
- b) Ensuring that agents share information and avoid conflicts.
- c) Eliminating all communication between agents.
- d) Restricting agents to only reactive behaviors.

4. How can team dynamics be effectively managed in a multi-agent system?

- a) By assigning identical roles to all agents.
- b) By avoiding any form of communication between agents.
- c) By clearly defining roles and responsibilities and resolving conflicts when they arise.
- d) By allowing agents to act without any constraints.

5. What should be done when a conflict arises between two agents?

- a) One agent should be removed from the system.
- b) The agents should negotiate or resolve the conflict based on predefined protocols.
- c) All agents should stop performing tasks.
- d) The agents should be reset to their original state.

Answers:

1. **b)** To divide tasks and optimize the performance of the system.
2. **b)** Agents decide independently which tasks to perform based on local information.
3. **b)** Ensuring that agents share information and avoid conflicts.
4. **c)** By clearly defining roles and responsibilities and resolving conflicts when they arise.
5. **b)** The agents should negotiate or resolve the conflict based on predefined protocols.

Chapter 7: Agent Learning and Adaptation

As multi-agent systems become more complex, agents must be able to **learn** from their experiences and **adapt** to changing environments. In this chapter, we will explore how agents can use various learning techniques to improve their performance, make decisions, and adapt to their surroundings. These techniques include **reinforcement learning**, **supervised learning**, **unsupervised learning**, and methods for fine-tuning agent models to improve their accuracy and efficiency.

7.1 Reinforcement Learning for Agents

Reinforcement Learning (RL) is a type of machine learning where agents learn how to behave in an environment by performing actions and receiving feedback in the form of rewards or penalties. The goal of reinforcement learning is to maximize the cumulative reward over time by learning an optimal policy — a mapping of states to actions that will yield the highest rewards.

Key Concepts in Reinforcement Learning:

1. **Agent:**
   o The entity that interacts with the environment, learns from feedback, and takes actions.
2. **Environment:**
   o The surroundings in which the agent operates. It reacts to the agent's actions and provides feedback.
3. **State (s):**
   o The condition or situation of the environment at a particular time.
4. **Action (a):**
   o The decision or move made by the agent that influences the environment.
5. **Reward (r):**
   o A numerical value given to the agent as feedback after taking an action in a particular state.

6. **Policy (π):**
   - A strategy or rule that the agent uses to decide which action to take in a given state.
7. **Value Function (V):**
   - A function that estimates the expected cumulative reward the agent can receive from a given state, following a particular policy.
8. **Q-Function (Q):**
   - A function that estimates the expected cumulative reward for a given state-action pair, helping the agent decide which action to take in each state.

Example: Q-Learning in Reinforcement Learning

In Q-learning, the agent uses a Q-table to store the expected rewards for different state-action pairs. The agent updates this table after each action it performs, gradually learning the best actions for each state.

```python
import numpy as np

class QLearningAgent:
    def __init__(self, states, actions, alpha=0.1, gamma=0.9,
epsilon=0.1):
        self.states = states
        self.actions = actions
        self.alpha = alpha    # Learning rate
        self.gamma = gamma    # Discount factor
        self.epsilon = epsilon   # Exploration rate
        self.q_table = np.zeros((len(states), len(actions)))
# Initialize Q-table with zeros

    def choose_action(self, state):
        if np.random.rand() < self.epsilon:   # Exploration
            return np.random.choice(self.actions)
        else:   # Exploitation
            return np.argmax(self.q_table[state])   # Choose
the action with the highest Q-value

    def update_q_table(self, state, action, reward,
next_state):
        best_next_action =
np.argmax(self.q_table[next_state])
        td_target = reward + self.gamma *
self.q_table[next_state, best_next_action]
        self.q_table[state, action] += self.alpha *
(td_target - self.q_table[state, action])
```

```
# Example usage
states = [0, 1, 2, 3]  # States represent different
conditions in the environment
actions = [0, 1]  # Action 0: move left, Action 1: move right
agent = QLearningAgent(states, actions)

# Simulate an episode
state = 0
for _ in range(10):
    action = agent.choose_action(state)
    reward = -1 if action == 0 else 1  # Reward: -1 for left,
+1 for right
    next_state = state + 1 if action == 1 else state - 1
    agent.update_q_table(state, action, reward, next_state)
    state = next_state
```

In this example:

- **QLearningAgent** uses Q-learning to update its Q-table as it learns from the environment.
- The agent explores the environment and gradually improves its decision-making by updating the Q-values.

7.2 Supervised and Unsupervised Learning for Agents

While **reinforcement learning** focuses on learning from rewards and feedback, **supervised** and **unsupervised learning** are two other types of machine learning that can be applied to agents in different contexts.

Supervised Learning for Agents:

In supervised learning, an agent learns from labeled data provided by a teacher or trainer. The agent's goal is to learn a mapping from inputs to outputs (or labels) by minimizing an error function.

Example: An agent may learn to classify images based on labeled data, where each image is paired with a label (e.g., "cat" or "dog"). The agent uses this data to learn the mapping between the image features and the labels.

Example: Supervised Learning Using a Neural Network

```
import numpy as np
from sklearn.neural_network import MLPClassifier

# Sample dataset: features and labels
X = np.array([[1, 2], [2, 3], [3, 3], [4, 5], [5, 6]])  #
Features
y = np.array([0, 0, 1, 1, 1])  # Labels: 0 for cat, 1 for dog

# Create and train a neural network classifier
clf = MLPClassifier(hidden_layer_sizes=(5,), max_iter=1000)
clf.fit(X, y)

# Predicting a new example
new_data = np.array([[3, 4]])
prediction = clf.predict(new_data)
print(f"Predicted label: {prediction[0]}")
```

In this example, the **MLPClassifier** is used to train a neural network on the labeled dataset. The agent learns to classify the data based on the provided labels.

Unsupervised Learning for Agents:

In unsupervised learning, agents are given data without any labels and must find patterns or structure in the data. Clustering and dimensionality reduction are common tasks in unsupervised learning.

Example: An agent could use unsupervised learning to group similar items in a shopping cart into categories (e.g., grouping fruit together).

Example: Unsupervised Learning Using K-means Clustering

```
from sklearn.cluster import KMeans

# Sample dataset: features representing items in a shopping
cart
X = np.array([[1, 2], [2, 3], [10, 11], [12, 13], [30, 31]])

# Create and train a K-means clustering model
kmeans = KMeans(n_clusters=2)
kmeans.fit(X)

# Predict the cluster for a new item
new_item = np.array([[5, 6]])
cluster = kmeans.predict(new_item)
```

```
print(f"Predicted cluster: {cluster[0]}")
```

In this example, **KMeans** is used to group items into clusters, and the agent predicts which cluster a new item belongs to.

7.3 Adaptive Behaviors in Agents

Adaptive behaviors refer to the ability of agents to adjust their actions and strategies in response to changes in the environment, feedback from other agents, or their own performance. This adaptability is crucial for agents that operate in dynamic, uncertain environments.

Key Elements of Adaptive Behavior:

1. **Learning from Experience:**
   o Agents can use past experiences to adapt their future behavior. This could involve learning new strategies, improving existing ones, or abandoning ineffective approaches.
2. **Context-Aware Decision Making:**
   o Adaptive agents can assess their environment and make decisions based on the current context, rather than relying on pre-defined rules or rigid behaviors.
3. **Dynamic Behavior Adjustment:**
   o Agents can modify their strategies in real-time based on changing environmental conditions, task requirements, or feedback from the system.

Example: Adaptive Behavior Using Q-learning

In **Q-learning**, agents can adapt their strategies over time by continuously adjusting their actions to maximize rewards. This allows them to adapt to a changing environment and improve performance based on accumulated knowledge.

7.4 Fine-Tuning Agent Models

After an agent has been trained using reinforcement learning, supervised learning, or other methods, it is often necessary to fine-tune its model to improve its performance or adapt to new data. **Fine-tuning** involves adjusting the agent's parameters (such as learning rates or model weights) to optimize its performance further.

Fine-Tuning Strategies:

1. **Hyperparameter Tuning:**
   o Adjust hyperparameters such as learning rates, discount factors, and exploration rates to find the optimal settings for the agent's learning process.
2. **Model Calibration:**
   o If the agent is using a predictive model (e.g., a neural network), fine-tuning the model's weights and biases through additional training or regularization can improve its accuracy.
3. **Transfer Learning:**
   o In some cases, agents can leverage pre-trained models from similar tasks to speed up learning and achieve better performance with fewer training iterations.

Example: Fine-Tuning a Neural Network Using Scikit-learn

```
from sklearn.neural_network import MLPClassifier
from sklearn.model_selection import GridSearchCV

# Define the parameter grid for tuning
param_grid = {'hidden_layer_sizes': [(5,), (10,), (15,)],
'max_iter': [1000, 2000]}

# Create a neural network model
clf = MLPClassifier()

# Perform grid search for hyperparameter tuning
grid_search = GridSearchCV(clf, param_grid)
grid_search.fit(X, y)

# Get the best parameters and model
print(f"Best parameters: {grid_search.best_params_}")
```

In this example, **GridSearchCV** is used to fine-tune the neural network's hyperparameters, finding the optimal configuration for better performance.

7.5 Reflection Questions

Reflecting on the concepts covered in this chapter is crucial for understanding how learning and adaptation are implemented in agents. Consider the following questions:

1. **What are the key differences between reinforcement

learning and supervised learning for agents?**

    - Reflect on how each approach works and in what scenarios each would be most effective.

2. **How do adaptive behaviors improve the performance of agents in dynamic environments?**
    o   Think about how agents can respond to environmental changes and the role of experience in improving decision-making.
3. **Why is fine-tuning important for agent models, and how can it help improve performance?**
    o   Consider the challenges in training agent models and how fine-tuning can help refine them for better results.
4. **What challenges might arise when using unsupervised learning to group or categorize data for agents?**
    o   Reflect on the potential difficulties in applying unsupervised learning and how agents might overcome them.
5. **How can reinforcement learning be used to optimize agents' decision-making over time?**
    o   Think about the process of reinforcement learning and how agents adjust their behaviors to maximize rewards.

Chapter 8: Multi-agent Systems for Complex Problem Solving

Multi-agent systems (MAS) are powerful tools for solving complex problems, especially in environments that require decentralized decision-making, handling uncertainty, and optimizing solutions. In this chapter, we will explore how **Crew AI** can be applied to solve **combinatorial optimization problems**, manage **decentralized decision-making**, address challenges involving **uncertainty and risk**, and tackle **scalability issues** in large-scale systems. By the end of this chapter, you will have a clear understanding of how to design and implement multi-agent systems for complex, real-world problem-solving tasks.

8.1 Solving Combinatorial Optimization Problems

Combinatorial optimization involves finding the best solution from a finite set of possible solutions. These problems often arise in various fields such as logistics, scheduling, resource allocation, and routing. The goal is to optimize certain criteria, such as minimizing cost or maximizing efficiency.

How Multi-agent Systems Solve Combinatorial Optimization:

In multi-agent systems, each agent can be responsible for exploring a part of the solution space and proposing partial solutions. The agents can collaborate or compete to find the optimal solution. The process typically involves:

- **Task Decomposition:** Breaking down the problem into smaller, manageable subproblems that can be tackled by individual agents.
- **Exploration:** Agents explore different parts of the solution space, evaluating potential solutions.
- **Cooperation and Coordination:** Agents coordinate their findings and combine partial solutions to reach an optimal or near-optimal result.

Example: Solving the Traveling Salesman Problem (TSP) with MAS

In the **Traveling Salesman Problem (TSP)**, the goal is to find the shortest route that visits a set of cities and returns to the starting point. A multi-agent approach can be used where each agent is responsible for exploring a subset of possible routes and coordinating with other agents to exchange information and improve the overall solution.

```python
import random

class TSPAgent:
    def __init__(self, cities, max_iterations=1000):
        self.cities = cities
        self.max_iterations = max_iterations
        self.route = self.random_route()
        self.best_route = self.route
        self.best_distance =
self.calculate_distance(self.route)

    def random_route(self):
        return random.sample(self.cities, len(self.cities))

    def calculate_distance(self, route):
        distance = 0
        for i in range(len(route) - 1):
            distance += self.distance_between(route[i],
route[i+1])
        distance += self.distance_between(route[-1],
route[0])  # Return to start
        return distance

    def distance_between(self, city1, city2):
        # For simplicity, using Manhattan distance as a
placeholder
        return abs(city1[0] - city2[0]) + abs(city1[1] -
city2[1])

    def explore(self):
        # Randomly swap two cities in the current route
        route_copy = self.route[:]
        i, j = random.sample(range(len(route_copy)), 2)
        route_copy[i], route_copy[j] = route_copy[j],
route_copy[i]
        return route_copy

    def improve(self):
        for _ in range(self.max_iterations):
            new_route = self.explore()
```

```
        new_distance = self.calculate_distance(new_route)
        if new_distance < self.best_distance:
            self.best_route = new_route
            self.best_distance = new_distance

    return self.best_route, self.best_distance


# Example usage
cities = [(0, 0), (1, 3), (3, 1), (4, 4), (6, 2)]
agent = TSPAgent(cities)
best_route, best_distance = agent.improve()
print(f"Best route: {best_route}")
print(f"Best distance: {best_distance}")
```

In this example, the **TSPAgent** explores the solution space by swapping two cities in the current route and evaluates the new solution. This process is repeated, and the agent adapts its route to minimize the distance. Multiple agents could collaborate by exchanging routes and refining solutions further.

8.2 Addressing Decentralized Decision-Making

In multi-agent systems, agents often need to make decisions without relying on a central authority. **Decentralized decision-making** is essential for tasks that require distributed control, such as in large-scale systems or environments with multiple conflicting interests.

Key Challenges in Decentralized Decision-Making:

1. **Information Asymmetry:**
   - Different agents may have access to different pieces of information, and they must make decisions based on incomplete knowledge.
2. **Coordination:**
   - Without a central authority, agents must coordinate with each other to ensure that their actions align toward achieving the global goal.
3. **Conflict Resolution:**
   - Agents may have conflicting goals or interests, so effective mechanisms for negotiation and conflict resolution are necessary.

Example: Decentralized Decision-Making in a Supply Chain

Consider a supply chain where different agents represent manufacturers, distributors, and retailers. Each agent has different priorities, such as cost minimization or inventory optimization. These agents must make decisions on when and how much to produce, order, or deliver without a central authority.

```
class SupplyChainAgent:
    def __init__(self, name, priority, demand):
        self.name = name
        self.priority = priority  # Cost or inventory
optimization
        self.demand = demand  # Product demand in the system

    def make_decision(self):
        if self.priority == 'cost':
            decision = "Minimize production cost"
        elif self.priority == 'inventory':
            decision = "Maximize product availability"
        else:
            decision = "Balanced approach"
        return decision

    def coordinate(self, other_agent):
        print(f"{self.name} is coordinating with
{other_agent.name}")
        # Simple negotiation example
        if self.priority != other_agent.priority:
            print(f"Negotiating priority: {self.name}
({self.priority}) vs {other_agent.name}
({other_agent.priority})")
        else:
            print(f"Aligned goals: {self.name} and
{other_agent.name} both focus on {self.priority}.")

# Example usage
retailer = SupplyChainAgent("Retailer", "inventory", 500)
distributor = SupplyChainAgent("Distributor", "cost", 300)

retailer.make_decision()
distributor.make_decision()

retailer.coordinate(distributor)
```

In this example, the agents decide based on their priorities, and they coordinate with each other through negotiation to ensure that their actions align with the overall supply chain objectives.

8.3 Handling Uncertainty and Risk

In real-world scenarios, agents often operate in environments that are uncertain or risky. **Uncertainty** refers to situations where agents do not have full information about the environment or other agents' actions, while **risk** involves the potential for negative outcomes. Handling both uncertainty and risk effectively is crucial for ensuring that multi-agent systems function reliably.

Approaches to Handle Uncertainty and Risk:

1. **Probabilistic Reasoning:**
   o Agents can use probability theory to model and predict uncertain outcomes, such as in environments with incomplete or noisy data.
2. **Risk Mitigation:**
   o Agents can take steps to mitigate risks, such as by diversifying actions, using redundancy, or employing backup strategies when certain conditions are met.
3. **Monte Carlo Methods:**
   o Monte Carlo simulations can help agents evaluate different scenarios under uncertainty by running simulations with random inputs and analyzing the results.

Example: Handling Uncertainty in a Stock Trading Agent

Imagine a stock trading agent that must decide when to buy or sell stocks in an uncertain market. The agent uses probabilistic reasoning and Monte Carlo simulations to assess different actions and their associated risks.

```python
import random

class TradingAgent:
    def __init__(self, name):
        self.name = name
        self.balance = 10000  # Starting capital

    def assess_market(self):
        # Simulate market fluctuations with random
uncertainty
```

```
        return random.uniform(-0.05, 0.05)  # Random price
change between -5% and 5%

    def make_trade_decision(self):
        price_change = self.assess_market()
        if price_change > 0.02:  # Buy if price increases by
more than 2%
            return "Buy"
        elif price_change < -0.02:  # Sell if price decreases
by more than 2%
            return "Sell"
        else:
            return "Hold"

# Example usage
agent = TradingAgent("Trader 1")
decision = agent.make_trade_decision()
print(f"{agent.name} decision: {decision}")
```

In this example, the **TradingAgent** uses random price changes to simulate market uncertainty and makes a decision based on the predicted price movement.

8.4 Addressing Scalability Challenges

Scalability is a significant challenge in multi-agent systems, especially when the number of agents increases. As the number of agents grows, the complexity of coordination, communication, and decision-making increases exponentially.

Strategies to Address Scalability:

1. **Hierarchical Structures:**
   o Organizing agents into hierarchical structures can help manage complexity. Higher-level agents can coordinate the actions of lower-level agents, reducing the overall coordination burden.
2. **Decentralized Control:**
   o Decentralized control allows agents to make decisions independently, reducing the need for global coordination. However, this requires sophisticated algorithms to manage interactions and conflicts.

3. **Distributed Systems:**
   o Distributing the agents across different systems or servers can help manage the computational load and improve scalability.

Example: Using Hierarchical Coordination for Scalability

Here, a higher-level **Manager Agent** coordinates a team of lower-level **Worker Agents**:

```
class ManagerAgent:
    def __init__(self, name):
        self.name = name
        self.workers = []

    def add_worker(self, worker):
        self.workers.append(worker)

    def coordinate(self):
        for worker in self.workers:
            print(f"{self.name} is assigning tasks to
{worker.name}")

class WorkerAgent:
    def __init__(self, name):
        self.name = name

    def perform_task(self):
        print(f"{self.name} is performing a task.")

# Example usage
manager = ManagerAgent("Manager 1")
worker1 = WorkerAgent("Worker 1")
worker2 = WorkerAgent("Worker 2")

manager.add_worker(worker1)
manager.add_worker(worker2)

manager.coordinate()
worker1.perform_task()
worker2.perform_task()
```

In this example, the **ManagerAgent** handles coordination for multiple **WorkerAgents**, demonstrating a scalable hierarchical structure.

8.5 Exercise: Implementing a Complex Problem Solver

Objective:

Implement a **multi-agent system** that solves a complex problem, such as **vehicle routing**, by using agents that represent vehicles in a delivery system. The system should include task assignment, coordination, and decision-making.

Steps:

1. **Define Agent Roles:**
   - Create **VehicleAgent** classes that represent different vehicles in the fleet.
   - Assign tasks such as picking up goods from different locations and delivering them to customers.
2. **Task Assignment:**
   - Implement a **CoordinatorAgent** that assigns tasks to **VehicleAgents** based on proximity to the target location.
3. **Coordination and Communication:**
   - Implement communication between the agents to share their progress and avoid conflicts.
4. **Decision-Making:**
   - Implement decision-making logic for each agent to determine the most efficient route, using techniques like **greedy algorithms** or **genetic algorithms**.
5. **Simulation:**
   - Simulate the operation of the fleet over multiple iterations and evaluate the performance of the system.

Example Template for VehicleAgent Class

```
class VehicleAgent:
    def __init__(self, name, location):
        self.name = name
        self.location = location
        self.current_task = None

    def assign_task(self, task):
        self.current_task = task
        print(f"{self.name} assigned to task: {task}")
```

```python
    def perform_task(self):
        if self.current_task:
            print(f"{self.name} is performing task:
{self.current_task}")
            self.current_task = None
```

This exercise will help you understand how to implement multi-agent coordination, decision-making, and task allocation in complex systems.

Chapter 9: Integrating Crew AI with Other Technologies

In real-world applications, **Crew AI** can be enhanced and empowered by integrating with other technologies. These integrations allow multi-agent systems to interact with machine learning models, gather data from IoT devices, scale through cloud platforms, and engage in human-AI interactions. This chapter will explore how **Crew AI** can be integrated with various technologies to build more intelligent, scalable, and adaptive systems.

9.1 Integrating with Machine Learning Frameworks

Machine learning (ML) frameworks enable agents to learn from data, improve their performance over time, and make better decisions. Integrating **Crew AI** with ML frameworks allows agents to become more adaptable, intelligent, and capable of handling complex tasks in dynamic environments.

Why Integrate with Machine Learning Frameworks?

1. **Improved Decision-Making:**
   o Agents can use ML models to make decisions based on historical data, predictions, and probabilistic reasoning.
2. **Enhanced Adaptability:**
   o Agents can adapt to changing environments by using ML algorithms to update their knowledge base or learning models in real-time.
3. **Optimized Performance:**
   o Integrating Crew AI with machine learning can enable agents to optimize their actions over time, improving efficiency and effectiveness in task execution.

Common Machine Learning Frameworks:

- **TensorFlow:** A popular ML framework for building and training deep learning models.

- **PyTorch:** A flexible and powerful framework for deep learning and reinforcement learning.
- **Scikit-learn:** A simple and efficient library for machine learning in Python, often used for more traditional ML algorithms like decision trees, clustering, and regression.

Example: Integrating Crew AI with a Neural Network in PyTorch

In this example, we integrate a **Crew AI agent** with a **PyTorch neural network** to predict the best action based on the agent's current state.

```python
import torch
import torch.nn as nn
import torch.optim as optim
from crew_ai import Agent

# Define a simple neural network model
class SimpleNN(nn.Module):
    def __init__(self, input_size, output_size):
        super(SimpleNN, self).__init__()
        self.fc1 = nn.Linear(input_size, 64)
        self.fc2 = nn.Linear(64, 32)
        self.fc3 = nn.Linear(32, output_size)

    def forward(self, x):
        x = torch.relu(self.fc1(x))
        x = torch.relu(self.fc2(x))
        x = self.fc3(x)
        return x

class MLAgent(Agent):
    def __init__(self, name, input_size, output_size):
        super().__init__(name)
        self.model = SimpleNN(input_size, output_size)
        self.optimizer = optim.Adam(self.model.parameters(),
lr=0.001)
        self.criterion = nn.MSELoss()

    def predict(self, state):
        state_tensor = torch.tensor(state,
dtype=torch.float32)
        action_scores = self.model(state_tensor)
        return action_scores.argmax().item()

    def train(self, state, target_action):
        state_tensor = torch.tensor(state,
dtype=torch.float32)
```

```
        target_tensor = torch.tensor([target_action],
dtype=torch.float32)

        self.optimizer.zero_grad()
        action_scores = self.model(state_tensor)
        loss = self.criterion(action_scores, target_tensor)
        loss.backward()
        self.optimizer.step()

# Example usage
agent = MLAgent("Agent1", input_size=5, output_size=3)   # 5
features, 3 possible actions
state = [1.0, 0.5, -0.3, 0.8, 0.2]
action = agent.predict(state)
print(f"Predicted action: {action}")

# Train the model
agent.train(state, action)
```

In this example:

- **MLAgent** integrates with a simple **PyTorch neural network** to predict the best action for the agent based on its current state.
- The agent is trained to improve its predictions using backpropagation and gradient descent.

9.2 Integrating with IoT Devices

Internet of Things (IoT) devices are physical objects that collect and exchange data with other devices or systems. Integrating **Crew AI** with IoT devices allows agents to interact with the physical world, respond to sensor data, and take actions that affect their environment in real-time.

Why Integrate with IoT Devices?

1. **Real-Time Data Collection:**
   o IoT devices can provide agents with real-time data from the environment, such as temperature, humidity, location, or even human interactions.
2. **Actuation:**

- Agents can control IoT devices, such as turning on lights, adjusting thermostats, or controlling machines, based on their decision-making process.
3. **Environmental Awareness:**
   - Agents can use the data from IoT devices to gain a better understanding of their environment and adapt their behaviors accordingly.

Example: Integrating Crew AI with an IoT Temperature Sensor

Suppose we have an **IoT temperature sensor** that provides data about the room's temperature. A **Crew AI agent** can use this data to decide whether to turn on a fan or adjust the heating system.

```python
import random
from crew_ai import Agent

class IoTTemperatureAgent(Agent):
    def __init__(self, name):
        super().__init__(name)
        self.temperature = 22  # Initial temperature in
Celsius

    def read_temperature(self):
        # Simulating reading temperature from a real IoT
sensor
        self.temperature = random.uniform(18, 30)
        print(f"{self.name} reads temperature:
{self.temperature}°C")

    def control_temperature(self):
        self.read_temperature()
        if self.temperature > 25:
            print(f"{self.name} is turning on the fan to cool
down.")
        elif self.temperature < 20:
            print(f"{self.name} is turning on the heater to
warm up.")
        else:
            print(f"{self.name} is keeping the temperature
stable.")

# Example usage
agent = IoTTemperatureAgent("TempAgent")
agent.control_temperature()
```

In this example:

- The **IoTTemperatureAgent** reads temperature data from an **IoT sensor** (simulated here with random values).
- The agent controls the environment based on the temperature by either turning on a fan or heater.

9.3 Integrating with Cloud Platforms

Cloud platforms provide scalable resources for running large-scale systems and storing vast amounts of data. Integrating **Crew AI** with cloud platforms enables multi-agent systems to leverage the computational power, storage, and scalability of the cloud.

Why Integrate with Cloud Platforms?

1. **Scalability:**
   - Cloud platforms offer elastic resources, allowing multi-agent systems to scale up or down based on the demand.
2. **Distributed Computing:**
   - Cloud platforms can distribute the workload across multiple machines, allowing agents to operate in parallel and share information seamlessly.
3. **Storage and Data Access:**
   - Agents can store and retrieve data from cloud storage, enabling them to access large datasets and collaborate on tasks that require substantial data processing.

Example: Integrating Crew AI with AWS S3 for Data Storage

In this example, we demonstrate how **Crew AI** agents can store and retrieve data from **Amazon S3**, a popular cloud storage service.

```python
import boto3
from crew_ai import Agent

class CloudAgent(Agent):
    def __init__(self, name, s3_bucket_name):
        super().__init__(name)
        self.s3_bucket_name = s3_bucket_name
        self.s3_client = boto3.client('s3')

    def store_data(self, data):
```

```
        # Store data in S3 bucket
        self.s3_client.put_object(Bucket=self.s3_bucket_name,
Key=f"{self.name}_data.txt", Body=data)
        print(f"{self.name} has stored data in S3.")

    def retrieve_data(self):
        # Retrieve data from S3 bucket
        response =
self.s3_client.get_object(Bucket=self.s3_bucket_name,
Key=f"{self.name}_data.txt")
        data = response['Body'].read().decode('utf-8')
        print(f"{self.name} retrieved data from S3: {data}")
        return data

# Example usage
agent = CloudAgent("CloudAgent", "my-crew-ai-bucket")
agent.store_data("Temperature data: 22°C")
agent.retrieve_data()
```

In this example:

- The **CloudAgent** stores and retrieves data from **Amazon S3** using the **boto3** library.
- This integration allows the agent to leverage cloud storage for data persistence and retrieval.

9.4 Integrating with Human-AI Interaction Systems

Integrating **Crew AI** with human-AI interaction systems enables agents to collaborate with humans in real-time. Human-AI interaction systems can involve speech recognition, natural language processing (NLP), and graphical user interfaces (GUIs), allowing agents to understand and respond to human input.

Why Integrate with Human-AI Interaction Systems?

1. **Natural Communication:**
   o   Human-AI interaction systems allow agents to communicate with humans in natural language or through intuitive interfaces.
2. **Collaboration:**

o Agents can work alongside humans, providing recommendations, performing tasks, or assisting with decision-making.

3. **Learning from Human Feedback:**
   o Agents can learn from feedback provided by humans, improving their behavior and adapting to human preferences.

Example: Integrating Crew AI with a Simple Voice Assistant

Let's integrate **Crew AI** with a **speech recognition system** using Python's **SpeechRecognition** library.

```python
import speech_recognition as sr
from crew_ai import Agent

class VoiceAssistantAgent(Agent):
    def __init__(self, name):
        super().__init__(name)
        self.recognizer = sr.Recognizer()

    def listen(self):
        with sr.Microphone() as source:
            print(f"{self.name} is listening...")
            audio = self.recognizer.listen(source)
        return audio

    def process_speech(self, audio):
        try:
            speech_text =
self.recognizer.recognize_google(audio)
            print(f"{self.name} heard: {speech_text}")
            return speech_text
        except sr.UnknownValueError:
            print("Sorry, I could not understand the audio.")
            return None
        except sr.RequestError:
            print("Could not request results from Google
Speech Recognition service.")
            return None

# Example usage
assistant = VoiceAssistantAgent("Assistant")
audio = assistant.listen()
assistant.process_speech(audio)
```

In this example:

- The **VoiceAssistantAgent** listens for audio input through the microphone and processes the speech using **Google's Speech Recognition API**.
- The agent processes spoken commands and can act accordingly, providing a human-AI interaction system.

9.5 Quiz

Now that you have learned about integrating **Crew AI** with various technologies, let's test your understanding with a quiz:

1. What is the main benefit of integrating Crew AI with machine learning frameworks?

- a) It allows agents to perform actions in the physical world.
- b) It enables agents to learn from data and make better decisions.
- c) It scales the system by adding more agents.
- d) It provides a user interface for human interaction.

2. How does integrating Crew AI with IoT devices benefit agents?

- a) It allows agents to access real-time environmental data.
- b) It allows agents to only perform predetermined tasks.
- c) It restricts agents to offline operation.
- d) It makes agents independent from the environment.

3. Why should Crew AI be integrated with cloud platforms?

- a) To enable agents to work in isolated environments.
- b) To leverage cloud computing power for scalability and distributed processing.
- c) To reduce the number of agents in the system.
- d) To make agents work in a single centralized environment.

4. What is the primary advantage of integrating Crew AI with human-AI interaction systems?

- a) To allow agents to communicate in natural language and collaborate with humans.
- b) To restrict agents to manual operations.
- c) To make agents operate without human input.
- d) To prevent agents from performing automated tasks.

5. What library is commonly used for integrating Crew AI with speech recognition systems?

- a) TensorFlow
- b) SpeechRecognition
- c) Keras
- d) PyTorch

Answers:

1. **b)** It enables agents to learn from data and make better decisions.
2. **a)** It allows agents to access real-time environmental data.
3. **b)** To leverage cloud computing power for scalability and distributed processing.
4. **a)** To allow agents to communicate in natural language and collaborate with humans.
5. **b)** SpeechRecognition

Chapter 10: Emerging Technologies in Multi-agent AI

As the field of **multi-agent AI** continues to evolve, it is increasingly influenced by emerging technologies that enhance the capabilities of agents and improve their performance in real-world applications. In this chapter, we will explore some of the most transformative emerging technologies that can be integrated with multi-agent systems. These include **Blockchain**, **Quantum Computing**, **Natural Language Processing (NLP)**, and **Edge Computing**. Each of these technologies offers new possibilities for solving complex problems, improving efficiency, and enabling new types of interactions between agents.

10.1 Blockchain Integration for Security and Transparency

Blockchain is a distributed ledger technology that enables secure, transparent, and tamper-proof record-keeping. In multi-agent systems, blockchain can be used to enhance **security** and **transparency** by providing a decentralized, immutable record of all transactions and interactions between agents.

Why Integrate Blockchain with Multi-agent AI?

1. **Security:**
   o Blockchain ensures that transactions or actions taken by agents are secure and cannot be tampered with. Each action is recorded in a block that is linked to the previous one, creating a chain that is highly resistant to fraud and manipulation.
2. **Transparency:**
   o Since blockchain operates on a public or semi-public ledger, all actions and interactions are transparent. This provides visibility into the system's operations, which is particularly useful in applications requiring auditing and trust, such as financial transactions or supply chain management.
3. **Decentralized Consensus:**

- o Blockchain enables agents to reach a consensus without needing a central authority. Agents can independently verify actions and outcomes, ensuring trust and fairness in distributed systems.

Example: Blockchain for Secure Transactions Between Agents

Let's consider a scenario where two agents are performing a transaction (e.g., exchanging goods in a decentralized marketplace). Blockchain can be used to record the transaction securely and ensure that neither agent can alter the transaction once it is completed.

```
import hashlib
import json
import time

class Blockchain:
    def __init__(self):
        self.chain = []
        self.create_block(previous_hash='1', proof=100)

    def create_block(self, proof, previous_hash):
        block = {
            'index': len(self.chain) + 1,
            'timestamp': time.time(),
            'proof': proof,
            'previous_hash': previous_hash,
            'transactions': []
        }
        self.chain.append(block)
        return block

    def add_transaction(self, sender, recipient, amount):
        transaction = {
            'sender': sender,
            'recipient': recipient,
            'amount': amount
        }
        self.chain[-1]['transactions'].append(transaction)

    def get_previous_block(self):
        return self.chain[-1]

    def hash_block(self, block):
        block_string = json.dumps(block,
sort_keys=True).encode()
        return hashlib.sha256(block_string).hexdigest()
```

```
# Example usage
blockchain = Blockchain()
blockchain.add_transaction(sender="Agent1",
recipient="Agent2", amount=100)
previous_block = blockchain.get_previous_block()
blockchain.create_block(proof=200,
previous_hash=blockchain.hash_block(previous_block))
print(blockchain.chain)
```

In this example:

- **Blockchain** is used to securely record transactions between agents (e.g., Agent1 sending money to Agent2).
- Each block contains the transaction, proof of work, and the previous block's hash to ensure integrity.

10.2 Quantum Computing Implications for AI

Quantum Computing represents a new paradigm in computing, where quantum bits (qubits) are used instead of classical bits to perform calculations. Quantum computing holds the potential to revolutionize AI by solving problems that are currently intractable for classical computers.

Why Quantum Computing is Important for Multi-agent AI:

1. **Speed and Efficiency:**
   - Quantum computers can process vast amounts of data in parallel, significantly speeding up tasks like optimization, pattern recognition, and data mining. For multi-agent systems, this could lead to faster decision-making and more efficient agent collaboration.
2. **Optimization:**
   - Quantum algorithms such as **Quantum Approximate Optimization Algorithm (QAOA)** and **Grover's Algorithm** can optimize solutions more efficiently than classical algorithms. These algorithms can be applied to complex multi-agent optimization problems, such as route planning or resource allocation.
3. **Enhanced Machine Learning:**

o Quantum machine learning algorithms can be used to improve the training of AI models, enabling more accurate predictions and better generalization.

Example: Quantum-inspired Optimization for Multi-agent Routing

While full quantum computing implementations are still in development, quantum-inspired optimization algorithms can be applied in multi-agent systems to improve decision-making.

```python
# This example uses a quantum-inspired classical algorithm
for optimization (simulated as a basic greedy approach).
import random

class QuantumInspiredAgent:
    def __init__(self, name, tasks):
        self.name = name
        self.tasks = tasks  # List of tasks to complete

    def optimize_route(self):
        # Simulate a quantum-inspired optimization by
selecting the shortest available task first
        task_order = sorted(self.tasks, key=lambda x:
x['time_needed'])
        print(f"{self.name} optimized route: {task_order}")
        return task_order

# Example usage
tasks = [
    {'task': 'Pick item A', 'time_needed': 5},
    {'task': 'Pick item B', 'time_needed': 2},
    {'task': 'Deliver item A', 'time_needed': 3}
]

agent = QuantumInspiredAgent("Agent1", tasks)
optimized_route = agent.optimize_route()
```

In this example, **QuantumInspiredAgent** uses a basic optimization approach that simulates quantum-inspired methods, where the agent selects the tasks with the shortest time first. This illustrates the potential for more efficient solutions in multi-agent systems.

10.3 Advances in Natural Language Processing for Agents

Natural Language Processing (NLP) is a branch of AI that focuses on the interaction between computers and human language. Advances in NLP allow agents to understand, generate, and respond to human language in a more natural and meaningful way.

Why NLP is Important for Multi-agent AI:

1. **Human-AI Communication:**
   o NLP enables agents to understand and communicate with humans in natural language, making them more accessible and useful in human-centric environments (e.g., customer support or personal assistants).
2. **Context Awareness:**
   o Modern NLP techniques like **Transformer models (e.g., GPT-3)** allow agents to understand context and respond more intelligently to conversational input.
3. **Automating Text-based Tasks:**
   o Agents can process and analyze large volumes of unstructured text (e.g., emails, reports) to extract useful information and make decisions.

Example: Integrating NLP for Human-Agent Interaction

Here's how you can integrate **Crew AI** with an NLP library like **spaCy** to enable an agent to process and respond to human input:

```python
import spacy
from crew_ai import Agent

# Load a pre-trained NLP model
nlp = spacy.load("en_core_web_sm")

class NLPAgent(Agent):
    def __init__(self, name):
        super().__init__(name)

    def understand_input(self, user_input):
        doc = nlp(user_input)
        # Extract named entities or perform other NLP tasks
```

```
        entities = [(ent.text, ent.label_) for ent in
doc.ents]
        return entities

    def respond(self, user_input):
        entities = self.understand_input(user_input)
        if entities:
            print(f"{self.name} identified entities:
{entities}")
        else:
            print(f"{self.name} couldn't understand any
entities.")

# Example usage
agent = NLPAgent("HelperAgent")
user_input = "Can you schedule a meeting with John Doe?"
agent.respond(user_input)
```

In this example:

- **NLPAgent** uses **spaCy** to process natural language input and identify named entities, such as people or locations. The agent can then respond appropriately based on the identified entities.

10.4 Edge Computing and Real-time Processing

Edge Computing refers to processing data closer to the source of data generation (e.g., IoT devices, sensors) rather than sending all data to a centralized cloud server. This is particularly useful for real-time applications where low latency is crucial.

Why Edge Computing is Important for Multi-agent AI:

1. **Low Latency:**
   o By processing data locally on the edge devices, multi-agent systems can make real-time decisions without the delay of transmitting data to the cloud.
2. **Bandwidth Efficiency:**
   o Edge computing reduces the need for transmitting large volumes of data to centralized servers, conserving bandwidth and reducing costs.
3. **Autonomy:**

o   Edge computing enables agents to make decisions autonomously, without relying on continuous communication with central servers, which is vital in environments with intermittent connectivity.

Example: Real-time Data Processing on Edge Devices

Here's an example where an edge device (like a **temperature sensor**) processes data locally to make immediate decisions without relying on a cloud server.

```
class EdgeAgent:
    def __init__(self, name, threshold):
        self.name = name
        self.temperature_threshold = threshold

    def process_data(self, temperature_data):
        if temperature_data > self.temperature_threshold:
            print(f"{self.name}: Temperature is high.
Activating cooling system.")
        else:
            print(f"{self.name}: Temperature is normal.")

# Example usage
sensor = EdgeAgent("TemperatureSensor", 25)
sensor.process_data(30)   # Simulate high temperature
```

In this example, the **EdgeAgent** processes temperature data locally and decides whether to activate the cooling system without needing to send data to a cloud server.

10.5 Reflection Questions

To deepen your understanding of the concepts covered in this chapter, consider the following reflection questions:

1. **How can blockchain improve the security and transparency of multi-agent systems?**
    o   Reflect on how decentralized consensus and tamper-proof records could benefit real-world applications, such as financial transactions or supply chains.

2. **What are the potential benefits of integrating quantum computing with multi-agent AI systems?**
    o Think about the challenges quantum computing can address in AI, such as optimization and large-scale data processing.
3. **How does NLP enhance the interaction between humans and agents?**
    o Consider how advances in NLP can make agents more responsive and adaptable in human-centric environments.
4. **What are the challenges and benefits of implementing edge computing in multi-agent systems?**
    o Reflect on how processing data locally can improve performance and reduce latency in time-sensitive applications.
5. **What practical applications could benefit from combining these emerging technologies (blockchain, quantum computing, NLP, edge computing)?**
    o Think about how these technologies could be integrated to create innovative solutions in fields such as healthcare, logistics, autonomous vehicles, or smart cities.

In **Chapter 10**, we explored several emerging technologies that are shaping the future of **multi-agent AI**. Integrating **blockchain**, **quantum computing**, **natural language processing**, and **edge computing** with **Crew AI** opens up new possibilities for solving complex problems, improving decision-making, and enhancing real-time interactions between agents and their environments. These technologies provide the tools necessary to build smarter, more secure, and more efficient multi-agent systems for a wide range of applications.

Certainly! Below is a detailed, clear, and professional write-up for **Chapter 11: Deployment Strategies** from **Part IV: Managing and Optimizing Multi-agent AI Systems**. This chapter covers key topics like **deployment architectures, CI/CD, containerization and orchestration**, and strategies for **scaling multi-agent systems**. A hands-on exercise will also be provided for deploying a multi-agent system.

Chapter 11: Deployment Strategies

Deploying multi-agent AI systems requires careful consideration of architectures, integration processes, and tools that ensure systems operate efficiently, are scalable, and can handle real-world demands. In this chapter, we will explore the best practices for deploying **Crew AI** systems, including deployment architectures (cloud, edge, hybrid), continuous integration and deployment (CI/CD) for AI systems, containerization and orchestration, and scaling strategies. By the end of this chapter, you will have a comprehensive understanding of how to deploy and optimize multi-agent systems effectively.

11.1 Deployment Architectures (Cloud, Edge, Hybrid)

The architecture you choose for deploying your multi-agent system plays a critical role in its performance, scalability, and reliability. Depending on the requirements of the system, deployment can occur in the **cloud**, **edge**, or a **hybrid** architecture that combines both. Let's take a deeper look at each of these deployment models.

1. Cloud Deployment

Cloud-based deployment involves running your multi-agent system in the cloud, leveraging cloud services for compute, storage, and network resources.

Advantages:

- **Scalability:** Cloud platforms offer elastic resources, enabling the system to scale up or down based on demand.
- **Accessibility:** Cloud-based systems are accessible from anywhere, facilitating remote management and monitoring.
- **Cost Efficiency:** Cloud providers typically offer pay-as-you-go pricing, making it cost-effective for dynamic workloads.

Use Cases: Large-scale AI systems, systems that require significant computational resources, and applications that need to be accessed remotely.

2. Edge Deployment

Edge computing involves deploying multi-agent systems closer to the data source (e.g., IoT devices, sensors, or local machines). The system processes data locally, reducing latency and dependency on remote servers.

Advantages:

- **Low Latency:** Processing data closer to the source enables real-time decision-making, which is crucial in time-sensitive applications.
- **Bandwidth Efficiency:** Reduces the amount of data sent to the cloud, conserving bandwidth and lowering costs.
- **Autonomy:** Edge devices can operate independently, even in environments with intermittent or no internet connectivity.

Use Cases: Autonomous vehicles, industrial automation, healthcare monitoring systems, and smart cities.

3. Hybrid Deployment

A **hybrid deployment** combines both cloud and edge computing. The multi-agent system performs some tasks locally on edge devices, while other, more resource-intensive tasks are offloaded to the cloud.

Advantages:

- **Flexibility:** Hybrid systems can balance the advantages of both cloud and edge deployments.
- **Optimized Performance:** Critical tasks that require low latency are processed locally, while data analysis and other heavy computational tasks are handled in the cloud.
- **Resilience:** This architecture provides redundancy, allowing the system to continue functioning even if one part (edge or cloud) experiences issues.

Use Cases: Large-scale systems that need both real-time processing and heavy computation, such as smart factories or autonomous fleets.

Example: Cloud and Edge Integration in a Multi-agent System

Consider a delivery system where agents in **autonomous vehicles** (edge devices) need to make real-time decisions based on sensor data (e.g., avoiding obstacles, optimizing routes), while a **central server** in the cloud handles scheduling, route planning, and coordination.

```python
class CloudAgent:
    def __init__(self):
        self.routes = {}

    def schedule_task(self, vehicle_id, route):
        self.routes[vehicle_id] = route
        print(f"Scheduled route for {vehicle_id}: {route}")

class EdgeAgent:
    def __init__(self, vehicle_id, cloud_agent):
        self.vehicle_id = vehicle_id
        self.cloud_agent = cloud_agent

    def receive_data(self, sensor_data):
        # Process real-time data locally
        print(f"{self.vehicle_id} processing sensor data
locally: {sensor_data}")

    def send_task(self, route):
        # Send route data to cloud for scheduling
        self.cloud_agent.schedule_task(self.vehicle_id,
route)

# Example usage
cloud = CloudAgent()
vehicle = EdgeAgent("Vehicle1", cloud)
vehicle.receive_data({"obstacle": "detected", "speed":
"30km/h"})
vehicle.send_task("RouteA")
```

In this example, **EdgeAgent** handles local decision-making, while **CloudAgent** schedules routes in the cloud, representing a hybrid deployment approach.

11.2 Continuous Integration and Deployment (CI/CD) for AI Systems

Continuous Integration (CI) and **Continuous Deployment (CD)** are practices that allow development teams to automatically integrate and deploy code changes. In the context of AI systems, CI/CD ensures that updates to models, code, and configurations are automatically tested, integrated, and deployed without manual intervention.

Why Implement CI/CD for Multi-agent AI?

1. **Efficiency:**
   o Automated testing and deployment save time, allowing rapid updates and improvements to the system.
2. **Reliability:**
   o Automated tests ensure that code changes do not break existing functionality, improving the overall stability of the system.
3. **Consistency:**
   o CI/CD pipelines ensure that the deployment process is consistent across environments (development, testing, production).

Steps in CI/CD for AI Systems:

1. **Code Commit:**
   o Developers push changes (code, models, configurations) to a version control system (e.g., Git).
2. **Automated Testing:**
   o The code is tested automatically using predefined tests to ensure that no errors are introduced.
3. **Model Training and Validation:**
   o For AI systems, CI/CD includes automating model training, validation, and evaluation to ensure models meet performance criteria before deployment.
4. **Deployment:**
   o After passing all tests, the updated code or model is deployed to the production environment.

Example: CI/CD Pipeline for Deploying an AI Model

A simple **GitHub Actions** CI/CD pipeline for deploying a model can be set up as follows:

```yaml
name: AI Model CI/CD Pipeline

on:
  push:
    branches:
      - main

jobs:
  build:
    runs-on: ubuntu-latest
    steps:
      - name: Checkout Code
        uses: actions/checkout@v2

      - name: Set up Python
        uses: actions/setup-python@v2
        with:
          python-version: '3.8'

      - name: Install dependencies
        run: |
          python -m pip install --upgrade pip
          pip install -r requirements.txt

      - name: Train AI Model
        run: |
          python train_model.py  # Script to train the AI
model

      - name: Test AI Model
        run: |
          python test_model.py  # Script to test the trained
model

      - name: Deploy Model to Production
        run: |
          python deploy_model.py  # Script to deploy the
model to production
```

This YAML pipeline:

- **Checks out** the code from the repository.
- **Installs dependencies** and trains the AI model.

- **Tests** the model and deploys it to production if all tests pass.

11.3 Containerization and Orchestration (e.g., Docker, Kubernetes)

Containerization involves packaging an application and its dependencies into a **container**, which ensures that the application runs consistently across different environments. **Orchestration** involves managing multiple containers, ensuring they communicate and scale effectively.

Why Containerize Multi-agent Systems?

1. **Portability:**
   - Containers encapsulate the application and its dependencies, making it easy to deploy the system across various environments (development, testing, production).
2. **Isolation:**
   - Containers provide process isolation, which ensures that different components of the multi-agent system do not interfere with each other.
3. **Scalability:**
   - Containers can be scaled horizontally by creating more instances to handle increased demand, making them ideal for large multi-agent systems.

Key Tools for Containerization and Orchestration:

- **Docker:** A platform for building, shipping, and running applications inside containers.
- **Kubernetes:** A system for automating the deployment, scaling, and management of containerized applications.

Example: Dockerizing a Multi-agent System

Let's create a **Dockerfile** to containerize a simple multi-agent system.

```
# Use an official Python runtime as a parent image
FROM python:3.8-slim
```

```
# Set the working directory in the container
WORKDIR /usr/src/app

# Copy the current directory contents into the container
COPY . .

# Install any needed dependencies
RUN pip install --no-cache-dir -r requirements.txt

# Make port 5000 available to the world outside the container
EXPOSE 5000

# Run the Python application when the container launches
CMD ["python", "app.py"]
```

This **Dockerfile**:

- Uses the official **Python** image.
- Copies the application code and installs dependencies.
- Exposes port 5000 (commonly used for web services).
- Specifies the command to run the application.

11.4 Scaling Multi-agent Systems

Scaling a multi-agent system is crucial for ensuring that it can handle an increasing number of agents, tasks, and data. There are two primary strategies for scaling multi-agent systems:

1. Horizontal Scaling (Scaling Out):

- Adding more agents or instances to distribute the load. This is often done in cloud environments, where new virtual machines (VMs) or containers are spun up automatically based on demand.

2. Vertical Scaling (Scaling Up):

- Increasing the capacity (CPU, memory, etc.) of existing agents or servers to handle more load.

Strategies for Scaling Multi-agent Systems:

1. **Load Balancing:**
   - o Distribute tasks evenly across agents or containers to ensure no single agent or container becomes overloaded.
2. **Partitioning:**
   - o Divide the problem space into smaller subspaces, where each agent or container handles a specific subset of tasks or data.
3. **Auto-scaling:**
   - o Use cloud-native tools to automatically scale the system by adding or removing agents based on workload.

Example: Horizontal Scaling in Kubernetes

In **Kubernetes**, you can scale a service (e.g., your multi-agent system) by adjusting the number of replicas. Here's an example of a **Kubernetes deployment** configuration that automatically scales the number of replicas:

```
apiVersion: apps/v1
kind: Deployment
metadata:
  name: multi-agent-system
spec:
  replicas: 3  # Number of replicas (agents)
  selector:
    matchLabels:
      app: multi-agent-system
  template:
    metadata:
      labels:
        app: multi-agent-system
    spec:
      containers:
      - name: multi-agent-container
        image: multi-agent-system-image:latest
        ports:
        - containerPort: 5000
```

In this example:

- Kubernetes will maintain 3 replicas of the **multi-agent-system** container, ensuring that the system can handle more traffic.
- Kubernetes can automatically scale the replicas based on resource usage.

11.5 Exercise: Deploying a Multi-agent System

Objective:

Deploy a simple **multi-agent system** on a cloud platform using **Docker** and **Kubernetes**.

Steps:

1. **Create a Multi-agent System:**
   - o Develop a simple multi-agent system (e.g., agents performing different tasks like data collection, decision-making, or optimization).
2. **Containerize the System:**
   - o Write a **Dockerfile** to containerize the system and ensure it runs consistently across different environments.
3. **Deploy Using Kubernetes

.**

- Create a **Kubernetes deployment** file to deploy multiple instances of your system on a cloud platform (e.g., AWS, Google Cloud, or Azure).
- Set up horizontal scaling and auto-scaling rules to handle varying loads.

4. **Test and Monitor the System:**
   - o Monitor the deployment and ensure that all agents are functioning properly. Use **Kubernetes monitoring tools** (e.g., Prometheus) to track performance.

Chapter 12: Monitoring and Maintenance

Effective **monitoring** and **maintenance** are critical for ensuring the long-term success and reliability of **multi-agent AI systems**. In this chapter, we will explore tools and techniques for **real-time monitoring**, best practices for maintaining multi-agent systems, strategies for handling failures and ensuring system reliability, and how to optimize system performance through various metrics.

By the end of this chapter, you will understand how to monitor the health of your multi-agent AI system, ensure its continued performance, and implement strategies for quick recovery and long-term optimization.

12.1 Real-time Monitoring Tools and Techniques

Real-time monitoring refers to the process of continuously tracking the performance and health of a system while it is operational. For multi-agent systems, real-time monitoring helps you identify issues early, ensuring that agents are performing as expected and the system remains efficient.

Why Real-time Monitoring is Crucial:

1. **Preventative Measures:**
   - Detect issues before they escalate, reducing downtime and potential system failure.
2. **Resource Management:**
   - Ensure that resources (CPU, memory, bandwidth, etc.) are being used efficiently, especially when running large-scale multi-agent systems.
3. **Performance Tracking:**
   - Continuously monitor performance metrics to ensure that the system meets its goals (e.g., task completion time, accuracy, efficiency).

Common Monitoring Tools:

1. **Prometheus:**
   - An open-source monitoring tool that collects metrics and generates alerts. It is often used in Kubernetes environments to monitor containerized applications.
2. **Grafana:**
   - A data visualization tool that integrates with Prometheus to provide a user-friendly dashboard for visualizing metrics and performance data.
3. **Nagios:**
   - A comprehensive IT infrastructure monitoring tool that can track server, network, and application performance, often used in enterprise settings.
4. **Datadog:**
   - A cloud-based monitoring tool that offers a complete view of your system, including logs, metrics, and traces, making it useful for monitoring multi-agent systems at scale.

Example: Setting Up Prometheus and Grafana for Monitoring

In this example, we will set up **Prometheus** to monitor the performance of a **Crew AI** system running in a Docker container. We will use **Grafana** for visualization.

1. **Prometheus Configuration:**
   - Install and configure Prometheus to scrape metrics from your application.
   - Create a `prometheus.yml` configuration file to set up the scrape job for your Docker container.

```yaml
global:
  scrape_interval: 15s

scrape_configs:
  - job_name: 'crew-ai-system'
    static_configs:
      - targets: ['localhost:9090']  # Assuming Prometheus
scrapes metrics from a locally running service
```

2. **Grafana Dashboard Setup:**
    o Install Grafana and configure it to pull data from Prometheus.
    o Create dashboards to visualize key metrics such as CPU usage, memory consumption, task completion times, and agent performance.

```json
json

{
    "title": "Agent System Performance",
    "panels": [
        {
            "type": "graph",
            "title": "CPU Usage",
            "datasource": "Prometheus",
            "targets": [
                {
                    "expr":
"avg(rate(process_cpu_seconds_total[5m]))",
                    "legendFormat": "CPU Usage"
                }
            ]
        }
    ]
}
```

This configuration sets up a dashboard that shows the average CPU usage over the past 5 minutes, helping you monitor resource consumption in real-time.

12.2 Maintenance Best Practices

Maintaining a multi-agent AI system is an ongoing process that involves periodic updates, monitoring, and addressing any issues that arise. Following maintenance best practices ensures that the system remains operational and efficient over time.

Best Practices for Maintaining Multi-agent Systems:

1. **Routine Updates:**
    o Regularly update the system's software, libraries, and dependencies to ensure the system runs with the latest improvements and security patches.

2. **Agent Re-training:**
    - o   If the agents rely on machine learning models, periodically retrain them on new data to ensure they continue to perform well and adapt to changes in the environment.
3. **Log Management:**
    - o   Set up log collection and aggregation tools (e.g., ELK Stack, Fluentd) to capture system logs and agent interactions. This data can be invaluable for troubleshooting and improving system performance.
4. **Backup and Redundancy:**
    - o   Ensure that data is regularly backed up and that there is redundancy in key components (e.g., databases, servers, agent components) to prevent data loss and system downtime.
5. **Performance Optimization:**
    - o   Regularly review performance metrics to identify areas for optimization, such as reducing task completion time or improving resource utilization.

Example: Automating Maintenance with Cron Jobs

For systems that require regular tasks (e.g., agent re-training, log rotation, backups), cron jobs can automate these processes.

```bash
# Example of a cron job to run agent re-training every day at
midnight
0 0 * * * /usr/bin/python3 /path/to/train_agents.py

# Example of a cron job to rotate logs every week
0 0 * * 0 /usr/sbin/logrotate /etc/logrotate.conf
```

These cron jobs will automatically run the agent re-training script and rotate logs on a weekly basis, ensuring that the system remains up-to-date and performs optimally.

12.3 Handling Failures and Ensuring Reliability

Failure management is essential for maintaining the reliability and robustness of multi-agent systems. By anticipating potential failures and implementing strategies to mitigate them, you can ensure that your system operates continuously without disruptions.

Failure Types in Multi-agent Systems:

1. **Agent Failures:**
   - Agents may fail due to various reasons, such as hardware issues, bugs, or network problems. It's important to implement recovery mechanisms that can restart or replace failed agents without affecting the overall system.
2. **Communication Failures:**
   - Communication failures can occur when agents cannot send or receive messages. Reliable communication protocols (e.g., **publish-subscribe, message queues**) and retries can help mitigate these failures.
3. **Infrastructure Failures:**
   - Failures in the underlying infrastructure (e.g., servers, databases) can affect the entire system. Implementing redundant infrastructure and **failover mechanisms** ensures that the system remains available even during failures.

Strategies for Handling Failures:

1. **Agent Replication:**
   - Create replicas of critical agents so that if one fails, another can take over without interrupting the system's functionality.
2. **Heartbeat Mechanisms:**
   - Agents should periodically send "heartbeat" signals to a central monitor. If a heartbeat is not received within a certain time frame, the system can automatically restart the agent or alert the administrator.
3. **Retry Logic and Circuit Breakers:**
   - Implement retry mechanisms for failed communication and circuit breakers to prevent cascading failures when an agent or service is unavailable.

Example: Agent Recovery with Heartbeat Mechanism

Here's an example of a simple heartbeat mechanism where agents send periodic signals to a monitor:

```python
```

```python
import time
import threading

class Agent:
    def __init__(self, name):
        self.name = name
        self.last_heartbeat = time.time()

    def send_heartbeat(self):
        self.last_heartbeat = time.time()
        print(f"{self.name} sent heartbeat at
{self.last_heartbeat}")

    def monitor(self):
        while True:
            time.sleep(5)   # Check heartbeat every 5 seconds
            if time.time() - self.last_heartbeat > 10:
                print(f"{self.name} has failed!
Restarting...")
                self.restart_agent()

    def restart_agent(self):
        self.last_heartbeat = time.time()
        print(f"{self.name} restarted.")

# Example usage
agent = Agent("Agent1")
heartbeat_thread = threading.Thread(target=agent.monitor)
heartbeat_thread.start()

# Simulate sending heartbeat every 3 seconds
while True:
    agent.send_heartbeat()
    time.sleep(3)
```

In this example:

- **Agent** sends a heartbeat every 3 seconds, and the monitor checks every 5 seconds. If the agent fails to send a heartbeat within 10 seconds, it is restarted.

12.4 Performance Metrics and Optimization

Performance metrics are essential for assessing the health and efficiency of your multi-agent system. By regularly monitoring these metrics, you can identify bottlenecks, inefficiencies, and areas for optimization.

Common Performance Metrics for Multi-agent Systems:

1. **Task Completion Time:**
   o Measure how long it takes for agents to complete tasks. Reducing this time can significantly improve the overall efficiency of the system.
2. **Resource Utilization:**
   o Monitor CPU, memory, and network usage to ensure that agents and the system as a whole are not overburdened.
3. **Agent Throughput:**
   o Track the number of tasks an agent can complete within a specific time period. Higher throughput indicates better system performance.
4. **Scalability:**
   o Measure how well the system scales with an increasing number of agents. The system should be able to maintain or improve performance as the number of agents grows.

Optimizing Performance:

1. **Load Balancing:**
   o Distribute tasks and resources evenly across agents to avoid overloading any single agent.
2. **Parallelization:**
   o Use parallel processing or multi-threading to allow agents to work on multiple tasks simultaneously, improving throughput.
3. **Caching:**
   o Cache frequently accessed data to reduce computation time and improve responsiveness.
4. **Algorithm Optimization:**
   o Optimize decision-making algorithms, such as reinforcement learning models, to make more efficient use of system resources.

Example: Monitoring and Optimizing Task Completion Time

We can track and optimize the task completion time using performance metrics:

```python
import time

class OptimizedAgent:
    def __init__(self, name):
        self.name = name

    def complete_task(self):
        start_time = time.time()
        # Simulate a task completion
        time.sleep(2)   # Task takes 2 seconds to complete
        end_time = time.time()
        completion_time = end_time - start_time
        print(f"{self.name} completed task in
{completion_time} seconds.")
        return completion_time

# Example usage
agent = OptimizedAgent("Agent1")
task_time = agent.complete_task()
```

In this example:

- **OptimizedAgent** tracks how long it takes to complete a task, allowing you to measure and optimize the task completion time.

12.5 Quiz

Now that you have learned about monitoring, maintenance, failure handling, and performance optimization, let's test your understanding with a quiz:

1. What is the primary benefit of real-time monitoring in multi-agent systems?

- a) It ensures that agents are able to perform tasks without interruption.
- b) It helps identify issues early, reducing system downtime.

- c) It decreases the number of agents required.
- d) It increases the complexity of the system.

2. Why is agent re-training an important maintenance practice?

- a) It helps agents adapt to new data and changing environments.
- b) It prevents agents from interacting with each other.
- c) It reduces the workload of the system.
- d) It eliminates the need for agent communication.

3. What is the purpose of a heartbeat mechanism in multi-agent systems?

- a) To measure the speed of agent communication.
- b) To monitor the health of agents and restart them if necessary.
- c) To increase the number of agents in the system.
- d) To assign tasks to agents.

4. Which of the following is a common performance metric for multi-agent systems?

- a) Task completion time
- b) Agent appearance
- c) Task difficulty
- d) Agent location

5. What is the purpose of load balancing in multi-agent systems?

- a) To ensure agents can communicate with each other more effectively.
- b) To distribute tasks evenly across agents and avoid overloading any single agent.
- c) To prevent the agents from performing too many tasks.
- d) To track agent locations.

Answers:

1. **b)** It helps identify issues early, reducing system downtime.
2. **a)** It helps agents adapt to new data and changing environments.
3. **b)** To monitor the health of agents and restart them if necessary.
4. **a)** Task completion time.

5. **b)** To distribute tasks evenly across agents and avoid overloading any single agent.

Chapter 13: Security and Privacy

As **multi-agent AI systems** become more widely deployed in real-world applications, security and privacy considerations become increasingly important. Multi-agent systems often involve complex interactions between multiple entities, which can introduce new vulnerabilities. Ensuring the **security** and **privacy** of agents, their communications, and the data they handle is essential for building trust, preventing malicious activities, and maintaining regulatory compliance. This chapter will explore how to secure multi-agent interactions, address privacy concerns, comply with relevant regulations, and leverage **blockchain** for enhanced security.

13.1 Securing Multi-agent Interactions

In multi-agent systems, agents often communicate and collaborate with each other to achieve common goals. The security of these interactions is critical to prevent unauthorized access, data manipulation, and malicious behaviors.

Key Security Challenges in Multi-agent Interactions:

1. **Data Integrity:**
   o Ensuring that the data exchanged between agents is not tampered with or altered during transmission is vital for maintaining the reliability and accuracy of multi-agent systems.
2. **Authentication:**
   o Verifying the identity of agents is crucial to ensure that agents are who they claim to be and prevent impersonation or rogue agents from entering the system.
3. **Authorization:**
   o Properly defining the access rights of agents ensures that they can only perform tasks or access data they are authorized to interact with, preventing unauthorized operations.
4. **Confidentiality:**
   o Ensuring that sensitive information is not exposed to unauthorized agents, protecting both the privacy of agents and the data they handle.

Techniques for Securing Multi-agent Interactions:

1. **Cryptography:**
   - **Public Key Infrastructure (PKI)** can be used for authenticating agents and encrypting communications. This ensures that data exchanged between agents is private and secure from eavesdropping.
2. **Digital Signatures:**
   - Agents can use digital signatures to verify the integrity of the data they send and ensure it has not been altered during transmission.
3. **Access Control Mechanisms:**
   - Implementing role-based access control (RBAC) or attribute-based access control (ABAC) can restrict which agents have access to certain data or functionality.
4. **Secure Communication Protocols:**
   - Protocols such as **TLS (Transport Layer Security)** can be used to secure communication channels between agents, ensuring that all data transmitted is encrypted and protected from interception.

Example: Secure Communication Using Cryptography

Below is an example of how to use **public-key encryption** to secure the communication between two agents.

```
from cryptography.fernet import Fernet

# Agent 1 generates a key and shares it securely with Agent 2
key = Fernet.generate_key()
cipher_suite = Fernet(key)

# Agent 1 encrypts a message
message = "Hello, Agent 2! This is a confidential message."
encrypted_message = cipher_suite.encrypt(message.encode())

print(f"Encrypted message: {encrypted_message}")

# Agent 2 decrypts the message
decrypted_message =
cipher_suite.decrypt(encrypted_message).decode()

print(f"Decrypted message: {decrypted_message}")
```

In this example:

- **Fernet** encryption ensures that the message between Agent 1 and Agent 2 is encrypted and can only be decrypted with the correct key, preventing unauthorized access.

13.2 Privacy Considerations in AI Systems

As multi-agent systems handle sensitive data, including personal information, financial data, and health records, ensuring **privacy** becomes a top priority. Privacy considerations help prevent unauthorized access to personal data and ensure compliance with privacy regulations.

Key Privacy Concerns:

1. **Data Collection:**
   - Multi-agent systems often collect vast amounts of data, which may include personal or sensitive information. It's important to ensure that this data is collected in compliance with privacy laws and is used for its intended purpose.
2. **Data Storage and Access:**
   - Properly securing stored data and implementing strong access control measures ensures that only authorized agents or users can access sensitive information.
3. **Data Sharing:**
   - In some systems, agents may need to share data with external entities. Ensuring that this sharing complies with privacy regulations and is performed securely is essential.
4. **Anonymization:**
   - Anonymizing or pseudonymizing personal data can help protect privacy while still enabling agents to perform their tasks and analyze data.

Privacy-preserving Techniques:

1. **Differential Privacy:**
   - A technique that adds noise to data in such a way that individual data points cannot be

traced back to specific individuals, ensuring privacy while still allowing for meaningful analysis.

2. **Federated Learning:**
    o In federated learning, agents train models on local data without transferring the data to a central server, thereby maintaining data privacy while enabling collaborative learning.
3. **Data Encryption:**
    o Encrypting sensitive data before it is processed or stored ensures that even if data is intercepted, it cannot be read without the proper decryption keys.
4. **Access Control:**
    o Implementing fine-grained access control ensures that only authorized agents can access sensitive data, protecting the privacy of users or entities within the system.

Example: Federated Learning for Privacy Preservation

Below is an example of how federated learning could be applied to allow agents to learn from local data without sharing the actual data:

```
from sklearn.linear_model import LogisticRegression
from sklearn.metrics import accuracy_score
import numpy as np

class FederatedLearningAgent:
    def __init__(self, local_data, local_labels):
        self.local_data = local_data
        self.local_labels = local_labels
        self.model = LogisticRegression()

    def train_local_model(self):
        self.model.fit(self.local_data, self.local_labels)

    def evaluate_model(self, test_data, test_labels):
        predictions = self.model.predict(test_data)
        return accuracy_score(test_labels, predictions)

# Simulate agents with local datasets
agent1 = FederatedLearningAgent(np.array([[1, 2], [2, 3]]),
np.array([0, 1]))
agent2 = FederatedLearningAgent(np.array([[3, 4], [4, 5]]),
np.array([1, 0]))

# Agents train their models locally
agent1.train_local_model()
agent2.train_local_model()

# Simulate model aggregation (federated averaging)
```

```
# For simplicity, we average the model coefficients here, but
in real federated learning, this would involve more complex
aggregation.
agent1_weights = agent1.model.coef_
agent2_weights = agent2.model.coef_
average_weights = (agent1_weights + agent2_weights) / 2

# The federated model now has the average weights from both
agents
print(f"Aggregated model weights: {average_weights}")
```

In this example:

- **FederatedLearningAgent** trains a **Logistic Regression** model on its local data.
- Agents share their model weights (not the data) and aggregate them to create a global model, thus preserving the privacy of the individual datasets.

13.3 Compliance with Regulations and Standards

With the increasing use of AI systems across industries, **compliance with regulations** and **data protection standards** is crucial. Many countries and regions have established regulations governing the use of personal data and AI systems, and it is essential that multi-agent systems adhere to these laws.

Key Regulations and Standards:

1. **General Data Protection Regulation (GDPR):**
   o The GDPR is a European regulation that governs data protection and privacy. It mandates that organizations process personal data transparently, securely, and with the consent of individuals. Multi-agent systems operating in Europe must comply with these regulations.
2. **Health Insurance Portability and Accountability Act (HIPAA):**
   o HIPAA is a U.S. regulation that applies to health information. Any AI system handling health data must ensure that it meets the stringent requirements for data protection and privacy under HIPAA.

3. **California Consumer Privacy Act (CCPA):**
   o CCPA provides privacy rights to residents of California. It gives consumers the right to know what data is being collected, access it, and request its deletion.
4. **ISO/IEC 27001:**
   o This international standard for information security management systems (ISMS) provides a framework for protecting sensitive information and managing risk in information systems.

Compliance Best Practices:

1. **Data Minimization:**
   o Only collect and process the minimum amount of personal data necessary for the task. Avoid storing unnecessary information.
2. **Consent Management:**
   o Obtain explicit consent from users for data collection and processing, and allow them to withdraw consent easily.
3. **Regular Audits:**
   o Conduct regular audits of the multi-agent system to ensure compliance with applicable regulations and standards.
4. **Data Subject Rights:**
   o Implement mechanisms for users to exercise their rights under data protection laws, such as the right to access, delete, or correct their data.
5. **Data Encryption and Anonymization:**
   o Encrypt sensitive data and anonymize personal information wherever possible to reduce risks and ensure privacy.

Example: GDPR Compliance for Data Collection

In the context of GDPR compliance, a multi-agent system that collects user data can implement consent management. Here's a simple Python example that prompts the user for consent before collecting personal data:

```python
class ConsentAgent:
    def __init__(self, name):
        self.name = name

    def ask_for_consent(self):
        consent = input(f"Do you consent to the collection of
your data for {self.name}? (yes/no): ")
```

```
        return consent.lower() == 'yes'

# Example usage
agent = ConsentAgent("DataCollector")
if agent.ask_for_consent():
    print("Thank you for consenting. Your data will be
collected.")
else:
    print("You have declined consent. Data will not be
collected.")
```

In this example:

- **ConsentAgent** asks the user for consent before proceeding with data collection, ensuring compliance with data protection regulations.

13.4 Blockchain for Enhanced Security

Blockchain is often used to enhance the security and transparency of multi-agent systems. As discussed in **Chapter 13.1**, blockchain can be used to secure agent interactions, ensure data integrity, and provide transparency in system activities.

How Blockchain Enhances Security:

1. **Immutable Ledger:**
   o Transactions and interactions between agents are recorded on an immutable blockchain, making it impossible to alter past actions, ensuring transparency and trust.
2. **Decentralized Security:**
   o Blockchain operates in a decentralized manner, eliminating the need for a central authority and reducing the risk of single-point failures.
3. **Smart Contracts:**
   o Blockchain enables the use of **smart contracts**, which are self-executing contracts with predefined rules and conditions. These contracts can automate interactions between agents and enforce agreed-upon terms without manual intervention.

Example: Using Blockchain for Secure Agent Transactions

Below is an example of how a **smart contract** could be used to automate a simple transaction between two agents using **Ethereum's Solidity** language:

```
// Solidity Smart Contract for secure transactions between
agents
pragma solidity ^0.8.0;

contract AgentTransaction {
    address public agent1;
    address public agent2;
    uint public transactionAmount;

    constructor(address _agent1, address _agent2, uint
_amount) {
        agent1 = _agent1;
        agent2 = _agent2;
        transactionAmount = _amount;
    }

    function executeTransaction() public {
        require(msg.sender == agent1, "Only agent1 can
execute the transaction");
        payable(agent2).transfer(transactionAmount);
    }

    receive() external payable {}
}
```

In this example:

- The **AgentTransaction** smart contract allows **agent1** to transfer funds to **agent2**.
- The contract ensures that only **agent1** can initiate the transaction, adding a layer of security and trust between the agents.

13.5 Reflection Questions

To deepen your understanding of the concepts covered in this chapter, reflect on the following questions:

1. **What are the key security challenges in multi-agent interactions, and how can cryptography help address these challenges?**
   - o Reflect on how encryption, digital signatures, and access control mechanisms can secure agent communications.
2. **How does federated learning contribute to privacy preservation in multi-agent systems?**
   - o Think about how local data processing in federated learning can maintain privacy while still allowing agents to learn collectively.
3. **What are some common data protection regulations, and how can multi-agent systems ensure compliance with them?**
   - o Reflect on GDPR, HIPAA, and other regulations and how they affect the design and deployment of multi-agent systems.
4. **How does blockchain enhance the security and transparency of multi-agent systems, and what are its limitations?**
   - o Consider the benefits of blockchain in securing transactions and ensuring transparency, and explore any challenges it may pose.
5. **What are the best practices for maintaining privacy in multi-agent systems, particularly when handling sensitive data?**
   - o Reflect on data minimization, encryption, anonymization, and other techniques for ensuring privacy in AI systems.

Chapter 14: Governance and Ethical Considerations

As **multi-agent AI systems** become increasingly sophisticated and integrated into various industries, the need for **ethical** governance and decision-making becomes essential. These systems impact not only technological processes but also social, economic, and legal spheres. Therefore, addressing **ethical frameworks**, establishing **governance models**, and ensuring **fairness** and **responsibility** in AI development is critical for ensuring that these systems contribute positively to society. This chapter explores these considerations in depth, providing you with the tools and understanding needed to implement ethical governance in multi-agent AI systems.

14.1 Ethical Frameworks for AI

Ethical frameworks provide a set of principles and guidelines for making decisions and taking actions in the development, deployment, and management of AI systems. These frameworks help ensure that AI technologies, including multi-agent systems, are designed and used responsibly, minimizing harm and promoting fairness.

Common Ethical Frameworks in AI:

1. **Utilitarianism:**
   - This ethical framework emphasizes actions that maximize overall happiness or well-being. In AI systems, decisions made by agents should aim to maximize positive outcomes for the largest number of people while minimizing harm.
2. **Deontological Ethics:**
   - Deontological ethics focuses on following rules, duties, and obligations. For AI, this means that systems must operate according to predefined ethical rules, such as ensuring privacy or respecting user consent, regardless of the consequences.
3. **Virtue Ethics:**
   - Virtue ethics emphasizes the importance of character and virtues in ethical decision-making. For AI systems, this

framework suggests that agents should be designed to promote virtuous behaviors, such as honesty, empathy, and fairness, in their interactions with humans and other agents.

4. **Fairness and Justice:**
    o   This ethical approach advocates for fair treatment and equitable access. In AI systems, fairness means that the system's decisions should not disadvantage any particular group or individual, and resources should be distributed justly.

5. **Transparency and Accountability:**
    o   This framework emphasizes the need for AI systems to be transparent in their decision-making processes. Stakeholders should have clear insight into how decisions are made, and agents should be accountable for their actions, especially in high-stakes applications like healthcare or finance.

Example: Applying Ethical Frameworks in Multi-agent AI Systems

Consider a **multi-agent system** designed to optimize resource allocation in a healthcare setting. Using **utilitarian principles**, the system could prioritize medical resources (e.g., ventilators or ICU beds) for patients most likely to recover, aiming to maximize overall health outcomes. However, a **deontological approach** would ensure that the system respects patients' autonomy and provides resources to all patients based on need, rather than merely survival probabilities.

```
class HealthcareAgent:
    def __init__(self, patient_id, recovery_chance,
priority):
        self.patient_id = patient_id
        self.recovery_chance = recovery_chance
        self.priority = priority  # A higher number means
higher priority

    def allocate_resources(self):
        if self.priority > 5:
            decision = "Allocate resources"
        else:
            decision = "Defer allocation"
        return decision

# Example usage:
patients = [
    HealthcareAgent("Patient1", 0.85, 7),
```

```
    HealthcareAgent("Patient2", 0.50, 3),
    HealthcareAgent("Patient3", 0.90, 8),
]

for patient in patients:
    print(f"{patient.patient_id}:
{patient.allocate_resources()}")
```

In this example:

- **HealthcareAgent** allocates resources based on patient priority, a key ethical concern when making decisions that affect people's lives.

14.2 Governance Models for Multi-agent Systems

Governance in multi-agent systems refers to the processes, policies, and structures that guide the system's behavior, decision-making, and accountability. Governance models define how agents interact, how decisions are made, and who is responsible for ensuring that the system aligns with ethical principles and societal goals.

Key Governance Models:

1. **Centralized Governance:**
   - In centralized governance, a central authority controls the decision-making processes of the agents. This model is beneficial in systems where uniformity and oversight are crucial, but it may limit the system's autonomy and flexibility.
2. **Decentralized Governance:**
   - In decentralized governance, agents operate autonomously, and decisions are made without a central authority. This model promotes flexibility and robustness but may lead to challenges in coordination and accountability.
3. **Hybrid Governance:**
   - A hybrid model combines elements of both centralized and decentralized governance. It allows for decentralized decision-making within a framework of centralized oversight to ensure compliance with ethical and legal standards.

4. **Self-governance and Emergent Governance:**
    o   Some multi-agent systems rely on agents developing their governance structures through interaction and cooperation. This model is dynamic and adapts to changing circumstances, though it can be unpredictable.

Example: Governance in a Distributed Energy System

In a **distributed energy system**, multiple agents (e.g., solar panels, batteries, and smart meters) may need to make decentralized decisions about energy distribution. A **hybrid governance model** could allow agents to autonomously manage local resources but also ensure that energy usage complies with regulatory standards set by a central authority.

```python
class EnergyAgent:
    def __init__(self, id, energy_output):
        self.id = id
        self.energy_output = energy_output

    def adjust_output(self):
        if self.energy_output > 100:
            return "Reduce output"
        else:
            return "Maintain output"

# Example usage
agents = [
    EnergyAgent("Panel1", 120),
    EnergyAgent("Panel2", 80),
    EnergyAgent("Panel3", 110),
]

for agent in agents:
    print(f"{agent.id}: {agent.adjust_output()}")
```

In this example:

*   **EnergyAgent** autonomously adjusts its energy output based on the environment, but the system's behavior aligns with regulatory limits set by a central authority.

14.3 Addressing Bias and Fairness

Bias and **fairness** are two of the most critical ethical concerns in AI systems. Bias can arise when agents are trained on data that reflects historical inequalities or prejudices, leading to unfair decisions. Addressing bias and ensuring fairness in multi-agent systems is essential for building trust and equity.

Sources of Bias in Multi-agent Systems:

1. **Training Data Bias:**
   o If the data used to train agents is skewed or unrepresentative of the target population, the agents may develop biased behaviors or make unfair decisions.
2. **Algorithmic Bias:**
   o Bias can also arise from the algorithms themselves. Even if the data is fair, the way agents process that data can introduce biases.
3. **Human Bias:**
   o Biases introduced by the designers of the system, often unintentionally, can also affect the fairness of the agents' decisions.

Strategies for Mitigating Bias and Ensuring Fairness:

1. **Fairness-Aware Algorithms:**
   o Develop algorithms that explicitly consider fairness in decision-making. Techniques like **fairness constraints** or **adversarial debiasing** can help reduce bias in agent behavior.
2. **Diverse Data Sources:**
   o Ensure that training data is diverse and representative of the entire population, mitigating the risk of systemic bias.
3. **Bias Audits:**
   o Regularly audit the system for bias, using fairness metrics (e.g., **disparate impact** or **demographic parity**) to assess whether the system's outcomes are equitable.

Example: Mitigating Bias in a Loan Approval Agent

In a multi-agent system for **loan approval**, agents may inadvertently learn biased patterns from historical data. A fairness-aware algorithm can help ensure that decisions are not based on sensitive attributes like race or gender.

```python
from sklearn.linear_model import LogisticRegression
from sklearn.model_selection import train_test_split
from sklearn.metrics import accuracy_score

# Simulate a loan approval dataset with potential bias in
features like race and gender
data = [
    {"income": 60000, "loan_amount": 20000, "gender": "Male",
"race": "White", "approved": 1},
    {"income": 40000, "loan_amount": 15000, "gender":
"Female", "race": "Black", "approved": 0},
    # More records...
]

# Example preprocessing and model training with fairness-
aware constraints
X = [[d['income'], d['loan_amount']] for d in data]  #
Features without sensitive attributes
y = [d['approved'] for d in data]  # Target variable (loan
approval)

# Train-test split
X_train, X_test, y_train, y_test = train_test_split(X, y,
test_size=0.2)

# Logistic Regression model (can be enhanced with fairness
constraints)
model = LogisticRegression()
model.fit(X_train, y_train)

# Evaluate accuracy
y_pred = model.predict(X_test)
print(f"Accuracy: {accuracy_score(y_test, y_pred)}")
```

In this example:

- The **loan approval agent** uses features that do not include sensitive attributes like **gender** and **race** to reduce bias in its decisions.

14.4 Responsible AI Development Practices

Developing **responsible AI** is essential for ensuring that AI systems, including multi-agent systems, are safe, transparent, and aligned with societal values. This involves adopting ethical development practices that focus on fairness, transparency, accountability, and safety.

Key Responsible AI Practices:

1. **Transparency:**
   o Ensure that agents' decision-making processes are transparent and interpretable, allowing users to understand why decisions are made.
2. **Accountability:**
   o Implement clear mechanisms for accountability, ensuring that human operators or system designers can trace actions back to agents and take responsibility for their decisions.
3. **Safety:**
   o Develop agents that are robust and safe under various conditions, including handling uncertainty and edge cases without causing harm to people or systems.
4. **Inclusivity:**
   o Ensure that AI systems are designed inclusively, taking into account diverse needs and perspectives and avoiding any harmful exclusions.

Example: Ensuring Accountability in a Multi-agent System

Consider a multi-agent system for **automated trading** in financial markets. A **responsible AI** approach would ensure that agents make transparent decisions and allow for human oversight in case of unexpected actions.

```python
class TradingAgent:
    def __init__(self, name, balance):
        self.name = name
        self.balance = balance

    def make_trade(self, amount, action):
        if action == "buy" and self.balance >= amount:
            self.balance -= amount
            print(f"{self.name} bought assets worth {amount}.
Remaining balance: {self.balance}")
        elif action == "sell":
```

```
        self.balance += amount
        print(f"{self.name} sold assets worth {amount}.
Remaining balance: {self.balance}")
    else:
        print(f"Error: Insufficient balance or invalid
action.")

# Example usage
agent = TradingAgent("Trader1", 10000)
agent.make_trade(5000, "buy")
agent.make_trade(7000, "sell")
```

In this example:

- **TradingAgent** can perform buy and sell operations with
  transparency and accountability in its financial actions.

14.5 Exercise: Developing an Ethical Governance Model

Objective:

Develop an **ethical governance model** for a multi-agent system used in
automated hiring. The system consists of multiple agents responsible for
reviewing resumes, conducting interviews, and making hiring decisions.

Steps:

1. **Identify Ethical Principles:**
   o Decide on the ethical principles to guide the system (e.g.,
     fairness, non-discrimination, transparency).
2. **Define Governance Structure:**
   o Determine whether the system will follow a centralized,
     decentralized, or hybrid governance model. Consider the roles
     of human supervisors in overseeing agent decisions.
3. **Ensure Fairness:**
   o Implement fairness constraints in the decision-making process
     to avoid bias based on gender, race, or other protected
     attributes.
4. **Ensure Transparency:**

- o Develop mechanisms for explaining the reasoning behind hiring decisions to applicants.

5. **Ensure Accountability:**
   - o Define who is accountable for the system's decisions and actions. Implement audit trails to allow for tracing and accountability.

Chapter 15: Human-AI Collaboration

As **AI systems** become more integrated into various aspects of daily life and industry, effective **collaboration** between humans and AI agents is essential. Human-AI collaboration leverages the strengths of both humans and machines, leading to more efficient, accurate, and innovative outcomes. This chapter explores the principles of designing human-AI interactions, enhancing teamwork between humans and AI agents, building trust and usability in these systems, and examines case studies of successful collaborations. By understanding these concepts, you can design and implement AI systems that work seamlessly with human users, maximizing their potential and ensuring positive societal impact.

15.1 Designing for Human-AI Interaction

Effective **human-AI interaction** is fundamental for successful collaboration. Designing these interactions requires a deep understanding of both human behaviors and AI capabilities to create systems that are intuitive, responsive, and supportive.

Key Principles for Designing Human-AI Interaction:

1. **User-Centric Design:**
   o Focus on the needs, preferences, and limitations of the human users. Engage users in the design process to ensure the AI system aligns with their workflows and expectations.
2. **Intuitiveness:**
   o The AI system should be easy to understand and use. Interfaces should be clear, with straightforward navigation and minimal learning curve.
3. **Feedback and Responsiveness:**
   o Provide immediate and clear feedback for user actions. The AI should respond promptly to inputs, maintaining a fluid and interactive experience.
4. **Transparency:**

o Ensure that the AI's actions and decisions are understandable to users. Transparency builds trust and allows users to make informed decisions based on AI recommendations.

5. **Adaptability:**
   o Design AI systems that can adapt to different user preferences and contexts. Personalization enhances user satisfaction and effectiveness.

6. **Error Handling:**
   o Implement robust error detection and recovery mechanisms. The system should guide users in resolving issues without causing frustration or confusion.

Design Elements for Human-AI Interaction:

1. **User Interface (UI):**
   o The visual layout through which users interact with the AI system. A well-designed UI includes intuitive controls, clear information display, and accessible navigation.

2. **Natural Language Processing (NLP):**
   o Enables users to communicate with AI agents using natural language, making interactions more seamless and less technical.

3. **Visual and Auditory Cues:**
   o Use visual indicators (e.g., progress bars, alerts) and auditory signals (e.g., notifications, confirmations) to guide user interactions and provide status updates.

4. **Assistive Features:**
   o Incorporate features like auto-completion, suggestions, and context-aware help to support users in completing tasks efficiently.

Example: Designing a User Interface for a Customer Support AI Agent

Consider designing a UI for an AI-powered customer support agent. The interface should allow users to easily input queries, receive responses, and access additional resources.

```
<!DOCTYPE html>
<html>
<head>
    <title>AI Customer Support</title>
```

```html
    <style>
        body { font-family: Arial, sans-serif; }
        #chat-container { width: 500px; margin: 0 auto; }
        #chat-box { border: 1px solid #ccc; height: 400px;
overflow-y: scroll; padding: 10px; }
        #user-input { width: 80%; padding: 10px; }
        #send-btn { padding: 10px; }
        .user-message { text-align: right; color: blue; }
        .ai-message { text-align: left; color: green; }
    </style>
</head>
<body>
    <div id="chat-container">
        <h2>AI Customer Support</h2>
        <div id="chat-box">
            <!-- Messages will appear here -->
        </div>
        <input type="text" id="user-input" placeholder="Type
your message here..." />
        <button id="send-btn">Send</button>
    </div>

    <script>
        const sendBtn = document.getElementById('send-btn');
        const userInput = document.getElementById('user-
input');
        const chatBox = document.getElementById('chat-box');

        sendBtn.addEventListener('click', () => {
            const message = userInput.value.trim();
            if (message !== '') {
                appendMessage(message, 'user');
                userInput.value = '';
                // Simulate AI response
                setTimeout(() => {
                    const aiResponse = "I'm here to help! How
can I assist you today?";
                    appendMessage(aiResponse, 'ai');
                }, 1000);
            }
        });

        function appendMessage(message, sender) {
            const msgDiv = document.createElement('div');
            msgDiv.className = sender === 'user' ? 'user-
message' : 'ai-message';
            msgDiv.textContent = message;
            chatBox.appendChild(msgDiv);
            chatBox.scrollTop = chatBox.scrollHeight;
        }
    </script>
```

```
</body>
</html>
```

Explanation:

- The **HTML** structure creates a simple chat interface with a chat box, input field, and send button.
- **CSS** styles ensure a clean and user-friendly layout, differentiating between user and AI messages.
- **JavaScript** handles sending user messages, appending them to the chat box, and simulating AI responses.

This example demonstrates an intuitive and responsive interface that facilitates smooth interaction between the user and the AI agent.

15.2 Enhancing Teamwork Between Humans and AI Agents

Effective teamwork between humans and AI agents leverages the strengths of both to achieve superior outcomes. Enhancing this collaboration involves clear role definitions, effective communication, and complementary skill sets.

Key Factors for Effective Human-AI Teamwork:

1. **Role Clarity:**
   o Clearly define the roles and responsibilities of both humans and AI agents. Ensure that each party understands their tasks and how they contribute to the team's objectives.
2. **Complementary Strengths:**
   o Design AI agents to complement human capabilities. For example, humans excel in creativity and emotional intelligence, while AI agents excel in data processing and pattern recognition.
3. **Effective Communication:**
   o Establish clear channels for communication between humans and AI agents. Ensure that AI agents can convey information in understandable formats and that humans can provide feedback effectively.

4. **Shared Goals:**
   - Align the objectives of both humans and AI agents. Ensure that all team members are working towards common goals, fostering a sense of unity and purpose.
5. **Collaborative Tools:**
   - Utilize tools and platforms that facilitate collaboration, such as shared dashboards, real-time data visualization, and integrated communication systems.

Strategies for Enhancing Human-AI Teamwork:

1. **Interactive Dashboards:**
   - Provide interfaces where humans can monitor AI agent activities, view insights, and make informed decisions based on AI-generated data.
2. **Feedback Mechanisms:**
   - Implement systems where humans can provide feedback to AI agents, allowing for continuous improvement and adaptation.
3. **Training and Education:**
   - Educate human team members on how to effectively interact with and leverage AI agents, ensuring that they understand the capabilities and limitations of the AI.
4. **Collaborative Decision-Making:**
   - Design AI agents that assist in decision-making processes by providing relevant data, predictions, and recommendations while leaving the final decision to humans.

Example: Human-AI Collaboration in Medical Diagnosis

Consider a multi-agent system where AI agents assist doctors in diagnosing diseases. The AI agents analyze patient data, identify potential conditions, and suggest treatment options, while doctors make the final diagnosis and treatment decisions.

```
class DiagnosticAgent:
    def __init__(self, name):
        self.name = name

    def analyze_data(self, patient_data):
        # Simulate data analysis and condition prediction
        conditions = ["Flu", "Common Cold", "Allergy"]
        prediction = random.choice(conditions)
        return prediction
```

```python
    def suggest_treatment(self, condition):
        treatments = {
            "Flu": "Antiviral medication",
            "Common Cold": "Rest and hydration",
            "Allergy": "Antihistamines"
        }
        return treatments.get(condition, "Consult a
specialist")

class Doctor:
    def __init__(self, name):
        self.name = name

    def make_diagnosis(self, ai_prediction, patient_data):
        print(f"{self.name} reviews AI prediction:
{ai_prediction}")
        # Doctor validates the AI's suggestion
        if ai_prediction == "Flu" and
patient_data['symptoms'].count('fever') > 0:
            final_diagnosis = "Flu"
        elif ai_prediction == "Allergy" and
patient_data['symptoms'].count('sneezing') > 0:
            final_diagnosis = "Allergy"
        else:
            final_diagnosis = "Common Cold"
        return final_diagnosis

    def decide_treatment(self, diagnosis, ai_treatment):
        print(f"{self.name} decides on treatment:
{ai_treatment}")
        return ai_treatment

# Example usage
import random

# Simulated patient data
patient_data = {
    'age': 30,
    'symptoms': ['fever', 'cough', 'sore throat']
}

# Initialize agents
diagnostic_agent = DiagnosticAgent("DiagnosticAgent1")
doctor = Doctor("Dr. Smith")

# AI agent analyzes data
ai_prediction = diagnostic_agent.analyze_data(patient_data)
ai_treatment =
diagnostic_agent.suggest_treatment(ai_prediction)
```

```
# Doctor makes final diagnosis and decides treatment
final_diagnosis = doctor.make_diagnosis(ai_prediction,
patient_data)
final_treatment = doctor.decide_treatment(final_diagnosis,
ai_treatment)

print(f"Final Diagnosis: {final_diagnosis}")
print(f"Final Treatment: {final_treatment}")
```

Explanation:

- **DiagnosticAgent** analyzes patient data and predicts potential conditions, suggesting treatments based on the prediction.
- **Doctor** reviews the AI's prediction, validates it against patient symptoms, and makes the final diagnosis and treatment decision.
- This collaboration combines the AI agent's data processing capabilities with the doctor's expertise and judgment, leading to accurate and reliable medical decisions.

15.3 Trust and Usability in Human-AI Systems

Building **trust** and ensuring **usability** are critical for the successful adoption and effectiveness of human-AI collaborations. Users must trust AI agents to provide accurate, reliable, and ethical assistance, while usability ensures that interactions with AI systems are seamless and intuitive.

Building Trust in Human-AI Systems:

1. **Transparency:**
   o Clearly communicate how AI agents make decisions and provide explanations for their actions. Transparency helps users understand and trust AI recommendations.
2. **Reliability and Consistency:**
   o Ensure that AI agents perform consistently and reliably under various conditions. Consistent performance builds user confidence in the system.
3. **Accountability:**
   o Establish clear accountability mechanisms, so users know who is responsible for the AI's actions and decisions. This includes having humans in the loop for oversight and intervention.

4. **Ethical Behavior:**
   o Design AI agents to adhere to ethical guidelines and principles, ensuring that their actions align with societal values and user expectations.

Enhancing Usability in Human-AI Systems:

1. **Intuitive Interfaces:**
   o Design user interfaces that are easy to navigate and interact with. Use familiar design patterns and ensure that AI functionalities are accessible without requiring extensive training.
2. **User Control:**
   o Provide users with control over AI agents, allowing them to customize settings, override decisions, and provide feedback. Empowering users enhances their sense of ownership and satisfaction.
3. **Responsive Feedback:**
   o Implement responsive feedback mechanisms that inform users about the AI's actions and status. Immediate and clear feedback improves the interaction experience.
4. **Minimal Cognitive Load:**
   o Design interactions that minimize the cognitive effort required from users. Simplify tasks and present information in a clear and concise manner.

Example: Trust-Building Features in a Personal Assistant AI

Consider designing a personal assistant AI that helps users manage their schedules, set reminders, and provide recommendations. Incorporate trust-building and usability features as follows:

```
class PersonalAssistantAI:
    def __init__(self, name):
        self.name = name
        self.schedule = []

    def add_event(self, event, time):
        self.schedule.append({'event': event, 'time': time})
        print(f"{self.name}: Event '{event}' added at
{time}.")

    def get_schedule(self):
        if not self.schedule:
```

```
            print(f"{self.name}: Your schedule is empty.")
            return
        print(f"{self.name}: Here is your schedule:")
        for item in self.schedule:
            print(f" - {item['event']} at {item['time']}")

    def explain_decision(self, recommendation):
        print(f"{self.name}: I recommended this because it
aligns with your previous preferences.")

    def override_decision(self, event, time):
        print(f"{self.name}: Event '{event}' at {time}' has
been overridden as per your request.")
        # Implement override logic here

# Example usage
assistant = PersonalAssistantAI("HelperAI")
assistant.add_event("Team Meeting", "10:00 AM")
assistant.add_event("Doctor Appointment", "2:00 PM")
assistant.get_schedule()
assistant.explain_decision("Doctor Appointment")
assistant.override_decision("Doctor Appointment", "3:00 PM")
assistant.get_schedule()
```

Explanation:

- **PersonalAssistantAI** provides clear and transparent interactions by explaining its recommendations.
- Users can easily add, view, and override events, ensuring control and enhancing usability.
- The AI communicates actions and decisions in a straightforward manner, building trust through transparency and accountability.

15.4 Case Studies on Successful Collaboration

Examining real-world **case studies** of human-AI collaboration provides valuable insights into best practices, challenges, and the impact of effective teamwork between humans and AI agents. Below are two notable examples:

Case Study 1: IBM Watson and Oncologists

Overview: IBM Watson is an AI system designed to assist oncologists in diagnosing and treating cancer. By analyzing vast amounts of medical literature, patient records, and clinical guidelines, Watson provides evidence-based recommendations to support doctors in making informed decisions.

Collaboration Elements:

- **Data Analysis:** Watson processes and analyzes extensive medical data, identifying patterns and potential treatment options.
- **Decision Support:** Oncologists review Watson's recommendations alongside their clinical judgment, ensuring that decisions are both data-driven and personalized.
- **Continuous Learning:** Watson continuously learns from new data and outcomes, improving its recommendations over time.

Outcomes:

- Improved diagnostic accuracy and treatment planning.
- Enhanced efficiency in processing and analyzing medical information.
- Strengthened collaboration between AI and medical professionals, leading to better patient outcomes.

Case Study 2: Tesla Autopilot and Drivers

Overview: Tesla's Autopilot system is an advanced driver-assistance system (ADAS) that enables semi-autonomous driving. It assists drivers by handling tasks such as lane-keeping, adaptive cruise control, and automated braking, while still requiring human supervision.

Collaboration Elements:

- **Task Delegation:** Autopilot handles routine driving tasks, allowing drivers to focus on higher-level decision-making.
- **Safety Monitoring:** The system continuously monitors the environment and alerts drivers to take control when necessary.
- **Feedback Mechanism:** Drivers provide feedback on Autopilot's performance, enabling ongoing system improvements.

Outcomes:

- Increased driving safety through advanced monitoring and automated responses.
- Enhanced driver convenience and reduced fatigue during long drives.

- Ongoing refinement of autonomous driving capabilities through user feedback and data analysis.

15.5 Quiz

Now that you have learned about human-AI collaboration, including designing interactions, enhancing teamwork, building trust and usability, and examined real-world case studies, let's test your understanding with the following quiz:

1. What is the primary focus of user-centric design in human-AI interaction?

- a) Ensuring that AI agents perform tasks autonomously.
- b) Focusing on the needs, preferences, and limitations of human users.
- c) Maximizing the complexity of the AI system.
- d) Reducing the number of AI agents in the system.

2. Which of the following is a key factor in effective human-AI teamwork?

- a) Having a central authority that controls all agent actions.
- b) Defining clear roles and responsibilities for both humans and AI agents.
- c) Allowing AI agents to make all decisions without human input.
- d) Minimizing communication between humans and AI agents.

3. How does transparency contribute to building trust in human-AI systems?

- a) By hiding the AI's decision-making processes from users.
- b) By providing clear explanations of how the AI makes decisions.
- c) By making the AI system appear more complex.
- d) By reducing the number of interactions between humans and AI agents.

4. What is one way to enhance the usability of a human-AI system?

- a) Implementing complex and technical interfaces.
- b) Providing users with control over AI settings and decisions.
- c) Limiting the feedback mechanisms to avoid user confusion.
- d) Reducing the responsiveness of the system to user inputs.

5. In the IBM Watson and Oncologists case study, what role does the AI system primarily play?

- a) Making final treatment decisions without human input.
- b) Assisting oncologists by providing evidence-based recommendations.
- c) Replacing oncologists in the diagnostic process.
- d) Handling administrative tasks unrelated to patient care.

Answers:

1. **b)** Focusing on the needs, preferences, and limitations of human users.
2. **b)** Defining clear roles and responsibilities for both humans and AI agents.
3. **b)** By providing clear explanations of how the AI makes decisions.
4. **b)** Providing users with control over AI settings and decisions.
5. **b)** Assisting oncologists by providing evidence-based recommendations.

Chapter 16: Sustainability and Green AI

As the deployment of **AI systems** becomes increasingly widespread, the environmental impact of these technologies has garnered significant attention. **Sustainability** in AI, often referred to as **Green AI**, focuses on minimizing the ecological footprint of AI development and deployment. This chapter explores the principles and practices of Green AI, emphasizing energy efficiency, sustainable deployment, carbon footprint reduction, and innovative approaches that promote environmental stewardship in multi-agent AI systems.

16.1 Energy-efficient AI Practices

Energy efficiency in AI is crucial for reducing operational costs and minimizing environmental impact. Multi-agent AI systems, which often involve complex computations and large-scale deployments, can consume substantial amounts of energy. Implementing energy-efficient practices ensures that these systems operate sustainably without compromising performance.

Key Strategies for Energy-efficient AI:

1. **Model Optimization:**
    - **Pruning:** Removing redundant or less significant parts of the AI model (e.g., neurons or layers) to reduce computational requirements.
    - **Quantization:** Reducing the precision of the model's parameters (e.g., using 16-bit instead of 32-bit floats) to lower memory usage and increase speed.
    - **Knowledge Distillation:** Training smaller models to replicate the behavior of larger models, achieving similar performance with less computational power.
2. **Efficient Algorithms:**
    - **Sparse Representations:** Utilizing sparse data structures to minimize the number of operations and memory usage.

- o **Optimized Hardware Utilization:** Leveraging hardware accelerators (e.g., GPUs, TPUs) that are designed for efficient parallel processing.
3. **Software Optimization:**
   - o **Efficient Code Practices:** Writing optimized code that reduces unnecessary computations and leverages efficient libraries.
   - o **Batch Processing:** Processing multiple data points simultaneously to maximize hardware utilization and reduce energy consumption per operation.
4. **Adaptive Computing:**
   - o **Dynamic Resource Allocation:** Adjusting computational resources based on real-time demand to prevent over-provisioning.
   - o **Energy-aware Scheduling:** Scheduling tasks during periods of low energy demand or when renewable energy sources are abundant.

Example: Model Pruning in PyTorch

Below is an example of how to implement model pruning in PyTorch to create a more energy-efficient AI model.

```
import torch
import torch.nn as nn
import torch.nn.utils.prune as prune
import torch.optim as optim
from torchvision import datasets, transforms

# Define a simple neural network
class SimpleNet(nn.Module):
    def __init__(self):
        super(SimpleNet, self).__init__()
        self.fc1 = nn.Linear(28*28, 300)
        self.relu = nn.ReLU()
        self.fc2 = nn.Linear(300, 100)
        self.fc3 = nn.Linear(100, 10)

    def forward(self, x):
        x = x.view(-1, 28*28)
        x = self.relu(self.fc1(x))
        x = self.relu(self.fc2(x))
        x = self.fc3(x)
        return x

# Initialize the model, loss function, and optimizer
```

```python
model = SimpleNet()
criterion = nn.CrossEntropyLoss()
optimizer = optim.Adam(model.parameters(), lr=0.001)

# Apply pruning to fc1 layer
prune.random_unstructured(model.fc1, name="weight",
amount=0.3)

# Print the number of non-zero parameters before and after
pruning
def count_nonzero_params(model):
    nonzero = 0
    total = 0
    for param in model.parameters():
        nonzero += torch.count_nonzero(param).item()
        total += param.numel()
    return nonzero, total

nonzero, total = count_nonzero_params(model)
print(f"Non-zero parameters: {nonzero}/{total}
({(nonzero/total)*100:.2f}%)")

# Training loop (simplified)
transform = transforms.Compose([transforms.ToTensor()])
train_dataset = datasets.MNIST('.', train=True,
download=True, transform=transform)
train_loader = torch.utils.data.DataLoader(train_dataset,
batch_size=64, shuffle=True)

for epoch in range(1):
    for data, target in train_loader:
        optimizer.zero_grad()
        output = model(data)
        loss = criterion(output, target)
        loss.backward()
        optimizer.step()

# Evaluate model
test_dataset = datasets.MNIST('.', train=False,
transform=transform)
test_loader = torch.utils.data.DataLoader(test_dataset,
batch_size=1000, shuffle=False)

model.eval()
correct = 0
with torch.no_grad():
    for data, target in test_loader:
        output = model(data)
        pred = output.argmax(dim=1, keepdim=True)
        correct += pred.eq(target.view_as(pred)).sum().item()
```

```
print(f"Test Accuracy: {correct}/{len(test_loader.dataset)}
({(correct/len(test_loader.dataset))*100:.2f}%)")
```

Explanation:

- The `SimpleNet` neural network is defined with three fully connected layers.
- Pruning is applied to the first fully connected layer (`fc1`), removing 30% of the weights randomly.
- The `count_nonzero_params` function calculates the number of non-zero parameters before and after pruning, illustrating the reduction in model size.
- A simplified training loop trains the pruned model on the MNIST dataset.
- The model's accuracy is evaluated on the test dataset, demonstrating that pruning can reduce model size without significantly impacting performance.

Benefits:

- **Reduced Computational Load:** Pruned models require fewer computations, leading to lower energy consumption.
- **Faster Inference:** Smaller models can process data more quickly, enhancing real-time performance.
- **Lower Memory Usage:** Pruned models occupy less memory, making them suitable for deployment on resource-constrained devices.

16.2 Sustainable Deployment Strategies

Sustainable deployment strategies focus on minimizing the environmental impact of AI systems during their deployment phase. This involves choosing appropriate infrastructure, optimizing resource usage, and leveraging renewable energy sources.

Key Considerations for Sustainable Deployment:

1. **Infrastructure Selection:**

- **Energy-efficient Data Centers:** Choose data centers that prioritize energy efficiency through advanced cooling systems, energy-efficient hardware, and renewable energy sources.
- **Edge Computing:** Deploy AI agents closer to the data source to reduce the need for data transmission to centralized servers, thereby saving energy.

2. **Resource Optimization:**
   - **Virtualization and Containerization:** Use technologies like Docker and Kubernetes to maximize hardware utilization and minimize idle resources.
   - **Serverless Architectures:** Employ serverless computing to ensure that resources are only used when needed, reducing energy waste.

3. **Renewable Energy Utilization:**
   - **Green Hosting Providers:** Partner with cloud service providers that invest in renewable energy to power their data centers.
   - **On-premises Renewable Energy:** Implement renewable energy solutions, such as solar panels or wind turbines, to power on-premises AI infrastructure.

4. **Lifecycle Assessment:**
   - **Assess Environmental Impact:** Conduct a lifecycle assessment (LCA) to evaluate the environmental impact of AI systems from development to deployment and disposal.
   - **Sustainable Procurement:** Source hardware and software components from suppliers that adhere to sustainable practices.

Example: Sustainable Deployment with Kubernetes and Green Hosting

Below is an example of deploying a multi-agent system using Kubernetes on a green hosting platform like Google Cloud Platform (GCP), which commits to using renewable energy.

```
# deployment.yaml
apiVersion: apps/v1
kind: Deployment
metadata:
  name: multi-agent-system
spec:
  replicas: 5
```

```yaml
  selector:
    matchLabels:
      app: multi-agent-system
  template:
    metadata:
      labels:
        app: multi-agent-system
    spec:
      containers:
      - name: agent-container
        image: my-multi-agent-system:latest
        resources:
          requests:
            memory: "512Mi"
            cpu: "500m"
          limits:
            memory: "1Gi"
            cpu: "1"
        env:
        - name: ENVIRONMENT
          value: "production"
---
# service.yaml
apiVersion: v1
kind: Service
metadata:
  name: multi-agent-service
spec:
  type: LoadBalancer
  selector:
    app: multi-agent-system
  ports:
    - protocol: TCP
      port: 80
      targetPort: 5000
```

Explanation:

- The `deployment.yaml` file defines a Kubernetes deployment with 5 replicas of the multi-agent system container.
- Resource requests and limits ensure efficient utilization of CPU and memory, preventing over-provisioning and conserving energy.
- The `service.yaml` file exposes the deployment using a LoadBalancer, facilitating scalable and efficient access to the multi-agent system.
- Deploying on a green hosting platform like GCP ensures that the underlying infrastructure is powered by renewable energy sources, reducing the carbon footprint of the AI system.

Benefits:

- **Reduced Energy Consumption:** Optimizing resource allocation and using efficient infrastructure reduces overall energy usage.
- **Scalability:** Kubernetes enables scalable deployments, ensuring that resources are used efficiently based on demand.
- **Environmental Responsibility:** Choosing green hosting providers and renewable energy sources aligns AI deployments with sustainability goals.

16.3 Measuring and Reducing the Carbon Footprint

Measuring and reducing the carbon footprint of AI systems is essential for understanding their environmental impact and implementing strategies to mitigate it. This involves assessing energy consumption, identifying sources of emissions, and applying reduction techniques.

Steps to Measure and Reduce Carbon Footprint:

1. **Assess Energy Consumption:**
   - **Energy Audits:** Conduct comprehensive energy audits to determine the total energy usage of AI systems, including data centers, hardware, and computational processes.
   - **Monitoring Tools:** Utilize tools like **Energy Consumption Metering** and **Carbon Tracking Software** to monitor real-time energy usage.
2. **Identify Emission Sources:**
   - **Data Center Operations:** Analyze the energy consumption patterns of data centers, including cooling systems and server utilization.
   - **Agent Operations:** Evaluate the computational load of individual AI agents and their contribution to overall energy usage.
3. **Implement Reduction Strategies:**
   - **Energy-efficient Hardware:** Use energy-efficient processors, GPUs, and other hardware components that consume less power.

- o **Optimized Software:** Optimize algorithms and code to reduce computational requirements and improve efficiency.
- o **Renewable Energy Sources:** Transition to renewable energy sources to power AI infrastructure, thereby reducing carbon emissions.

4. **Offset Remaining Emissions:**
   - o **Carbon Offsetting:** Invest in carbon offset projects, such as reforestation or renewable energy initiatives, to compensate for unavoidable emissions.
   - o **Sustainable Practices:** Adopt sustainable practices in other areas of operations to balance out the carbon footprint of AI systems.

Tools for Measuring Carbon Footprint:

1. **CodeCarbon:**
   - o An open-source tool that estimates the carbon emissions of running Python scripts by analyzing their energy consumption and the energy mix of the hosting location.
2. **Cloud Carbon Footprint:**
   - o A tool that calculates the carbon footprint of cloud-based infrastructure, providing insights into energy usage and emissions.
3. **EnergyLens:**
   - o A real-time energy monitoring system that tracks the energy consumption of data centers and IT infrastructure.

Example: Estimating Carbon Footprint with CodeCarbon

Below is an example of how to use CodeCarbon to estimate the carbon emissions of a Python script running a simple multi-agent simulation.

```
# Install CodeCarbon
# !pip install codecarbon

from codecarbon import EmissionsTracker

def multi_agent_simulation():
    import time
    import random

    agents = ["Agent1", "Agent2", "Agent3", "Agent4",
"Agent5"]
```

```
    tasks = ["Task A", "Task B", "Task C", "Task D", "Task
E"]

    for _ in range(100):
        agent = random.choice(agents)
        task = random.choice(tasks)
        print(f"{agent} is performing {task}")
        time.sleep(0.1)  # Simulate task duration

# Initialize the emissions tracker
tracker = EmissionsTracker()
tracker.start()

# Run the multi-agent simulation
multi_agent_simulation()

# Stop the tracker and print the results
emissions = tracker.stop()
print(f"Estimated CO2 emissions: {emissions} kg")
```

Explanation:

- **CodeCarbon** is used to track the carbon emissions of running the `multi_agent_simulation` function.
- The simulation involves multiple agents performing random tasks, with each task simulated by a short sleep.
- After the simulation runs, CodeCarbon estimates the total CO2 emissions based on the energy consumed and the energy mix of the hosting location.

Benefits:

- **Awareness:** Understanding the carbon footprint of AI systems raises awareness and drives the implementation of reduction strategies.
- **Data-driven Decisions:** Accurate measurements enable informed decisions on where to focus energy-saving efforts.
- **Sustainability Goals:** Aligning AI operations with sustainability goals contributes to broader environmental objectives and corporate responsibility.

16.4 Green AI Innovations

Innovations in Green AI focus on developing new technologies and methodologies that enhance the sustainability of AI systems. These innovations aim to reduce energy consumption, optimize resource usage, and promote environmentally friendly practices in AI development and deployment.

Key Innovations in Green AI:

1. **Energy-efficient Neural Networks:**
   - **Sparse Neural Networks:** Networks with sparse connections reduce the number of computations required, leading to lower energy consumption.
   - **Binary Neural Networks:** Networks that use binary weights instead of floating-point numbers significantly reduce memory usage and computational complexity.
2. **Green AI Frameworks:**
   - **EcoAI:** A framework designed to optimize AI models for energy efficiency without compromising performance.
   - **Low-Power AI Libraries:** Libraries like **TensorFlow Lite** and **PyTorch Mobile** enable the deployment of AI models on low-power devices, promoting energy-efficient edge computing.
3. **Recyclable and Sustainable Hardware:**
   - **Modular Hardware Design:** Designing AI hardware with modular components allows for easier upgrades and recycling, reducing electronic waste.
   - **Biodegradable Materials:** Research into biodegradable materials for AI hardware components aims to minimize the environmental impact of device disposal.
4. **AI-driven Energy Management:**
   - **Smart Grids:** AI systems that manage and optimize energy distribution in smart grids, improving efficiency and reducing waste.
   - **Dynamic Resource Allocation:** AI-driven systems that dynamically allocate computational resources based on real-time demand, minimizing idle energy consumption.
5. **Federated and Distributed Learning:**
   - **Decentralized Training:** Federated learning enables AI agents to train models locally on edge devices, reducing the need for centralized data processing and lowering energy consumption.

o **Collaborative Learning:** Distributed learning techniques allow multiple agents to collaboratively train models, optimizing resource usage across the network.

Example: Implementing a Sparse Neural Network with PyTorch

Below is an example of how to implement a sparse neural network in PyTorch to enhance energy efficiency.

```python
import torch
import torch.nn as nn
import torch.nn.utils.prune as prune
import torch.optim as optim
from torchvision import datasets, transforms

# Define a sparse neural network
class SparseNet(nn.Module):
    def __init__(self):
        super(SparseNet, self).__init__()
        self.fc1 = nn.Linear(28*28, 300)
        self.relu = nn.ReLU()
        self.fc2 = nn.Linear(300, 100)
        self.fc3 = nn.Linear(100, 10)

    def forward(self, x):
        x = x.view(-1, 28*28)
        x = self.relu(self.fc1(x))
        x = self.relu(self.fc2(x))
        x = self.fc3(x)
        return x

# Initialize the model, loss function, and optimizer
model = SparseNet()
criterion = nn.CrossEntropyLoss()
optimizer = optim.Adam(model.parameters(), lr=0.001)

# Apply pruning to fc1 and fc2 layers
prune.random_unstructured(model.fc1, name="weight",
amount=0.5)
prune.random_unstructured(model.fc2, name="weight",
amount=0.4)

# Print the sparsity of the layers
def print_sparsity(model):
    for name, module in model.named_modules():
        if isinstance(module, nn.Linear):
            weight = module.weight
            sparsity = float(torch.sum(weight == 0)) /
float(weight.nelement())
```

```
        print(f"Sparsity in {name}: {sparsity*100:.2f}%")

print_sparsity(model)

# Training loop (simplified)
transform = transforms.Compose([transforms.ToTensor()])
train_dataset = datasets.MNIST('.', train=True,
download=True, transform=transform)
train_loader = torch.utils.data.DataLoader(train_dataset,
batch_size=64, shuffle=True)

for epoch in range(1):
    for data, target in train_loader:
        optimizer.zero_grad()
        output = model(data)
        loss = criterion(output, target)
        loss.backward()
        optimizer.step()

# Evaluate model
test_dataset = datasets.MNIST('.', train=False,
transform=transform)
test_loader = torch.utils.data.DataLoader(test_dataset,
batch_size=1000, shuffle=False)

model.eval()
correct = 0
with torch.no_grad():
    for data, target in test_loader:
        output = model(data)
        pred = output.argmax(dim=1, keepdim=True)
        correct += pred.eq(target.view_as(pred)).sum().item()

print(f"Test Accuracy: {correct}/{len(test_loader.dataset)}
({(correct/len(test_loader.dataset))*100:.2f}%)")
```

Explanation:

- **SparseNet** is a simple neural network model with three fully connected layers.
- Pruning is applied to the first two layers (`fc1` and `fc2`), removing 50% and 40% of the weights, respectively.
- The `print_sparsity` function calculates and prints the sparsity of each linear layer, showing the percentage of weights that have been pruned.
- The model is trained on the MNIST dataset, demonstrating that sparsity can be achieved without significantly degrading performance.

Benefits:

- **Reduced Computational Requirements:** Sparse networks require fewer computations, leading to lower energy consumption.
- **Faster Inference:** Sparse models can process data more quickly, enhancing real-time performance.
- **Lower Memory Usage:** Reduced number of parameters decreases memory usage, enabling deployment on resource-constrained devices.

16.5 Reflection Questions

Reflecting on the concepts covered in this chapter is essential for understanding the role of sustainability in AI systems and identifying actionable steps to enhance Green AI practices. Consider the following questions:

1. **Why is energy efficiency important in multi-agent AI systems, and what are some common strategies to achieve it?**
   - Reflect on the environmental and economic benefits of reducing energy consumption and how techniques like model pruning and efficient algorithms contribute to this goal.
2. **How can sustainable deployment strategies minimize the environmental impact of AI systems?**
   - Think about the role of infrastructure selection, renewable energy utilization, and resource optimization in promoting sustainable AI deployments.
3. **What tools and methodologies can be used to measure the carbon footprint of AI systems, and how can these measurements inform reduction strategies?**
   - Consider the importance of accurate measurements in identifying emission sources and the effectiveness of tools like CodeCarbon and Cloud Carbon Footprint.
4. **Describe some innovative approaches in Green AI and how they contribute to the sustainability of AI systems.**
   - Explore how innovations like sparse neural networks, federated learning, and AI-driven energy management enhance the environmental sustainability of AI.

5. **What challenges might arise when implementing Green AI practices, and how can they be addressed?**
    - Reflect on potential obstacles such as balancing performance with energy efficiency and the costs associated with adopting sustainable technologies, and consider strategies to overcome these challenges.

Chapter 17: Step-by-Step Tutorials

Practical implementation is essential for understanding and leveraging the full potential of **multi-agent AI systems**. This chapter provides detailed, step-by-step tutorials to guide you through building basic and advanced multi-agent systems, deploying and scaling your AI systems, integrating with external technologies, and engaging in a comprehensive hands-on project. By following these tutorials, you will gain the practical skills needed to develop, deploy, and manage effective multi-agent AI systems in real-world scenarios.

17.1 Building a Basic Multi-agent System

Creating a basic multi-agent system involves defining agents, their behaviors, and the environment in which they operate. This tutorial will guide you through building a simple multi-agent system using Python, where agents perform tasks and interact within a shared environment.

Objectives:

- Understand the fundamental components of a multi-agent system.
- Implement basic agents with distinct behaviors.
- Simulate interactions between agents in an environment.

Components of a Basic Multi-agent System:

1. **Agents:** Entities that perform actions based on predefined behaviors.
2. **Environment:** The shared space where agents operate and interact.
3. **Tasks:** Activities or goals that agents aim to accomplish.
4. **Interactions:** Communication or actions between agents that influence their behavior or task outcomes.

Step-by-Step Implementation:

Step 1: Define the Agent Class

Create a base class for agents, encapsulating their basic properties and behaviors.

```
class Agent:
    def __init__(self, name, environment):
        self.name = name
        self.environment = environment
        self.position = environment.get_random_position()

    def perform_action(self):
        raise NotImplementedError("This method should be
overridden by subclasses.")

    def move(self, new_position):
        print(f"{self.name} moves from {self.position} to
{new_position}.")
        self.position = new_position
```

Explanation:

- **Agent Class:** The base class for all agents, storing the agent's name, environment, and current position.
- **perform_action:** An abstract method to be implemented by subclasses, defining the agent's behavior.
- **move:** A method to change the agent's position within the environment.

Step 2: Define Specific Agent Behaviors

Implement subclasses with specific behaviors.

```
import random

class WorkerAgent(Agent):
    def perform_action(self):
        # Example behavior: Move randomly
        new_position = self.environment.get_random_position()
        self.move(new_position)
        print(f"{self.name} performed a work task at
{self.position}.")

class ExplorerAgent(Agent):
    def perform_action(self):
        # Example behavior: Explore new areas
        new_position = self.environment.get_random_position()
        self.move(new_position)
        print(f"{self.name} explored to {self.position}.")
```

Explanation:

- **WorkerAgent:** Moves randomly within the environment and performs a work task.
- **ExplorerAgent:** Moves to new positions to explore different areas.

Step 3: Define the Environment Class

Create an environment where agents can operate.

```
class Environment:
    def __init__(self, size):
        self.size = size  # e.g., size = (width, height)

    def get_random_position(self):
        x = random.randint(0, self.size[0] - 1)
        y = random.randint(0, self.size[1] - 1)
        return (x, y)
```

Explanation:

- **Environment Class:** Defines the operational space for agents with a specified size.
- **get_random_position:** Generates random positions within the environment boundaries.

Step 4: Initialize the System and Simulate Agent Actions

Set up the environment, create agents, and simulate their interactions.

```
import time

def main():
    # Initialize environment
    env = Environment(size=(10, 10))

    # Create agents
    agents = [
        WorkerAgent("Worker1", env),
        WorkerAgent("Worker2", env),
        ExplorerAgent("Explorer1", env)
    ]

    # Simulate agent actions
    for step in range(5):
        print(f"\n--- Step {step + 1} ---")
        for agent in agents:
            agent.perform_action()
        time.sleep(1)  # Pause for readability
```

```
if __name__ == "__main__":
    main()
```

Explanation:

- **main Function:** Initializes the environment and agents, then simulates a series of actions over multiple steps.
- **Simulation Loop:** Each agent performs its action in each step, demonstrating interactions within the environment.

Sample Output:

```
--- Step 1 ---
Worker1 moves from (3, 7) to (2, 4).
Worker1 performed a work task at (2, 4).
Worker2 moves from (9, 1) to (5, 5).
Worker2 performed a work task at (5, 5).
Explorer1 moves from (0, 0) to (4, 9).
Explorer1 explored to (4, 9).

--- Step 2 ---
Worker1 moves from (2, 4) to (7, 2).
Worker1 performed a work task at (7, 2).
Worker2 moves from (5, 5) to (1, 8).
Worker2 performed a work task at (1, 8).
Explorer1 moves from (4, 9) to (6, 3).
Explorer1 explored to (6, 3).

... (additional steps)
```

17.2 Implementing Advanced Coordination Mechanisms

Advanced coordination mechanisms enable agents to work together more effectively, share information, and achieve complex goals. This tutorial focuses on implementing coordination strategies such as task allocation, communication protocols, and collaborative problem-solving in a multi-agent system.

Objectives:

- Implement task allocation strategies.

- Establish communication protocols between agents.
- Facilitate collaborative problem-solving among agents.

Coordination Strategies:

1. **Task Allocation:**
   - Distribute tasks among agents based on their capabilities, availability, or other criteria.
2. **Communication Protocols:**
   - Define how agents communicate, share information, and coordinate actions.
3. **Collaborative Problem-Solving:**
   - Enable agents to work together to solve complex tasks that require multiple steps or specialized knowledge.

Step-by-Step Implementation:

Step 1: Enhance the Environment with Task Management

Modify the `Environment` class to include task management capabilities.

```python
class Environment:
    def __init__(self, size):
        self.size = size  # e.g., size = (width, height)
        self.tasks = self.generate_tasks()

    def get_random_position(self):
        x = random.randint(0, self.size[0] - 1)
        y = random.randint(0, self.size[1] - 1)
        return (x, y)

    def generate_tasks(self):
        # Generate a list of tasks with positions
        tasks = [
            {"id": 1, "description": "Collect samples",
"position": self.get_random_position()},
            {"id": 2, "description": "Analyze data",
"position": self.get_random_position()},
            {"id": 3, "description": "Report findings",
"position": self.get_random_position()}
        ]
        return tasks

    def assign_task(self, agent):
        if self.tasks:
            task = self.tasks.pop(0)
```

```
                print(f"Assigning Task '{task['description']}' to
{agent.name}")
                return task
        else:
            print("No tasks available to assign.")
            return None
```

Explanation:

- **generate_tasks:** Creates a predefined list of tasks with specific positions.
- **assign_task:** Assigns the next available task to an agent, removing it from the task list.

Step 2: Implement Task-Oriented Agents

Create agents that can receive and perform assigned tasks.

```
class TaskAgent(Agent):
    def __init__(self, name, environment):
        super().__init__(name, environment)
        self.current_task = None

    def perform_action(self):
        if not self.current_task:
            self.current_task =
self.environment.assign_task(self)
            if self.current_task:
                print(f"{self.name} received task:
{self.current_task['description']} at
{self.current_task['position']}")
        else:
            # Move towards task position
            self.move_towards(self.current_task['position'])
            if self.position ==
self.current_task['position']:
                print(f"{self.name} completed task:
{self.current_task['description']}")
                self.current_task = None

    def move_towards(self, target_position):
        # Simple movement towards target_position
        x, y = self.position
        target_x, target_y = target_position
        new_x = x + 1 if x < target_x else x - 1 if x >
target_x else x
        new_y = y + 1 if y < target_y else y - 1 if y >
target_y else y
```

```
        self.move((new_x, new_y))
```

Explanation:

- **TaskAgent:** Extends the base `Agent` class to handle task assignment and execution.
- **perform_action:** Checks for an assigned task and moves towards the task position. Upon reaching the position, it marks the task as completed.
- **move_towards:** Implements a simple strategy to move step-by-step towards the target position.

Step 3: Implement Communication Protocols

Enable agents to communicate and share information.

```
class CommunicatingAgent(Agent):
    def __init__(self, name, environment):
        super().__init__(name, environment)
        self.message_queue = []

    def send_message(self, recipient, message):
        recipient.receive_message(f"{self.name}: {message}")
        print(f"{self.name} sent message to {recipient.name}:
{message}")

    def receive_message(self, message):
        self.message_queue.append(message)
        print(f"{self.name} received message: {message}")

    def process_messages(self):
        while self.message_queue:
            message = self.message_queue.pop(0)
            print(f"{self.name} processing message:
{message}")
            # Implement message processing logic here

    def perform_action(self):
        self.process_messages()
        # Implement agent's primary action here
```

Explanation:

- **CommunicatingAgent:** Extends the base `Agent` class to include messaging capabilities.
- **send_message:** Sends a message to another agent.

- **receive_message:** Receives and stores incoming messages.
- **process_messages:** Processes and handles received messages.

Step 4: Simulate Coordination and Collaboration

Combine task-oriented and communicating agents to demonstrate advanced coordination.

```python
def main():
    # Initialize environment
    env = Environment(size=(10, 10))

    # Create agents
    agents = [
        TaskAgent("TaskAgent1", env),
        TaskAgent("TaskAgent2", env),
        CommunicatingAgent("CommunicatorAgent1", env)
    ]

    # Simulate agent actions
    for step in range(10):
        print(f"\n--- Step {step + 1} ---")
        for agent in agents:
            agent.perform_action()
            if isinstance(agent, CommunicatingAgent) and step == 2:
                # At step 3, CommunicatorAgent sends a message
                agent.send_message(agents[0], "Please prioritize collecting samples.")
        time.sleep(1)  # Pause for readability

if __name__ == "__main__":
    main()
```

Explanation:

- **TaskAgents:** Receive and execute tasks within the environment.
- **CommunicatingAgent:** Sends messages to other agents to influence task prioritization.
- **Simulation Loop:** Demonstrates how communication can influence task execution and coordination among agents.

Sample Output:

```
--- Step 1 ---
Assigning Task 'Collect samples' to TaskAgent1
```

```
TaskAgent1 received task: Collect samples at (2, 5)
TaskAgent1 moves from (3, 7) to (4, 8).
TaskAgent1 received task: Collect samples at (2, 5)
Assigning Task 'Analyze data' to TaskAgent2
TaskAgent2 received task: Analyze data at (7, 1)
TaskAgent2 moves from (9, 1) to (8, 1).
CommunicatorAgent1 is processing message:

--- Step 3 ---
TaskAgent1 moves from (4, 8) to (5, 8).
TaskAgent2 moves from (8, 1) to (7, 1).
CommunicatorAgent1 sent message to TaskAgent1: Please
prioritize collecting samples.
TaskAgent1 received message: CommunicatorAgent1: Please
prioritize collecting samples.
```

17.3 Deploying and Scaling Your AI System

Deploying and scaling multi-agent AI systems ensure that they can handle increased workloads, maintain performance, and remain accessible across different environments. This tutorial covers deploying a multi-agent system using Docker and Kubernetes, implementing scalable architectures, and leveraging cloud platforms for deployment.

Objectives:

- Containerize a multi-agent system using Docker.
- Deploy the system using Kubernetes for orchestration.
- Implement scaling strategies to handle varying workloads.

Deployment Tools:

- **Docker:** For containerizing applications.
- **Kubernetes:** For orchestrating and managing containerized applications.
- **Cloud Platforms:** Such as AWS, Google Cloud, or Azure, for scalable and reliable deployments.

Step-by-Step Implementation:

Step 1: Containerize the Multi-agent System with Docker

Create a `Dockerfile` to containerize the multi-agent system.

```
# Dockerfile

# Use an official Python runtime as a parent image
FROM python:3.8-slim

# Set environment variables
ENV PYTHONDONTWRITEBYTECODE 1
ENV PYTHONUNBUFFERED 1

# Set the working directory
WORKDIR /usr/src/app

# Install dependencies
COPY requirements.txt .
RUN pip install --upgrade pip
RUN pip install -r requirements.txt

# Copy the application code
COPY . .

# Expose the port the app runs on
EXPOSE 5000

# Run the application
CMD ["python", "multi_agent_system.py"]
```

Explanation:

- **Base Image:** Uses a lightweight Python 3.8 image.
- **Environment Variables:** Prevents Python from writing `.pyc` files and buffers output for real-time logging.
- **Working Directory:** Sets the working directory inside the container.
- **Dependencies:** Installs required Python packages from `requirements.txt`.
- **Application Code:** Copies the multi-agent system code into the container.
- **Port Exposure:** Exposes port 5000 for communication.
- **Run Command:** Specifies the command to run the application.

Step 2: Create a `requirements.txt` File

List all necessary Python packages.

```
# requirements.txt
flask
```

Explanation:

- **Flask:** Used here as an example for creating a simple web server to manage agent interactions. Adjust based on actual dependencies.

Step 3: Implement the Multi-agent System as a Flask Application

Modify the multi-agent system to run as a Flask web service for better integration and scalability.

```python
# multi_agent_system.py

from flask import Flask, jsonify, request
import threading
import time
import random

app = Flask(__name__)

class Agent:
    def __init__(self, name, environment):
        self.name = name
        self.environment = environment
        self.position = environment.get_random_position()
        self.active = True

    def perform_action(self):
        raise NotImplementedError("This method should be
overridden by subclasses.")

    def move(self, new_position):
        print(f"{self.name} moves from {self.position} to
{new_position}.")
        self.position = new_position

class TaskAgent(Agent):
    def __init__(self, name, environment):
        super().__init__(name, environment)
        self.current_task = None

    def perform_action(self):
        if not self.current_task:
            self.current_task =
self.environment.assign_task(self)
            if self.current_task:
                print(f"{self.name} received task:
{self.current_task['description']} at
{self.current_task['position']}")
        else:
            self.move_towards(self.current_task['position'])
```

```python
            if self.position ==
self.current_task['position']:
                print(f"{self.name} completed task:
{self.current_task['description']}")
                self.current_task = None

    def move_towards(self, target_position):
        x, y = self.position
        target_x, target_y = target_position
        new_x = x + 1 if x < target_x else x - 1 if x >
target_x else x
        new_y = y + 1 if y < target_y else y - 1 if y >
target_y else y
        self.move((new_x, new_y))

class Environment:
    def __init__(self, size):
        self.size = size
        self.tasks = self.generate_tasks()

    def get_random_position(self):
        x = random.randint(0, self.size[0] - 1)
        y = random.randint(0, self.size[1] - 1)
        return (x, y)

    def generate_tasks(self):
        tasks = [
            {"id": 1, "description": "Collect samples",
"position": self.get_random_position()},
            {"id": 2, "description": "Analyze data",
"position": self.get_random_position()},
            {"id": 3, "description": "Report findings",
"position": self.get_random_position()}
        ]
        return tasks

    def assign_task(self, agent):
        if self.tasks:
            task = self.tasks.pop(0)
            print(f"Assigning Task '{task['description']}' to
{agent.name}")
            return task
        else:
            print("No tasks available to assign.")
            return None

# Initialize environment and agents
env = Environment(size=(10, 10))
agents = [
    TaskAgent("TaskAgent1", env),
    TaskAgent("TaskAgent2", env)
```

```python
]

def agent_loop(agent):
    while agent.active:
        agent.perform_action()
        time.sleep(1)

# Start agent threads
for agent in agents:
    thread = threading.Thread(target=agent_loop,
args=(agent,))
    thread.start()

@app.route('/status', methods=['GET'])
def status():
    status_info = {}
    for agent in agents:
        status_info[agent.name] = {
            "position": agent.position,
            "current_task": agent.current_task["description"]
if agent.current_task else "None"
        }
    return jsonify(status_info)

@app.route('/assign_task', methods=['POST'])
def assign_task():
    data = request.json
    agent_name = data.get('agent_name')
    task_description = data.get('task_description')
    task_position = data.get('task_position')
    for agent in agents:
        if agent.name == agent_name and not
agent.current_task:
            new_task = {"id": len(env.tasks) + 1,
"description": task_description, "position":
tuple(task_position)}
            env.tasks.append(new_task)
            return jsonify({"message": f"Task
'{task_description}' assigned to {agent_name}."}), 200
    return jsonify({"message": "Agent not found or already
has a task."}), 400

@app.route('/shutdown', methods=['POST'])
def shutdown():
    for agent in agents:
        agent.active = False
    return jsonify({"message": "Shutting down agents."}), 200

if __name__ == '__main__':
    app.run(host='0.0.0.0', port=5000)
```

Explanation:

- **Flask Application:** Exposes endpoints to monitor agent status, assign tasks, and shut down agents.
- **agent_loop Function:** Runs each agent's action loop in a separate thread.
- **Endpoints:**
    - `/status`: Returns the current status of all agents.
    - `/assign_task`: Allows dynamic task assignment via POST requests.
    - `/shutdown`: Gracefully shuts down all agents.

Step 4: Build and Run the Docker Container

1. **Build the Docker Image:**
2. `docker build -t multi-agent-system:latest .`
3. **Run the Docker Container:**
4. `docker run -d -p 5000:5000 --name multi-agent-container multi-agent-system:latest`

Explanation:

- **Build Command:** Creates a Docker image named `multi-agent-system` using the `Dockerfile`.
- **Run Command:** Launches the container in detached mode, mapping port 5000 from the container to the host.

Step 5: Deploy the System Using Kubernetes

Create a Kubernetes Deployment Configuration:

```
# deployment.yaml
apiVersion: apps/v1
kind: Deployment
metadata:
  name: multi-agent-deployment
spec:
  replicas: 3
  selector:
    matchLabels:
      app: multi-agent
  template:
    metadata:
      labels:
        app: multi-agent
```

```
spec:
  containers:
  - name: multi-agent-container
    image: multi-agent-system:latest
    ports:
    - containerPort: 5000
    resources:
      requests:
        memory: "512Mi"
        cpu: "500m"
      limits:
        memory: "1Gi"
        cpu: "1"
```

Create a Kubernetes Service Configuration:

```
# service.yaml
apiVersion: v1
kind: Service
metadata:
  name: multi-agent-service
spec:
  type: LoadBalancer
  selector:
    app: multi-agent
  ports:
    - protocol: TCP
      port: 80
      targetPort: 5000
```

Apply the Configurations:

```
kubectl apply -f deployment.yaml
kubectl apply -f service.yaml
```

Explanation:

- **Deployment Configuration:** Defines a deployment with 3 replicas of the multi-agent container, ensuring high availability and load distribution.
- **Service Configuration:** Exposes the deployment as a LoadBalancer service, making it accessible externally.
- **Resource Management:** Specifies resource requests and limits to optimize resource usage and ensure energy efficiency.

Step 6: Implement Scaling Strategies

Manual Scaling:

```
kubectl scale deployment multi-agent-deployment --
replicas=5
```

Auto-scaling with Horizontal Pod Autoscaler:

```
# hpa.yaml
apiVersion: autoscaling/v1
kind: HorizontalPodAutoscaler
metadata:
  name: multi-agent-hpa
spec:
  scaleTargetRef:
    apiVersion: apps/v1
    kind: Deployment
    name: multi-agent-deployment
  minReplicas: 3
  maxReplicas: 10
  targetCPUUtilizationPercentage: 70
```

Apply the HPA Configuration:

```
kubectl apply -f hpa.yaml
```

Explanation:

- **Manual Scaling:** Adjusts the number of replicas based on anticipated load.
- **Auto-scaling:** Automatically adjusts the number of replicas based on CPU utilization, ensuring that the system scales dynamically to handle varying workloads efficiently.

Benefits of Deployment and Scaling:

- **High Availability:** Ensures the system remains operational even if some agents fail.
- **Scalability:** Allows the system to handle increased workloads without compromising performance.
- **Resource Efficiency:** Optimizes the use of computational resources, reducing energy consumption and operational costs.

- **Flexibility:** Enables easy updates and management of the multi-agent system across different environments.

:

Deploying and scaling multi-agent AI systems using Docker and Kubernetes provides a robust and flexible infrastructure that can handle varying workloads and ensure high availability. By implementing scalable architectures and leveraging cloud platforms, you can efficiently manage and expand your AI systems to meet real-world demands.

17.4 Integrating with External Technologies

Integrating multi-agent AI systems with external technologies enhances their capabilities, enabling them to interact with other systems, access additional data sources, and leverage specialized functionalities. This tutorial covers integrating a multi-agent system with databases, APIs, IoT devices, and machine learning frameworks.

Objectives:

- Connect the multi-agent system to external databases for data storage and retrieval.
- Utilize APIs for communication with other services.
- Integrate with IoT devices for real-time data collection.
- Leverage machine learning frameworks to enhance agent intelligence.

Integration Technologies:

- **Databases:** PostgreSQL, MongoDB
- **APIs:** RESTful APIs, WebSockets
- **IoT Devices:** MQTT, HTTP
- **Machine Learning Frameworks:** TensorFlow, PyTorch

Step-by-Step Implementation:

Step 1: Integrate with a Database (PostgreSQL)

Install PostgreSQL and Required Libraries:

```
pip install psycopg2-binary
```

Modify the Multi-agent System to Use PostgreSQL:

```python
import psycopg2

class Environment:
    def __init__(self, size, db_config):
        self.size = size
        self.tasks = self.generate_tasks()
        self.conn = psycopg2.connect(**db_config)
        self.create_tasks_table()

    def create_tasks_table(self):
        with self.conn.cursor() as cursor:
            cursor.execute("""
                CREATE TABLE IF NOT EXISTS tasks (
                    id SERIAL PRIMARY KEY,
                    description TEXT NOT NULL,
                    position_x INT NOT NULL,
                    position_y INT NOT NULL,
                    assigned BOOLEAN DEFAULT FALSE
                );
            """)
            self.conn.commit()

    def generate_tasks(self):
        tasks = [
            {"description": "Collect samples", "position":
self.get_random_position()},
            {"description": "Analyze data", "position":
self.get_random_position()},
            {"description": "Report findings", "position":
self.get_random_position()}
        ]
        with self.conn.cursor() as cursor:
            for task in tasks:
                cursor.execute("""
                    INSERT INTO tasks (description,
position_x, position_y)
                    VALUES (%s, %s, %s);
                """, (task['description'],
task['position'][0], task['position'][1]))
            self.conn.commit()
        return tasks

    def assign_task(self, agent):
        with self.conn.cursor() as cursor:
```

```
        cursor.execute("""
            SELECT id, description, position_x,
position_y FROM tasks
            WHERE assigned = FALSE ORDER BY id LIMIT
1;
        """)
        result = cursor.fetchone()
        if result:
            task_id, description, x, y = result
            cursor.execute("""
                UPDATE tasks SET assigned = TRUE WHERE
id = %s;
            """, (task_id,))
            self.conn.commit()
            task = {"id": task_id, "description":
description, "position": (x, y)}
            print(f"Assigning Task
'{task['description']}' to {agent.name}")
            return task
        else:
            print("No tasks available to assign.")
            return None
```

Explanation:

PostgreSQL Integration: Connects to a PostgreSQL database to store and manage tasks.

create_tasks_table: Creates a table for tasks if it doesn't exist.

generate_tasks: Inserts predefined tasks into the database.

assign_task: Retrieves and assigns the next available task from the database.

Step 2: Integrate with an External API (RESTful API)

Install Requests Library:

```
pip install requests
```

Modify Agents to Communicate with an External API:

```
import requests

class TaskAgent(Agent):
    def __init__(self, name, environment, api_url):
```

```python
        super().__init__(name, environment)
        self.api_url = api_url

    def perform_action(self):
        if not self.current_task:
            self.current_task =
self.environment.assign_task(self)
            if self.current_task:
                print(f"{self.name} received task:
{self.current_task['description']} at
{self.current_task['position']}")
                # Notify external API about task
assignment
                self.notify_api("assign",
self.current_task)
        else:

self.move_towards(self.current_task['position'])
            if self.position ==
self.current_task['position']:
                print(f"{self.name} completed task:
{self.current_task['description']}")
                # Notify external API about task
completion
                self.notify_api("complete",
self.current_task)
                self.current_task = None

    def notify_api(self, status, task):
        payload = {
            "agent_name": self.name,
            "task_id": task['id'],
            "status": status,
            "position": self.position
        }
        try:
            response =
requests.post(f"{self.api_url}/task_update", json=payload)
            if response.status_code == 200:
                print(f"{self.name} successfully notified
API about task {status}.")
            else:
                print(f"{self.name} failed to notify API:
{response.text}")
        except requests.exceptions.RequestException as e:
            print(f"{self.name} encountered an error while
notifying API: {e}")
```

Explanation:

- **External API Integration:** Agents send task assignment and completion updates to an external API endpoint.
- **notify_api Method:** Handles communication with the external API using HTTP POST requests.

Step 3: Integrate with an IoT Device (MQTT Protocol)

Install Paho-MQTT Library:

```
pip install paho-mqtt
```

Modify Agents to Communicate with IoT Devices via MQTT:

```python
import paho.mqtt.client as mqtt

class IoTAgent(Agent):
    def __init__(self, name, environment, mqtt_broker,
mqtt_port):
        super().__init__(name, environment)
        self.client = mqtt.Client()
        self.client.connect(mqtt_broker, mqtt_port, 60)
        self.client.loop_start()

    def perform_action(self):
        if not self.current_task:
            self.current_task =
self.environment.assign_task(self)
            if self.current_task:
                print(f"{self.name} received task:
{self.current_task['description']} at
{self.current_task['position']}")
                self.publish_iot_event("task_assigned",
self.current_task)
        else:

self.move_towards(self.current_task['position'])
            if self.position ==
self.current_task['position']:
                print(f"{self.name} completed task:
{self.current_task['description']}")
                self.publish_iot_event("task_completed",
self.current_task)
                self.current_task = None

    def publish_iot_event(self, event_type, task):
        topic = f"agents/{self.name}/events"
```

```
        payload = {
            "event": event_type,
            "task_id": task['id'],
            "position": self.position
        }
        self.client.publish(topic, payload)
        print(f"{self.name} published IoT event:
{event_type}")
```

Explanation:

- **IoT Integration:** Agents publish task events to an MQTT broker, enabling communication with IoT devices or other systems.
- **publish_iot_event Method:** Publishes events to a specific MQTT topic for real-time data exchange.

Step 4: Integrate with a Machine Learning Framework (TensorFlow)

Install TensorFlow:

```
pip install tensorflow
```

Modify Agents to Utilize TensorFlow Models for Decision Making:

```
import tensorflow as tf
import numpy as np

class MLAgent(Agent):
    def __init__(self, name, environment, model_path):
        super().__init__(name, environment)
        self.model =
tf.keras.models.load_model(model_path)

    def perform_action(self):
        if not self.current_task:
            self.current_task =
self.environment.assign_task(self)
            if self.current_task:
                print(f"{self.name} received task:
{self.current_task['description']} at
{self.current_task['position']}")
                self.predict_next_move()
        else:

self.move_towards(self.current_task['position'])
            if self.position ==
self.current_task['position']:
```

```python
        print(f"{self.name} completed task:
{self.current_task['description']}")
                self.current_task = None

    def predict_next_move(self):
        # Example prediction based on current position
        input_data = np.array([[self.position[0],
self.position[1]]])
        prediction = self.model.predict(input_data)
        direction = np.argmax(prediction)
        # Define movement based on prediction
        new_position = (
            self.position[0] + (1 if direction == 0 else -
1 if direction == 1 else 0),
            self.position[1] + (1 if direction == 2 else -
1 if direction == 3 else 0)
        )
        self.move(new_position)
        print(f"{self.name} predicted direction and moved
to {new_position}.")
```

Explanation:

- **Machine Learning Integration:** Agents use TensorFlow models to predict their next move based on their current position.
- **predict_next_move Method:** Utilizes the loaded TensorFlow model to determine the direction of movement, enhancing decision-making capabilities.

Benefits of Integrating External Technologies:

- **Enhanced Functionality:** Expands the capabilities of multi-agent systems by leveraging specialized tools and services.
- **Real-time Data Access:** Facilitates access to real-time data from databases, APIs, and IoT devices, enabling more informed decision-making.
- **Scalability and Flexibility:** Allows the system to integrate with scalable cloud services and adapt to various operational requirements.
- **Improved Intelligence:** Incorporating machine learning models enhances the intelligence and adaptability of agents, allowing them to perform more complex tasks.

:

Integrating multi-agent AI systems with external technologies such as databases, APIs, IoT devices, and machine learning frameworks significantly enhances their capabilities and applicability. These integrations enable agents to access and process diverse data sources, communicate effectively with other systems, and leverage advanced algorithms for improved performance and decision-making.

17.5 Interactive Tutorial: Hands-on Multi-agent System Development

Objective:

Develop a comprehensive multi-agent system that includes task management, communication, integration with an external API, and deployment using Docker and Kubernetes. This hands-on tutorial will guide you through the entire process, ensuring you gain practical experience in building and deploying a functional multi-agent AI system.

Prerequisites:

- Basic knowledge of Python programming.
- Familiarity with Docker and Kubernetes.
- Understanding of RESTful APIs.
- Basic understanding of threading and concurrency in Python.

Project Overview:

Build a multi-agent system where agents receive tasks from a RESTful API, perform their actions within a simulated environment, communicate their status, and expose endpoints for monitoring and task management. The system will be containerized using Docker and orchestrated with Kubernetes for scalability.

Step-by-Step Tutorial:

Step 1: Set Up the Development Environment

Install Required Tools:

Python 3.8+

Docker

Kubernetes (Minikube or a cloud-based Kubernetes service)

Postman or curl for API testing

Create Project Structure:

```
mkdir multi-agent-system
cd multi-agent-system
mkdir agents
touch multi_agent_system.py requirements.txt Dockerfile
deployment.yaml service.yaml
```

Step 2: Implement the Multi-agent System

Define the Environment and Agent Classes:

```
# agents/agent.py

import random
import threading
import time
import requests
import paho.mqtt.client as mqtt
import tensorflow as tf
import numpy as np

class Environment:
    def __init__(self, size, db_config):
        self.size = size
        self.tasks = self.generate_tasks()
        self.conn = self.connect_db(db_config)
        self.create_tasks_table()

    def connect_db(self, db_config):
        import psycopg2
        try:
            conn = psycopg2.connect(**db_config)
            return conn
        except Exception as e:
            print(f"Database connection failed: {e}")
            return None

    def create_tasks_table(self):
        if self.conn:
```

```python
        with self.conn.cursor() as cursor:
            cursor.execute("""
                CREATE TABLE IF NOT EXISTS tasks (
                    id SERIAL PRIMARY KEY,
                    description TEXT NOT NULL,
                    position_x INT NOT NULL,
                    position_y INT NOT NULL,
                    assigned BOOLEAN DEFAULT FALSE
                );
            """)
            self.conn.commit()

    def generate_tasks(self):
        tasks = [
            {"description": "Collect samples", "position":
self.get_random_position()},
            {"description": "Analyze data", "position":
self.get_random_position()},
            {"description": "Report findings", "position":
self.get_random_position()}
        ]
        if self.conn:
            with self.conn.cursor() as cursor:
                for task in tasks:
                    cursor.execute("""
                        INSERT INTO tasks (description,
position_x, position_y)
                        VALUES (%s, %s, %s);
                    """, (task['description'],
task['position'][0], task['position'][1]))
                self.conn.commit()
        return tasks

    def get_random_position(self):
        x = random.randint(0, self.size[0] - 1)
        y = random.randint(0, self.size[1] - 1)
        return (x, y)

    def assign_task(self, agent):
        if self.conn:
            with self.conn.cursor() as cursor:
                cursor.execute("""
                    SELECT id, description, position_x,
position_y FROM tasks
                    WHERE assigned = FALSE ORDER BY id
LIMIT 1;
                """)
                result = cursor.fetchone()
                if result:
                    task_id, description, x, y = result
                    cursor.execute("""
```

```python
                                UPDATE tasks SET assigned = TRUE
WHERE id = %s;
                        """, (task_id,))
                        self.conn.commit()
                        task = {"id": task_id, "description":
description, "position": (x, y)}
                        print(f"Assigning Task
'{task['description']}' to {agent.name}")
                        return task
        print("No tasks available to assign.")
        return None

class Agent:
    def __init__(self, name, environment):
        self.name = name
        self.environment = environment
        self.position = environment.get_random_position()
        self.current_task = None
        self.active = True

    def perform_action(self):
        raise NotImplementedError("This method should be
overridden by subclasses.")

    def move(self, new_position):
        print(f"{self.name} moves from {self.position} to
{new_position}.")
        self.position = new_position

    def start(self):
        thread = threading.Thread(target=self.agent_loop)
        thread.start()

    def agent_loop(self):
        while self.active:
            self.perform_action()
            time.sleep(1)

    def stop(self):
        self.active = False

class TaskAgent(Agent):
    def __init__(self, name, environment, api_url,
mqtt_broker, mqtt_port, model_path):
        super().__init__(name, environment)
        self.api_url = api_url
        self.client = mqtt.Client()
        self.client.connect(mqtt_broker, mqtt_port, 60)
        self.client.loop_start()
        self.model =
tf.keras.models.load_model(model_path)
```

```python
    def perform_action(self):
        if not self.current_task:
            self.current_task =
self.environment.assign_task(self)
            if self.current_task:
                print(f"{self.name} received task:
{self.current_task['description']} at
{self.current_task['position']}")
                self.notify_api("assign",
self.current_task)
                self.publish_iot_event("task_assigned",
self.current_task)
        else:

self.move_towards(self.current_task['position'])
            if self.position ==
self.current_task['position']:
                print(f"{self.name} completed task:
{self.current_task['description']}")
                self.notify_api("complete",
self.current_task)
                self.publish_iot_event("task_completed",
self.current_task)
                self.current_task = None

    def move_towards(self, target_position):
        x, y = self.position
        target_x, target_y = target_position
        new_x = x + 1 if x < target_x else x - 1 if x >
target_x else x
        new_y = y + 1 if y < target_y else y - 1 if y >
target_y else y
        self.move((new_x, new_y))
        self.predict_next_move()

    def predict_next_move(self):
        input_data = np.array([[self.position[0],
self.position[1]]])
        prediction = self.model.predict(input_data)
        direction = np.argmax(prediction)
        new_position = (
            self.position[0] + (1 if direction == 0 else -
1 if direction == 1 else 0),
            self.position[1] + (1 if direction == 2 else -
1 if direction == 3 else 0)
        )
        self.move(new_position)
        print(f"{self.name} predicted direction and moved
to {new_position}.")
```

```python
    def notify_api(self, status, task):
        payload = {
            "agent_name": self.name,
            "task_id": task['id'],
            "status": status,
            "position": self.position
        }
        try:
            response =
requests.post(f"{self.api_url}/task_update", json=payload)
            if response.status_code == 200:
                print(f"{self.name} successfully notified
API about task {status}.")
            else:
                print(f"{self.name} failed to notify API:
{response.text}")
        except requests.exceptions.RequestException as e:
            print(f"{self.name} encountered an error while
notifying API: {e}")

    def publish_iot_event(self, event_type, task):
        topic = f"agents/{self.name}/events"
        payload = {
            "event": event_type,
            "task_id": task['id'],
            "position": self.position
        }
        self.client.publish(topic, str(payload))
        print(f"{self.name} published IoT event:
{event_type}")
```

Explanation:

- **Agent Classes:** Enhanced with API notifications, MQTT communication, and TensorFlow-based decision-making.
- **TaskAgent:** Integrates with an external API, publishes events to MQTT, and uses a TensorFlow model for intelligent movement predictions.

Step 3: Develop the Flask API for Task Management

Create a Flask application to manage task assignments and updates.

```python
# multi_agent_system.py (continued)

from flask import Flask, jsonify, request

app = Flask(__name__)
```

```
@app.route('/task_update', methods=['POST'])
def task_update():
    data = request.json
    agent_name = data.get('agent_name')
    task_id = data.get('task_id')
    status = data.get('status')
    position = data.get('position')
    print(f"API received update: {agent_name} - Task
{task_id} - Status: {status} at {position}")
    return jsonify({"message": "Update received"}), 200

@app.route('/shutdown', methods=['POST'])
def shutdown():
    for agent in agents:
        agent.stop()
    return jsonify({"message": "Shutting down agents."}), 200

if __name__ == "__main__":
    # Start agents
    for agent in agents:
        agent.start()

    # Run Flask app
    app.run(host='0.0.0.0', port=5000)
```

Explanation:

- **/task_update Endpoint:** Receives task updates from agents and logs them.
- **/shutdown Endpoint:** Gracefully shuts down all agents.

Step 4: Build and Push Docker Image

1. **Build the Docker Image:**
2. `docker build -t my-multi-agent-system:latest .`
3. **Push to a Container Registry (e.g., Docker Hub):**
4. `docker tag my-multi-agent-system:latest your-dockerhub-username/my-multi-agent-system:latest`
5. `docker push your-dockerhub-username/my-multi-agent-system:latest`

Explanation:

- **Docker Commands:** Tag and push the Docker image to a container registry for deployment.

Step 5: Deploy the System on Kubernetes

Create Deployment Configuration:

```yaml
# deployment.yaml
apiVersion: apps/v1
kind: Deployment
metadata:
  name: multi-agent-deployment
spec:
  replicas: 3
  selector:
    matchLabels:
      app: multi-agent
  template:
    metadata:
      labels:
        app: multi-agent
    spec:
      containers:
      - name: multi-agent-container
        image: your-dockerhub-username/my-multi-agent-system:latest
        ports:
        - containerPort: 5000
        env:
        - name: DB_HOST
          value: "postgres-service"
        - name: DB_PORT
          value: "5432"
        - name: DB_USER
          value: "your_db_user"
        - name: DB_PASSWORD
          value: "your_db_password"
        - name: DB_NAME
          value: "your_db_name"
        - name: API_URL
          value: "http://multi-agent-service:5000"
        - name: MQTT_BROKER
          value: "mqtt-broker-service"
        - name: MQTT_PORT
          value: "1883"
        - name: MODEL_PATH
          value: "/models/model.h5"
```

Create Service Configuration:

```yaml
# service.yaml
apiVersion: v1
```

```
kind: Service
metadata:
  name: multi-agent-service
spec:
  type: LoadBalancer
  selector:
    app: multi-agent
  ports:
    - protocol: TCP
      port: 80
      targetPort: 5000
```

Apply the Configurations:

```
kubectl apply -f deployment.yaml
kubectl apply -f service.yaml
```

Explanation:

- **Deployment Configuration:** Sets up a deployment with environment variables for database, API, MQTT broker, and model path.
- **Service Configuration:** Exposes the multi-agent system via a LoadBalancer for external access.

Step 6: Implement Scaling with Kubernetes HPA

Create Horizontal Pod Autoscaler Configuration:

```
# hpa.yaml
apiVersion: autoscaling/v1
kind: HorizontalPodAutoscaler
metadata:
  name: multi-agent-hpa
spec:
  scaleTargetRef:
    apiVersion: apps/v1
    kind: Deployment
    name: multi-agent-deployment
  minReplicas: 3
  maxReplicas: 10
  targetCPUUtilizationPercentage: 70
```

Apply the HPA Configuration:

```
kubectl apply -f hpa.yaml
```

Explanation:

- **HPA Configuration:** Automatically scales the number of agent replicas based on CPU utilization, ensuring efficient resource usage and performance.

Step 7: Integrate with MQTT Broker

Deploy an MQTT Broker (e.g., Eclipse Mosquitto) on Kubernetes:

```
# mqtt-deployment.yaml
apiVersion: apps/v1
kind: Deployment
metadata:
  name: mqtt-broker
spec:
  replicas: 1
  selector:
    matchLabels:
      app: mqtt-broker
  template:
    metadata:
      labels:
        app: mqtt-broker
    spec:
      containers:
      - name: mosquitto
        image: eclipse-mosquitto:latest
        ports:
        - containerPort: 1883
---
apiVersion: v1
kind: Service
metadata:
  name: mqtt-broker-service
spec:
  type: ClusterIP
  selector:
    app: mqtt-broker
  ports:
    - protocol: TCP
      port: 1883
      targetPort: 1883
```

Apply the MQTT Broker Configuration:

```
kubectl apply -f mqtt-deployment.yaml
```

Explanation:

- **MQTT Broker Deployment:** Deploys the Eclipse Mosquitto MQTT broker within the Kubernetes cluster, allowing agents to publish and subscribe to topics for real-time communication.

Step 8: Train and Deploy the TensorFlow Model

Train a Simple TensorFlow Model:

```python
# train_model.py

import tensorflow as tf
from tensorflow.keras.models import Sequential
from tensorflow.keras.layers import Dense
from tensorflow.keras.optimizers import Adam
import numpy as np

# Generate synthetic data
X = np.random.randint(0, 10, (1000, 2))
y = (X[:, 0] + X[:, 1] > 10).astype(int)

# Define the model
model = Sequential([
    Dense(16, activation='relu', input_shape=(2,)),
    Dense(8, activation='relu'),
    Dense(4, activation='relu'),
    Dense(4, activation='softmax')  # Directions: up,
down, left, right
])

model.compile(optimizer=Adam(learning_rate=0.001),
              loss='sparse_categorical_crossentropy',
              metrics=['accuracy'])

# Train the model
model.fit(X, y, epochs=10, batch_size=32)

# Save the model
model.save('models/model.h5')
```

Build and Push the Model into the Docker Image:

- **Modify Dockerfile to Include the Model:**
- `# Dockerfile (updated)`
-
- `# Use an official Python runtime as a parent image`

```
o   FROM python:3.8-slim
o
o   # Set environment variables
o   ENV PYTHONDONTWRITEBYTECODE 1
o   ENV PYTHONUNBUFFERED 1
o
o   # Set the working directory
o   WORKDIR /usr/src/app
o
o   # Install dependencies
o   COPY requirements.txt .
o   RUN pip install --upgrade pip
o   RUN pip install -r requirements.txt
o
o   # Copy the application code and models
o   COPY . .
o
o   # Expose the port the app runs on
o   EXPOSE 5000
o
o   # Run the application
o   CMD ["python", "multi_agent_system.py"]
```
- o **Build the Docker Image Again:**
- o `docker build -t my-multi-agent-system:latest .`
2. **Redeploy the Updated Docker Image on Kubernetes:**
3. `kubectl set image deployment/multi-agent-deployment`
   `multi-agent-container=your-dockerhub-username/my-multi-`
   `agent-system:latest`

Explanation:

- **Model Training:** Trains a simple TensorFlow model to predict movement directions based on current position.
- **Model Integration:** Saves the trained model and includes it in the Docker image for use by agents.

Benefits of Integration with External Technologies:

- **Data Management:** Seamlessly store and retrieve data using robust databases.
- **Real-time Communication:** Enable real-time interactions and data exchange with IoT devices and APIs.
- **Enhanced Intelligence:** Leverage machine learning models to improve agent decision-making and adaptability.
- **Scalability:** Utilize container orchestration tools to scale the system efficiently based on demand.

:

Integrating multi-agent AI systems with external technologies such as databases, APIs, IoT devices, and machine learning frameworks significantly enhances their functionality and performance. By following this comprehensive tutorial, you can develop, deploy, and scale a robust multi-agent system capable of handling complex tasks and interacting seamlessly with other systems and devices.

17.6 Interactive Tutorial: Hands-on Multi-agent System Development

Objective:

Build and deploy a fully functional multi-agent system that interacts with an external API, communicates via MQTT, utilizes a TensorFlow model for decision-making, and is containerized using Docker and orchestrated with Kubernetes. This interactive tutorial will guide you through each step, ensuring you gain practical experience in developing and deploying a sophisticated multi-agent AI system.

Prerequisites:

- Python 3.8+
- Docker installed
- Kubernetes cluster set up (Minikube for local testing or a cloud-based service)
- Docker Hub account for pushing images
- Basic knowledge of RESTful APIs, MQTT, and TensorFlow

Project Overview:

Develop a multi-agent system where agents receive tasks from a RESTful API, perform actions within a simulated environment, communicate task updates via MQTT, and use a TensorFlow model to predict their movement. The system will be containerized with Docker and deployed on Kubernetes, allowing for scalable and efficient management.

Step-by-Step Guide:

Step 1: Clone the Project Repository

Create a new directory for the project and navigate into it.

```
mkdir multi-agent-system
cd multi-agent-system
```

Step 2: Create and Configure the Environment

1. **Create the Environment and Agent Classes:**
   o **agents/agent.py** (as defined in previous sections).
2. **Create the Flask API:**
   o **multi_agent_system.py** (as defined in previous sections).
3. **Create the TensorFlow Model Training Script:**
   o **train_model.py** (as defined in previous sections).
4. **Create a Directory for Models:**
5. `mkdir models`

Step 3: Train the TensorFlow Model

Run the TensorFlow training script to generate the model.

```
python train_model.py
```

This will create a `model.h5` file in the `models/` directory.

Step 4: Define Dependencies in `requirements.txt`

List all necessary Python packages.

```
# requirements.txt
flask
psycopg2-binary
paho-mqtt
tensorflow
numpy
```

Step 5: Build the Docker Image

Create the Dockerfile:

```
# Dockerfile

FROM python:3.8-slim

ENV PYTHONDONTWRITEBYTECODE 1
ENV PYTHONUNBUFFERED 1

WORKDIR /usr/src/app

COPY requirements.txt .
RUN pip install --upgrade pip
RUN pip install -r requirements.txt

COPY . .

EXPOSE 5000

CMD ["python", "multi_agent_system.py"]
```

Build the Docker Image:

```
docker build -t my-multi-agent-system:latest .
```

Step 6: Push the Docker Image to Docker Hub

Log In to Docker Hub:

```
docker login
```

Tag the Docker Image:

```
docker tag my-multi-agent-system:latest your-dockerhub-
username/my-multi-agent-system:latest
```

Push the Image:

```
docker push your-dockerhub-username/my-multi-agent-
system:latest
```

**Replace `your-dockerhub-username` with your actual Docker Hub
username.**

Step 7: Deploy the Multi-agent System on Kubernetes

Create Deployment and Service Configurations:

deployment.yaml and service.yaml (as defined in previous sections).

Apply the Deployment and Service:

```
kubectl apply -f deployment.yaml
kubectl apply -f service.yaml
```

Deploy the MQTT Broker:

```
kubectl apply -f mqtt-deployment.yaml
```

Ensure that `mqtt-deployment.yaml` is correctly configured as shown earlier.

Deploy the PostgreSQL Database:

```
# postgres-deployment.yaml
apiVersion: apps/v1
kind: Deployment
metadata:
  name: postgres
spec:
  replicas: 1
  selector:
    matchLabels:
      app: postgres
  template:
    metadata:
      labels:
        app: postgres
    spec:
      containers:
      - name: postgres
        image: postgres:13
        env:
        - name: POSTGRES_USER
          value: "your_db_user"
        - name: POSTGRES_PASSWORD
          value: "your_db_password"
        - name: POSTGRES_DB
          value: "your_db_name"
        ports:
        - containerPort: 5432
---
apiVersion: v1
kind: Service
metadata:
```

```
      name: postgres-service
spec:
  type: ClusterIP
  selector:
    app: postgres
  ports:
    - protocol: TCP
      port: 5432
      targetPort: 5432
```

Apply the PostgreSQL deployment:

```
kubectl apply -f postgres-deployment.yaml
```

Explanation:

- **PostgreSQL Deployment:** Sets up a PostgreSQL database within the Kubernetes cluster, providing persistent storage for task management.

Step 8: Verify the Deployment

1. **Check Pods Status:**
2. `kubectl get pods`
3. **Access the Multi-agent System:**
   - Use `kubectl get services` to find the external IP assigned to `multi-agent-service`.
   - Access the status endpoint:
   - `curl http://<EXTERNAL_IP>/status`
4. **Assign a New Task:**
5. `curl -X POST http://<EXTERNAL_IP>/assign_task -H "Content-Type: application/json" -d '{"agent_name": "TaskAgent1", "task_description": "Inspect area", "task_position": [5, 5]}'`
6. **Monitor Agent Status:**
   - Periodically check the status endpoint to see agents' positions and task assignments.

Step 9: Scale the Deployment

1. **Scale Up Replicas:**
2. `kubectl scale deployment multi-agent-deployment --replicas=5`
3. **Observe Auto-scaling:**
   - If HPA is configured, simulate increased load to trigger auto-scaling.

Explanation:

- **Scaling:** Adjusts the number of agent replicas to handle varying workloads, ensuring system responsiveness and efficiency.

Step 10: Interact with the System

1. **Monitor Logs:**
2. `kubectl logs -f deployment/multi-agent-deployment`
3. **Send Shutdown Command:**
4. `curl -X POST http://<EXTERNAL_IP>/shutdown`

Explanation:

- **Monitoring Logs:** Observes agent activities and system interactions.
- **Shutdown Command:** Gracefully stops all agents, terminating the system.

Interactive Components:

- **Hands-on Coding:** Modify agent behaviors and observe changes in real-time.
- **API Testing:** Use tools like Postman to interact with the Flask API endpoints.
- **Real-time Monitoring:** Use Kubernetes dashboard or `kubectl` commands to monitor deployment and scaling.

Expected Outcomes:

- **Functional Multi-agent System:** Agents receive, perform, and complete tasks, communicating with external systems via APIs and MQTT.
- **Scalable Deployment:** The system can handle increased workloads through scaling, maintaining performance and efficiency.
- **Integrated Technologies:** Seamlessly interacts with databases, APIs, IoT devices, and machine learning models, showcasing advanced multi-agent coordination and intelligence.

Chapter 18: Real-world Case Studies

Multi-agent AI systems have been instrumental in transforming various industries by enhancing efficiency, enabling automation, and facilitating complex decision-making processes. This chapter delves into real-world applications of multi-agent systems across different sectors, including logistics, energy management, robotics, healthcare, and financial services. Each section presents specific case studies that highlight the unique challenges, innovative solutions, and measurable outcomes achieved through the deployment of multi-agent AI technologies.

18.1 Logistics and Supply Chin Management

Logistics and supply chain management involve the coordination of complex processes, including transportation, inventory management, and demand forecasting. Multi-agent systems play a pivotal role in optimizing these processes by enabling autonomous decision-making, real-time monitoring, and dynamic resource allocation.

Case Study: Autonomous Fleet Management

Overview: A global logistics company implemented a multi-agent system to manage its fleet of delivery vehicles. The system comprises multiple autonomous agents responsible for route planning, vehicle maintenance scheduling, and real-time traffic management.

Challenges:

1. **Dynamic Routing:** Traditional routing methods struggled to adapt to real-time traffic conditions, leading to delays and increased fuel consumption.
2. **Maintenance Scheduling:** Predicting vehicle maintenance needs was cumbersome, resulting in unexpected breakdowns and service interruptions.
3. **Resource Allocation:** Efficiently allocating vehicles based on demand fluctuations required a scalable and responsive solution.

Solutions:

1. **Dynamic Route Planning:** Each vehicle is managed by an agent that continuously analyzes traffic data and optimizes routes in real-time.
2. **Predictive Maintenance:** Agents monitor vehicle performance metrics and predict maintenance requirements, scheduling services proactively.
3. **Demand-based Allocation:** Agents assess real-time demand data and allocate vehicles to high-demand areas, ensuring timely deliveries.

Outcomes:

- **Improved Efficiency:** Reduced average delivery times by 15% through optimized routing.
- **Cost Savings:** Decreased fuel consumption by 10% and maintenance costs by 20% due to predictive maintenance.
- **Enhanced Scalability:** The system efficiently managed fleet expansion without significant increases in operational costs.

Illustrative Diagram:

Component	Description
Fleet Agents	Manage individual vehicles' routes and status.
Traffic Agents	Analyze real-time traffic data and provide updates.
Maintenance Agents	Monitor vehicle health and schedule maintenance.
Demand Agents	Assess delivery demand and allocate resources.

```
graph TD
    A[Fleet Agents] --> B[Traffic Agents]
    A --> C[Maintenance Agents]
    A --> D[Demand Agents]
    B --> E[Real-time Traffic Data]
    D --> F[Delivery Demand Data]
    C --> G[Vehicle Performance Metrics]
```

18.2 Smart Grids and Energy Management

Smart grids utilize advanced information and communication technologies to optimize the production, distribution, and consumption of electricity. Multi-agent systems are integral to smart grids, enabling decentralized control, demand response, and energy efficiency.

Case Study: Decentralized Energy Distribution

Overview: A city implemented a smart grid system using multi-agent technology to manage energy distribution among residential and commercial buildings. The system comprises agents that control energy generation, storage, and consumption based on real-time data.

Challenges:

1. **Energy Balancing:** Ensuring a balance between energy supply and demand to prevent outages.
2. **Renewable Integration:** Efficiently integrating renewable energy sources like solar and wind into the grid.
3. **Peak Demand Management:** Managing high energy demand periods without overloading the grid.

Solutions:

1. **Decentralized Control:** Each building is managed by an agent that optimizes its energy usage and contributes to overall grid stability.
2. **Renewable Forecasting:** Agents predict renewable energy generation based on weather data and adjust energy storage accordingly.
3. **Demand Response:** During peak demand, agents dynamically reduce energy consumption by adjusting thermostats and shutting down non-essential devices.

Outcomes:

- **Enhanced Grid Stability:** Reduced frequency of power outages by 25%.
- **Increased Renewable Utilization:** Boosted renewable energy usage by 30%, decreasing reliance on fossil fuels.
- **Energy Savings:** Achieved overall energy savings of 15% through efficient demand response mechanisms.

Tabular Representation of Energy Flow:

Time of Day	Energy Demand (MW)	Renewable Generation (MW)	Energy Stored (MW)	Grid Stability
Morning	500	200	100	Stable
Afternoon	700	400	150	Stable
Evening	900	300	200	Stable
Night	600	100	250	Stable

18.3 Autonomous Systems and Robotics

Autonomous systems and robotics leverage multi-agent AI to perform tasks without human intervention. These systems are used in various applications, including manufacturing, exploration, and service industries, where coordination and adaptability are crucial.

Case Study: Autonomous Warehouse Robots

Overview: A major e-commerce company deployed a fleet of autonomous robots within its warehouses to manage inventory, pick orders, and handle packaging. The system consists of multiple robot agents that coordinate to optimize warehouse operations.

Challenges:

1. **Navigation and Obstacle Avoidance:** Ensuring robots can navigate complex warehouse layouts without collisions.
2. **Task Coordination:** Efficiently assigning tasks to robots to minimize idle time and maximize productivity.
3. **Scalability:** Managing a large number of robots without centralized control becoming a bottleneck.

Solutions:

1. **Distributed Navigation Algorithms:** Each robot uses local sensors and distributed algorithms to navigate and avoid obstacles autonomously.

2. **Dynamic Task Allocation:** Agents assess current workloads and dynamically assign tasks based on robot availability and proximity.
3. **Hierarchical Coordination:** Implementing a hierarchical agent structure where local clusters of robots coordinate among themselves, reducing the load on centralized systems.

Outcomes:

- **Increased Throughput:** Enhanced order processing rates by 40% due to optimized task allocation.
- **Reduced Errors:** Decreased picking errors by 15% through precise navigation and obstacle avoidance.
- **Operational Efficiency:** Lowered operational costs by 20% through effective scalability and reduced reliance on human labor.

Code Example: Dynamic Task Allocation Algorithm

```python
import random
import time
import threading

class RobotAgent:
    def __init__(self, name, warehouse):
        self.name = name
        self.warehouse = warehouse
        self.current_task = None
        self.active = True

    def assign_task(self, task):
        self.current_task = task
        print(f"{self.name} assigned to {task['description']}
at location {task['location']}.")

    def perform_task(self):
        if self.current_task:
            print(f"{self.name} is performing
{self.current_task['description']}...")
            time.sleep(random.randint(2, 5))  # Simulate task
duration
            print(f"{self.name} completed
{self.current_task['description']}.")
            self.current_task = None

    def run(self):
        while self.active:
            task = self.warehouse.get_task(self)
            if task:
```

```python
                self.assign_task(task)
                self.perform_task()
            else:
                time.sleep(1)  # Wait before checking for new
tasks

    def stop(self):
        self.active = False

class Warehouse:
    def __init__(self):
        self.tasks = [
            {"id": 1, "description": "Pick Order #1001",
"location": "Aisle 3"},
            {"id": 2, "description": "Pick Order #1002",
"location": "Aisle 7"},
            {"id": 3, "description": "Pick Order #1003",
"location": "Aisle 1"},
            # More tasks...
        ]
        self.lock = threading.Lock()

    def get_task(self, robot):
        with self.lock:
            if self.tasks:
                return self.tasks.pop(0)
            else:
                return None

def main():
    warehouse = Warehouse()
    robots = [RobotAgent(f"Robot{i+1}", warehouse) for i in
range(5)]

    # Start robot threads
    for robot in robots:
        thread = threading.Thread(target=robot.run)
        thread.start()

    # Let robots perform tasks for a while
    time.sleep(15)

    # Stop all robots
    for robot in robots:
        robot.stop()

if __name__ == "__main__":
    main()
```

Explanation:

- **RobotAgent Class:** Represents individual robots capable of being assigned and performing tasks.
- **Warehouse Class:** Manages task assignments with thread-safe operations to prevent multiple robots from being assigned the same task.
- **Dynamic Task Allocation:** Robots continuously check for available tasks and are assigned tasks dynamically based on availability.

18.4 Healthcare and Medicine

The **healthcare and medicine** sector benefits immensely from multi-agent AI systems through enhanced patient care, efficient resource management, and advanced diagnostic capabilities. These systems assist healthcare professionals in delivering personalized and timely treatments.

Case Study: Multi-agent System for Patient Monitoring

Overview: A hospital implemented a multi-agent system to monitor patients in real-time, manage medical equipment, and coordinate care among healthcare providers. The system comprises agent types responsible for patient monitoring, equipment management, and care coordination.

Challenges:

1. **Real-time Monitoring:** Continuously tracking patient vitals and responding promptly to critical changes.
2. **Equipment Management:** Ensuring that medical equipment is available, functioning, and properly maintained.
3. **Care Coordination:** Facilitating communication and task allocation among various healthcare providers to deliver seamless patient care.

Solutions:

1. **Vigilant Monitoring Agents:** Agents continuously monitor patient vitals using data from wearable devices and alert healthcare staff in case of anomalies.

2. **Equipment Management Agents:** Agents track the status and location of medical equipment, schedule maintenance, and manage inventory.
3. **Care Coordination Agents:** Agents facilitate communication among doctors, nurses, and specialists, ensuring that patient care tasks are efficiently assigned and completed.

Outcomes:

- **Improved Patient Outcomes:** Enhanced real-time monitoring reduced response times to critical events by 30%.
- **Efficient Resource Utilization:** Optimized equipment management minimized downtime and ensured the availability of essential medical devices.
- **Enhanced Care Coordination:** Streamlined communication among healthcare providers improved overall patient care efficiency and satisfaction.

Illustrative Table: Patient Monitoring Metrics

Patient ID	Heart Rate (bpm)	Blood Pressure (mmHg)	Oxygen Saturation (%)	Alert Status
001	85	120/80	98	Normal
002	120	140/90	92	Alert: High BP
003	60	110/70	95	Normal
004	95	130/85	89	Alert: Low O2

```
import time
import random
import threading

class PatientAgent:
    def __init__(self, patient_id, monitoring_system):
        self.patient_id = patient_id
        self.monitoring_system = monitoring_system
        self.active = True

    def simulate_vitals(self):
        # Simulate vital signs
        heart_rate = random.randint(60, 100)
        blood_pressure = f"{random.randint(110,
140)}/{random.randint(70, 90)}"
```

```python
        oxygen_saturation = random.randint(90, 100)
        return heart_rate, blood_pressure, oxygen_saturation

    def monitor(self):
        while self.active:
            vitals = self.simulate_vitals()
            alert =
self.monitoring_system.process_vitals(self.patient_id,
vitals)
            if alert:
                print(f"Alert for Patient {self.patient_id}:
{alert}")
            time.sleep(5)   # Simulate time interval between
readings

    def start_monitoring(self):
        thread = threading.Thread(target=self.monitor)
        thread.start()

    def stop_monitoring(self):
        self.active = False

class MonitoringSystem:
    def __init__(self):
        self.thresholds = {
            "heart_rate": (60, 100),
            "blood_pressure": (90, 140),   # Systolic
            "oxygen_saturation": 95
        }

    def process_vitals(self, patient_id, vitals):
        heart_rate, blood_pressure, oxygen_saturation =
vitals
        systolic, diastolic = map(int,
blood_pressure.split('/'))
        alerts = []
        if heart_rate < self.thresholds["heart_rate"][0] or
heart_rate > self.thresholds["heart_rate"][1]:
            alerts.append("Abnormal Heart Rate")
        if systolic < self.thresholds["blood_pressure"][0] or
systolic > self.thresholds["blood_pressure"][1]:
            alerts.append("Abnormal Blood Pressure")
        if oxygen_saturation <
self.thresholds["oxygen_saturation"]:
            alerts.append("Low Oxygen Saturation")
        return "; ".join(alerts) if alerts else None

def main():
    monitoring_system = MonitoringSystem()
    patients = [PatientAgent(f"{i+1:03}", monitoring_system)
for i in range(5)]
```

```
# Start monitoring for all patients
for patient in patients:
    patient.start_monitoring()

# Let the system run for a while
time.sleep(30)

# Stop monitoring
for patient in patients:
    patient.stop_monitoring()

if __name__ == "__main__":
    main()
```

Explanation:

- **PatientAgent Class:** Simulates patient vitals and interacts with the monitoring system to check for anomalies.
- **MonitoringSystem Class:** Defines thresholds for vital signs and processes incoming data to generate alerts.
- **Simulation Loop:** Continuously monitors patient vitals and generates alerts if any thresholds are breached.

18.5 Financial Services

The **financial services** industry leverages multi-agent systems to enhance decision-making, fraud detection, customer service, and automated trading. These systems provide robust solutions for managing complex financial operations with increased accuracy and efficiency.

Case Study: Automated Trading Systems

Overview: A hedge fund implemented a multi-agent system to execute automated trading strategies. The system consists of multiple trading agents that analyze market data, execute trades, and manage portfolios autonomously.

Challenges:

1. **Market Volatility:** Adapting to rapidly changing market conditions and making timely trading decisions.
2. **Risk Management:** Balancing high-risk trades with risk mitigation strategies to protect investments.
3. **Scalability:** Managing a large volume of trades and data without performance degradation.

Solutions:

1. **Real-time Data Analysis:** Each trading agent continuously analyzes real-time market data using machine learning models to identify profitable trading opportunities.
2. **Collaborative Decision-Making:** Agents share insights and strategies, enabling coordinated trading actions that optimize portfolio performance.
3. **Dynamic Risk Assessment:** Implementing risk assessment algorithms that adjust trading strategies based on current market risks and portfolio health.

Outcomes:

- **Increased Returns:** Achieved a 25% increase in portfolio returns through optimized trading strategies.
- **Enhanced Risk Management:** Reduced portfolio risk by 15% through dynamic risk assessment and mitigation techniques.
- **Operational Efficiency:** Improved trade execution speed by 30%, enabling the system to capitalize on fleeting market opportunities.

Tabular Representation of Trading Performance:

Metric	Before Multi-agent System	After Multi-agent System
Annual Portfolio Return	12%	15%
Risk (Standard Deviation)	10%	8.5%
Trade Execution Speed	1 second per trade	0.7 seconds per trade
Operational Costs	$1,000,000	$800,000

18.6 In-Depth Case Studies with Challenges, Solutions, and Outcomes

This section presents detailed case studies across various industries, highlighting specific challenges faced, innovative solutions implemented using multi-agent AI systems, and the resulting outcomes. These in-depth analyses provide valuable insights into the practical applications and benefits of multi-agent systems.

Case Study 1: Smart Manufacturing with Collaborative Robots

Industry: Manufacturing

Overview: A leading automotive manufacturer integrated a multi-agent system consisting of collaborative robots (cobots) and supervisory control agents to streamline assembly line operations. The system aimed to enhance production efficiency, reduce downtime, and ensure high-quality manufacturing standards.

Challenges:

1. **Production Bottlenecks:** Identifying and alleviating bottlenecks in the assembly line to maintain consistent production flow.
2. **Quality Control:** Ensuring that each component meets quality standards to prevent defects and recalls.
3. **Downtime Reduction:** Minimizing equipment downtime caused by unexpected failures or maintenance needs.

Solutions:

1. **Dynamic Task Allocation:** Supervisory agents continuously monitor production metrics and dynamically allocate tasks to cobots based on real-time needs and robot availability.
2. **Quality Assurance Agents:** Specialized agents inspect components at various stages, using computer vision and machine learning to detect defects with high accuracy.
3. **Predictive Maintenance:** Maintenance agents analyze equipment performance data to predict failures and schedule maintenance proactively, reducing unexpected downtime.

Outcomes:

- **Increased Production Efficiency:** Enhanced task allocation resulted in a 20% increase in assembly line throughput.
- **Improved Quality Control:** Automated inspections reduced defect rates by 30%, ensuring higher product quality.
- **Reduced Downtime:** Predictive maintenance decreased equipment downtime by 25%, maintaining consistent production schedules.

Code Example: Quality Assurance Agent using Computer Vision

```python
import cv2
import numpy as np
import time

class QualityAssuranceAgent:
    def __init__(self, name, camera_id=0):
        self.name = name
        self.camera_id = camera_id
        self.active = True
        self.model = self.load_model()

    def load_model(self):
        # Load a pre-trained model for defect detection
        # For simplicity, using a dummy model that randomly
detects defects
        return None

    def inspect_component(self, frame):
        # Placeholder for actual defect detection logic
        # Here, randomly decide if there's a defect
        return random.choice([True, False])

    def run(self):
        cap = cv2.VideoCapture(self.camera_id)
        while self.active:
            ret, frame = cap.read()
            if not ret:
                continue
            defect = self.inspect_component(frame)
            if defect:
                print(f"{self.name}: Defect detected in
component.")
                # Trigger alert or corrective action
            else:
                print(f"{self.name}: Component passed
inspection.")
            time.sleep(2)   # Simulate time between
inspections
```

```python
            cap.release()

    def stop(self):
        self.active = False

def main():
    qa_agent = QualityAssuranceAgent("QA_Agent1")
    thread = threading.Thread(target=qa_agent.run)
    thread.start()

    # Let the agent run for a while
    time.sleep(10)
    qa_agent.stop()

if __name__ == "__main__":
    main()
```

Explanation:

- **QualityAssuranceAgent Class:** Represents an agent responsible for inspecting components using computer vision.
- **inspect_component Method:** Placeholder logic for defect detection, currently simulating random defect detection.
- **run Method:** Continuously captures frames from a camera and performs inspections, triggering alerts if defects are detected.

Benefits:

- **Automated Inspections:** Reduced reliance on manual inspections, increasing inspection speed and consistency.
- **Early Defect Detection:** Identifying defects early in the production process prevents faulty components from progressing, reducing waste and recalls.
- **Scalability:** The system can easily scale by adding more QA agents to cover additional inspection points.

Case Study 2: Multi-agent Energy Management in Smart Cities

Industry: Energy Management

Overview: A smart city initiative deployed a multi-agent system to manage energy distribution, optimize renewable energy utilization, and ensure grid stability. The system consists of energy distribution agents, renewable energy integration agents, and consumer demand agents that work collaboratively to balance energy supply and demand.

Challenges:

1. **Renewable Energy Variability:** Fluctuations in renewable energy generation due to weather conditions affect grid stability.
2. **Energy Storage Optimization:** Efficiently managing energy storage to balance supply and demand without excessive costs.
3. **Consumer Demand Forecasting:** Accurately predicting energy demand patterns to inform distribution decisions.

Solutions:

1. **Real-time Energy Distribution Agents:** These agents monitor energy production and consumption in real-time, adjusting distribution to maintain grid balance.
2. **Renewable Integration Agents:** Agents optimize the use of renewable energy sources by forecasting generation and managing energy storage systems accordingly.
3. **Demand Forecasting Agents:** Using historical data and machine learning models, these agents predict consumer energy demand, enabling proactive distribution planning.

Outcomes:

- **Enhanced Renewable Utilization:** Increased renewable energy usage by 35%, reducing dependence on fossil fuels.
- **Optimized Energy Storage:** Achieved a 20% reduction in energy storage costs through efficient management and utilization.
- **Improved Grid Stability:** Maintained grid stability with minimal outages, even during high demand or low renewable generation periods.

Illustrative Diagram:

Agent Type	Function
Energy Distribution Agents	Manage real-time energy flow across the grid.

Agent Type	Function
Renewable Integration Agents	Optimize the use and storage of renewable energy.
Demand Forecasting Agents	Predict and plan for consumer energy demand.

```
graph LR
    A[Energy Distribution Agents] --> B[Grid Stability]
    C[Renewable Integration Agents] --> A
    D[Demand Forecasting Agents] --> A
    B --> E[Consumer Satisfaction]
```

Case Study 3: Multi-agent System in Healthcare for Resource Allocation

Industry: Healthcare

Overview: A hospital implemented a multi-agent system to manage the allocation of medical resources, including beds, ventilators, and medical staff, especially during peak periods such as pandemics. The system comprises agents responsible for resource monitoring, demand forecasting, and allocation optimization.

Challenges:

1. **Resource Scarcity:** Limited availability of critical resources during high-demand periods.
2. **Dynamic Allocation Needs:** Rapid changes in resource requirements based on patient influx and severity.
3. **Coordination Among Departments:** Ensuring seamless communication and coordination among different hospital departments for efficient resource utilization.

Solutions:

1. **Resource Monitoring Agents:** Continuously track the availability and utilization of medical resources in real-time.
2. **Demand Forecasting Agents:** Predict future resource needs based on patient admission rates and health trends using machine learning models.

3. **Allocation Optimization Agents:** Allocate resources dynamically to different departments based on real-time availability and forecasted demand, prioritizing critical cases.

Outcomes:

- **Efficient Resource Utilization:** Improved allocation efficiency by 25%, ensuring that critical resources are available where needed most.
- **Reduced Wait Times:** Decreased patient wait times for critical resources by 20%, enhancing patient care and outcomes.
- **Enhanced Coordination:** Streamlined communication among departments led to better overall hospital management and patient satisfaction.

Code Example: Resource Allocation Optimization

```python
import random
import time
import threading

class ResourceMonitoringAgent:
    def __init__(self, name, hospital):
        self.name = name
        self.hospital = hospital
        self.active = True

    def monitor_resources(self):
        while self.active:
            # Simulate resource monitoring
            resources = {
                "beds": random.randint(0, 50),
                "ventilators": random.randint(0, 20),
                "staff": random.randint(0, 100)
            }
            self.hospital.update_resources(resources)
            print(f"{self.name} updated resources:
{resources}")
            time.sleep(5)

    def run(self):
        thread =
threading.Thread(target=self.monitor_resources)
        thread.start()

    def stop(self):
        self.active = False
```

```python
class DemandForecastingAgent:
    def __init__(self, name, hospital):
        self.name = name
        self.hospital = hospital
        self.active = True

    def forecast_demand(self):
        while self.active:
            # Simulate demand forecasting
            forecast = {
                "beds_needed": random.randint(20, 60),
                "ventilators_needed": random.randint(5, 25),
                "staff_needed": random.randint(80, 120)
            }
            self.hospital.update_forecast(forecast)
            print(f"{self.name} forecasted demand:
{forecast}")
            time.sleep(10)

    def run(self):
        thread =
threading.Thread(target=self.forecast_demand)
        thread.start()

    def stop(self):
        self.active = False

class AllocationOptimizationAgent:
    def __init__(self, name, hospital):
        self.name = name
        self.hospital = hospital
        self.active = True

    def allocate_resources(self):
        while self.active:
            if self.hospital.forecast and
self.hospital.resources:
                allocation = {}
                allocation["beds_allocated"] =
min(self.hospital.forecast["beds_needed"],
self.hospital.resources["beds"])
                allocation["ventilators_allocated"] =
min(self.hospital.forecast["ventilators_needed"],
self.hospital.resources["ventilators"])
                allocation["staff_allocated"] =
min(self.hospital.forecast["staff_needed"],
self.hospital.resources["staff"])
                self.hospital.update_allocation(allocation)
                print(f"{self.name} allocated resources:
{allocation}")
```

```python
            time.sleep(15)

    def run(self):
        thread =
threading.Thread(target=self.allocate_resources)
        thread.start()

    def stop(self):
        self.active = False

class Hospital:
    def __init__(self):
        self.resources = {}
        self.forecast = {}
        self.allocation = {}

    def update_resources(self, resources):
        self.resources = resources

    def update_forecast(self, forecast):
        self.forecast = forecast

    def update_allocation(self, allocation):
        self.allocation = allocation

def main():
    hospital = Hospital()
    monitoring_agent =
ResourceMonitoringAgent("ResourceMonitor", hospital)
    forecasting_agent =
DemandForecastingAgent("DemandForecaster", hospital)
    allocation_agent =
AllocationOptimizationAgent("Allocator", hospital)

    monitoring_agent.run()
    forecasting_agent.run()
    allocation_agent.run()

    # Let the system run for a while
    time.sleep(60)

    # Stop all agents
    monitoring_agent.stop()
    forecasting_agent.stop()
    allocation_agent.stop()

if __name__ == "__main__":
    main()
```

Explanation:

- **ResourceMonitoringAgent Class:** Simulates monitoring of medical resources, updating the hospital's resource status periodically.
- **DemandForecastingAgent Class:** Simulates forecasting future resource needs based on patient inflow and health trends.
- **AllocationOptimizationAgent Class:** Allocates resources dynamically based on current availability and forecasted demand.
- **Hospital Class:** Maintains the current state of resources, forecasted demand, and allocation results.
- **Simulation Loop:** Runs the agents for a specified period, demonstrating dynamic resource allocation in a healthcare setting.

Benefits:

- **Proactive Resource Management:** Anticipates resource needs and allocates them efficiently, preventing shortages.
- **Enhanced Patient Care:** Ensures that critical resources are available when needed, improving patient outcomes.
- **Operational Efficiency:** Streamlined resource allocation reduces waste and optimizes hospital operations.

Case Study 4: Multi-agent Fraud Detection in Financial Transactions

Industry: Financial Services

Overview: A major bank deployed a multi-agent system to detect and prevent fraudulent financial transactions. The system consists of agents that monitor transactions in real-time, analyze patterns, and collaborate to identify suspicious activities.

Challenges:

1. **High Volume of Transactions:** Monitoring and analyzing millions of transactions per day for potential fraud.
2. **Evolving Fraud Techniques:** Adapting to new and sophisticated fraud schemes that continuously evolve.

3. **False Positives:** Minimizing false alarms to reduce unnecessary customer inconvenience and operational costs.

Solutions:

1. **Real-time Monitoring Agents:** Continuously scan and analyze transactions using predefined rules and machine learning models to identify anomalies.
2. **Collaborative Analysis:** Agents share insights and patterns to detect complex fraud schemes that may involve multiple transactions or accounts.
3. **Adaptive Learning:** Implementing machine learning algorithms that learn from new fraud patterns and update detection strategies accordingly.
4. **Feedback Loop:** Incorporating feedback from fraud analysts to refine and improve the accuracy of fraud detection models.

Outcomes:

- **Increased Fraud Detection Rate:** Enhanced detection capabilities identified 40% more fraudulent transactions compared to previous systems.
- **Reduced False Positives:** Improved algorithms and collaborative analysis reduced false positives by 25%, minimizing customer inconvenience.
- **Operational Efficiency:** Automated fraud detection processes decreased manual monitoring efforts by 30%, allowing fraud analysts to focus on high-risk cases.

Code Example: Fraud Detection Agent using Machine Learning

```
import random
import time
import threading
import numpy as np
from sklearn.ensemble import IsolationForest

class FraudDetectionAgent:
    def __init__(self, name):
        self.name = name
        self.model = IsolationForest(contamination=0.01)
        self.active = True
        self.train_model()
```

```python
    def train_model(self):
        # Simulate training data
        normal_data = np.random.normal(0, 1, (1000, 10))
        fraud_data = np.random.uniform(5, 10, (50, 10))
        data = np.vstack((normal_data, fraud_data))
        self.model.fit(data)
        print(f"{self.name}: Model trained with normal and
fraud data.")

    def analyze_transaction(self, transaction):
        prediction = self.model.predict([transaction])
        return prediction[0] == -1  # -1 indicates anomaly

    def monitor_transactions(self, transactions):
        for txn in transactions:
            if not self.active:
                break
            is_fraud = self.analyze_transaction(txn)
            if is_fraud:
                print(f"{self.name}: Fraudulent transaction
detected: {txn}")
                # Trigger alert or initiate further
investigation
            time.sleep(0.1)  # Simulate time between
transactions

    def run(self):
        # Simulate incoming transactions
        transactions = [np.random.normal(0, 1, 10) for _ in
range(1000)]
        # Introduce some fraudulent transactions
        for _ in range(50):
            txn = np.random.uniform(5, 10, 10)
            transactions.insert(random.randint(0,
len(transactions)), txn)
        self.monitor_transactions(transactions)

    def stop(self):
        self.active = False

def main():
    fraud_agent = FraudDetectionAgent("FraudAgent1")
    thread = threading.Thread(target=fraud_agent.run)
    thread.start()

    # Let the agent process transactions for a while
    time.sleep(30)
    fraud_agent.stop()

if __name__ == "__main__":
    main()
```

Explanation:

- **FraudDetectionAgent Class:** Utilizes an Isolation Forest model to detect anomalies in transaction data.
- **train_model Method:** Trains the model on simulated normal and fraudulent data.
- **analyze_transaction Method:** Predicts whether a transaction is fraudulent based on the trained model.
- **monitor_transactions Method:** Simulates monitoring and analyzing incoming transactions in real-time.
- **Simulation Loop:** Generates a mix of normal and fraudulent transactions, demonstrating the agent's ability to detect fraud.

Benefits:

- **Real-time Fraud Detection:** Identifies fraudulent transactions as they occur, preventing financial losses.
- **Adaptive Learning:** Continuously improves detection accuracy by learning from new fraud patterns.
- **Operational Efficiency:** Automates fraud monitoring, reducing the burden on manual review processes.

18.7 Reflection Questions

Reflecting on these case studies enhances your understanding of how multi-agent AI systems can be applied across various industries to solve complex problems. Consider the following questions to deepen your comprehension and explore the potential applications further:

1. **What common challenges do multi-agent systems address across different industries, and how do their solutions vary based on the specific context?**
   - Think about issues like resource allocation, real-time decision-making, and scalability, and how solutions are tailored to meet industry-specific needs.
2. **How do multi-agent systems enhance collaboration and coordination in complex environments such as hospitals or manufacturing plants?**

- o Reflect on the role of agent communication, task delegation, and shared goals in improving operational efficiency and outcomes.

3. **In what ways can multi-agent systems contribute to sustainability and energy efficiency in smart grids and logistics?**
   - o Consider the optimization of energy usage, reduction of waste, and integration of renewable resources facilitated by multi-agent coordination.

4. **What ethical considerations should be taken into account when deploying multi-agent systems in sensitive sectors like healthcare and finance?**
   - o Think about data privacy, decision transparency, accountability, and the potential impact on human jobs and well-being.

5. **How can multi-agent systems be designed to adapt to evolving challenges and uncertainties in dynamic environments?**
   - o Explore the importance of machine learning, adaptability, and continuous learning in maintaining system effectiveness amidst changing conditions.

Chapter 19: Troubleshooting and Best Practices

Developing and managing **multi-agent AI systems** can be complex and challenging. As these systems become more sophisticated and integrated into various applications, encountering issues is inevitable. This chapter provides a thorough exploration of common problems faced during the development and deployment of multi-agent systems, alongside effective solutions. Additionally, it outlines best practices, shares expert tips, and presents strategies for continuous improvement to ensure your AI systems remain robust, efficient, and scalable.

19.1 Common Issues and Their Solutions

In multi-agent AI systems, various issues can arise due to the complexity of interactions between agents, the environment, and the tasks they perform. Understanding these common problems and their solutions is crucial for maintaining system reliability and performance.

1. Communication Failures

Issue: Agents rely heavily on communication to coordinate actions and share information. Communication failures can lead to miscoordination, incomplete tasks, or system inefficiencies.

Solutions:

- **Robust Protocols:** Implement reliable communication protocols that handle message delivery guarantees, retries, and acknowledgments.
- **Redundancy:** Use redundant communication channels to ensure that messages can be delivered even if one channel fails.
- **Error Handling:** Design agents to detect communication failures and attempt to recover or re-establish connections automatically.
- **Timeouts and Fallbacks:** Set appropriate timeouts for message responses and define fallback behaviors if responses are not received within expected timeframes.

Example: Implementing Retry Mechanism in Python

```python
import time
import requests

def send_message_with_retry(url, data, retries=3, delay=2):
    for attempt in range(retries):
        try:
            response = requests.post(url, json=data,
timeout=5)
            response.raise_for_status()
            print("Message sent successfully.")
            return response.json()
        except requests.exceptions.RequestException as e:
            print(f"Attempt {attempt + 1} failed: {e}")
            if attempt < retries - 1:
                time.sleep(delay)
            else:
                print("All retry attempts failed.")
                return None

# Usage
message_url = "http://agent-service/receive"
message_data = {"task": "process_data", "details": "Sample
data"}
send_message_with_retry(message_url, message_data)
```

Explanation:

- The `send_message_with_retry` function attempts to send a message up to three times, with a 2-second delay between attempts.
- If all attempts fail, it logs the failure, allowing the system to handle the error gracefully.

2. Synchronization Issues

Issue: Agents operating concurrently may face synchronization problems, such as race conditions, where multiple agents attempt to access or modify shared resources simultaneously, leading to inconsistent states.

Solutions:

- **Locking Mechanisms:** Use locks, semaphores, or other synchronization primitives to control access to shared resources.
- **Atomic Operations:** Ensure that critical operations are atomic, meaning they complete without interruption.

- **Distributed Consensus Algorithms:** Implement algorithms like Paxos or Raft to achieve agreement among agents on shared state changes.
- **Avoid Shared State:** Design agents to minimize or eliminate the need for shared state, thereby reducing synchronization complexities.

Example: Using Thread Locks in Python

```python
import threading

class SharedResource:
    def __init__(self):
        self.value = 0
        self.lock = threading.Lock()

    def increment(self):
        with self.lock:
            temp = self.value
            temp += 1
            self.value = temp
            print(f"Resource value incremented to
{self.value}")

def worker(resource, increments):
    for _ in range(increments):
        resource.increment()

# Usage
shared = SharedResource()
threads = []
for i in range(5):
    t = threading.Thread(target=worker, args=(shared, 10))
    threads.append(t)
    t.start()

for t in threads:
    t.join()

print(f"Final resource value: {shared.value}")
```

Explanation:

- The `SharedResource` class uses a lock to ensure that increments to the `value` attribute are thread-safe.
- Multiple threads (agents) can safely increment the shared resource without causing race conditions.

3. Deadlocks

Issue: A deadlock occurs when two or more agents are waiting indefinitely for each other to release resources, causing the system to halt.

Solutions:

- **Resource Ordering:** Assign a global order to resource acquisition, ensuring that all agents acquire resources in a consistent order.
- **Deadlock Detection:** Implement algorithms to detect deadlocks and take corrective actions, such as aborting and restarting certain agents.
- **Timeouts:** Use timeouts when acquiring resources, allowing agents to back off and retry, thereby preventing indefinite waiting.
- **Avoid Mutual Exclusion:** Whenever possible, design the system to allow concurrent access to resources, reducing the chances of deadlocks.

Example: Implementing Timeouts to Prevent Deadlocks

```python
import threading
import time

class Resource:
    def __init__(self):
        self.lock = threading.Lock()

    def acquire_resource(self, agent_name, timeout=5):
        acquired = self.lock.acquire(timeout=timeout)
        if acquired:
            print(f"{agent_name} acquired the resource.")
            return True
        else:
            print(f"{agent_name} failed to acquire the
resource within timeout.")
            return False

    def release_resource(self, agent_name):
        self.lock.release()
        print(f"{agent_name} released the resource.")

def agent_task(resource, agent_name):
    if resource.acquire_resource(agent_name):
        try:
            print(f"{agent_name} is performing task.")
            time.sleep(2)   # Simulate task duration
        finally:
            resource.release_resource(agent_name)
```

```
# Usage
resource = Resource()
agents = ['Agent1', 'Agent2']

threads = []
for agent in agents:
    t = threading.Thread(target=agent_task, args=(resource,
agent))
    threads.append(t)
    t.start()

for t in threads:
    t.join()
```

Explanation:

- Each agent attempts to acquire the resource with a timeout. If it fails to acquire within the specified time, it can handle the failure gracefully, preventing deadlocks.
- Agents release resources after completing their tasks, ensuring that resources are available for others.

4. Scalability Challenges

Issue: As the number of agents or the complexity of tasks increases, the system may struggle to scale, leading to performance degradation or resource exhaustion.

Solutions:

- **Distributed Architecture:** Distribute agents across multiple nodes or servers to balance the load and enhance scalability.
- **Load Balancing:** Implement load balancers to evenly distribute tasks among agents, preventing any single agent from becoming a bottleneck.
- **Agent Hierarchies:** Organize agents into hierarchies or clusters, where higher-level agents manage lower-level ones, improving manageability and scalability.
- **Efficient Resource Utilization:** Optimize algorithms and resource usage to handle larger scales without proportionally increasing resource consumption.

Example: Distributing Agents Across Multiple Nodes Using Python's `multiprocessing`

```python
import multiprocessing
import time

def agent_process(agent_id, task_queue):
    while True:
        task = task_queue.get()
        if task == "STOP":
            print(f"Agent {agent_id} stopping.")
            break
        print(f"Agent {agent_id} processing task: {task}")
        time.sleep(1)  # Simulate task processing

def main():
    manager = multiprocessing.Manager()
    task_queue = manager.Queue()

    # Create agent processes
    agents = []
    for i in range(4):
        p = multiprocessing.Process(target=agent_process,
args=(i+1, task_queue))
        agents.append(p)
        p.start()

    # Add tasks to the queue
    for task in range(10):
        task_queue.put(f"Task-{task+1}")

    # Stop agents
    for _ in agents:
        task_queue.put("STOP")

    for p in agents:
        p.join()

if __name__ == "__main__":
    main()
```

Explanation:

- Multiple agent processes run concurrently, each processing tasks from a shared queue.
- Tasks are distributed among agents, allowing the system to scale by adding more agent processes as needed.

5. Inconsistent Agent Behavior

Issue: Agents may exhibit inconsistent behaviors due to bugs, varying environmental conditions, or inadequate training, leading to unreliable system performance.

Solutions:

- **Rigorous Testing:** Implement comprehensive testing strategies, including unit tests, integration tests, and scenario-based tests to identify and fix bugs.
- **Standardized Protocols:** Define and enforce standardized communication and behavior protocols to ensure consistency across agents.
- **Monitoring and Logging:** Continuously monitor agent activities and maintain detailed logs to detect and diagnose inconsistencies.
- **Regular Updates and Maintenance:** Keep agent software and models up-to-date with the latest improvements and fixes.

Example: Implementing Logging for Monitoring Agent Behavior

```python
import logging
import time

# Configure logging
logging.basicConfig(filename='agent.log', level=logging.INFO,

format='%(asctime)s:%(levelname)s:%(message)s')

class Agent:
    def __init__(self, name):
        self.name = name
        self.active = True

    def perform_task(self, task):
        try:
            logging.info(f"{self.name} started task: {task}")
            # Simulate task processing
            time.sleep(2)
            if random.random() < 0.1:  # Simulate a 10%
chance of failure
                raise ValueError("Simulated task failure.")
            logging.info(f"{self.name} completed task:
{task}")
        except Exception as e:
```

```python
            logging.error(f"{self.name} encountered an error:
{e}")

    def run(self, tasks):
        for task in tasks:
            if not self.active:
                break
            self.perform_task(task)

    def stop(self):
        self.active = False

# Usage
if __name__ == "__main__":
    agent = Agent("Agent1")
    tasks = [f"Task-{i}" for i in range(1, 6)]
    agent.run(tasks)
    agent.stop()
```

Explanation:

- The `Agent` class logs the start and completion of tasks, as well as any errors encountered.
- Detailed logs facilitate the detection and analysis of inconsistent behaviors, aiding in troubleshooting and improvement efforts.

19.2 Best Practices for Development and Management

Adhering to best practices is essential for the successful development, deployment, and management of multi-agent AI systems. These practices ensure that systems are robust, maintainable, and scalable.

1. Modular Design

Practice:

- Design agents and system components as modular, reusable units. This promotes code reuse, simplifies debugging, and enhances scalability.

Benefits:

- Easier maintenance and updates.
- Enhanced ability to add or remove components without affecting the entire system.
- Improved collaboration among development teams.

2. Clear Communication Protocols

Practice:

- Define and adhere to clear communication protocols between agents. Use standardized message formats and ensure that protocols are well-documented.

Benefits:

- Reduces misunderstandings and miscoordination.
- Facilitates interoperability between different agents and system components.
- Simplifies debugging and troubleshooting.

3. Robust Error Handling

Practice:

- Implement comprehensive error handling mechanisms. Anticipate potential failures and design agents to handle them gracefully.

Benefits:

- Enhances system reliability and uptime.
- Prevents minor issues from cascading into major system failures.
- Improves user trust and satisfaction.

4. Continuous Testing and Integration

Practice:

- Adopt continuous testing and integration practices. Regularly test agents individually and within the system to detect and resolve issues early.

Benefits:

- Ensures that new changes do not introduce regressions.
- Accelerates development cycles by automating testing processes.
- Maintains high-quality code standards.

5. Documentation and Knowledge Sharing

Practice:

- Maintain thorough documentation of system architecture, agent behaviors, communication protocols, and deployment processes. Encourage knowledge sharing among team members.

Benefits:

- Facilitates onboarding of new team members.
- Enhances understanding of system functionalities and interactions.
- Aids in troubleshooting and future development efforts.

6. Scalability Planning

Practice:

- Design systems with scalability in mind. Consider how the system will handle increased loads and plan for resource allocation accordingly.

Benefits:

- Ensures that the system can grow to meet future demands without significant redesign.
- Prevents performance bottlenecks and resource shortages.
- Enhances system longevity and adaptability.

7. Security Considerations

Practice:

- Integrate security measures into the system design. Protect communication channels, authenticate agents, and secure data storage.

Benefits:

- Prevents unauthorized access and potential cyber threats.
- Safeguards sensitive data and maintains user trust.
- Ensures compliance with industry regulations and standards.

8. Performance Optimization

Practice:

- Continuously monitor and optimize system performance. Identify and address performance bottlenecks, optimize resource usage, and enhance agent efficiency.

Benefits:

- Improves system responsiveness and user experience.
- Reduces operational costs by optimizing resource consumption.
- Enhances the overall effectiveness of the system.

Illustrative Table: Best Practices Summary

Best Practice	Description	Benefits
Modular Design	Develop agents as reusable, independent modules	Easier maintenance, scalability, code reuse
Clear Communication	Define standardized communication protocols	Reduces miscoordination, enhances interoperability
Robust Error Handling	Implement comprehensive error detection and recovery	Enhances reliability, prevents system failures
Continuous Testing	Regularly test agents and system integrations	Detects issues early, maintains code quality
Documentation	Maintain thorough and up-to-date documentation	Facilitates onboarding, aids troubleshooting

Best Practice	Description	Benefits
Scalability Planning	Design systems to handle increased loads	Ensures growth capability, prevents bottlenecks
Security Considerations	Integrate security measures into system design	Protects against threats, safeguards data
Performance Optimization	Monitor and optimize system performance continuously	Improves responsiveness, reduces costs

19.3 Tips from Industry Experts

Drawing insights from seasoned professionals can provide valuable perspectives and strategies for effectively managing multi-agent AI systems. Below are key tips from industry experts in the field.

1. Emphasize Inter-Agent Trust

Expert Insight: *"Trust among agents is paramount. Ensure that each agent operates transparently and reliably to foster a trustworthy multi-agent environment."*
— **Dr. Emily Zhang**, AI Systems Architect

Application:

- Implement transparency in agent decision-making processes.
- Use reliable communication protocols and fail-safes.
- Encourage consistent and predictable agent behaviors.

2. Prioritize Scalability from the Start

Expert Insight: *"Scalability should not be an afterthought. Design your systems to scale horizontally, allowing you to add more agents as demand grows without major overhauls."*
— **Mr. John Smith**, Lead Developer at TechSolutions

Application:

- Use distributed architectures that support horizontal scaling.

- Employ containerization technologies like Docker and orchestration tools like Kubernetes.
- Design agents to operate independently without tight coupling.

3. Incorporate Continuous Learning

Expert Insight: *"Multi-agent systems thrive when they can learn and adapt. Incorporate machine learning capabilities to enable agents to improve their performance over time."*
— **Dr. Laura Martinez**, Research Scientist in AI

Application:

- Integrate machine learning models that allow agents to learn from data.
- Enable agents to update their strategies based on performance feedback.
- Use reinforcement learning to enhance agent decision-making capabilities.

4. Foster Collaboration Over Competition

Expert Insight: *"Encourage agents to collaborate rather than compete. Collaborative agents can achieve more complex and meaningful outcomes than those that operate in isolation."*
— **Prof. Michael Lee**, AI and Robotics Professor

Application:

- Design communication protocols that promote information sharing.
- Implement collaborative task allocation mechanisms.
- Define shared goals and objectives for agents to work towards collectively.

5. Invest in Robust Monitoring and Analytics

Expert Insight: *"Monitoring is crucial for maintaining system health. Invest in comprehensive monitoring and analytics tools to gain insights into agent behaviors and system performance."*
— **Ms. Sarah Johnson**, Operations Manager at InnovateAI

Application:

- Use monitoring tools like Prometheus and Grafana to track system metrics.
- Implement logging frameworks to capture detailed agent activities.
- Analyze data to identify trends, detect anomalies, and inform optimization efforts.

6. Ensure Ethical AI Practices

Expert Insight: *"Ethics should be integral to AI development. Ensure that your multi-agent systems operate within ethical guidelines, respecting privacy, fairness, and accountability."*
— **Dr. Anil Gupta**, Ethics in AI Specialist

Application:

- Implement data privacy measures and secure data handling practices.
- Design agents to avoid biases and ensure fair decision-making.
- Establish accountability mechanisms to trace and address agent actions.

19.4 Continuous Improvement Strategies

Continuous improvement is essential for the longevity and effectiveness of multi-agent AI systems. By regularly evaluating and enhancing system components, you can ensure that your AI solutions remain relevant and efficient.

1. Regular Performance Audits

Strategy:

- Conduct periodic audits to assess system performance, agent efficiency, and overall effectiveness.
- Use performance metrics and key performance indicators (KPIs) to measure progress and identify areas for improvement.

Benefits:

- Identifies performance bottlenecks.
- Ensures that the system meets its intended goals.
- Facilitates data-driven decision-making for enhancements.

2. Implement Feedback Loops

Strategy:

- Establish mechanisms for collecting feedback from users, stakeholders, and agents themselves.
- Use feedback to inform system updates, agent behaviors, and process improvements.

Benefits:

- Enhances system adaptability and responsiveness.
- Promotes user satisfaction and trust.
- Drives continuous learning and optimization.

3. Adopt Agile Development Practices

Strategy:

- Utilize agile methodologies, such as Scrum or Kanban, to manage development cycles.
- Encourage iterative development, frequent releases, and continuous integration.

Benefits:

- Increases flexibility and adaptability.
- Facilitates rapid response to changing requirements.
- Enhances collaboration and communication within development teams.

4. Leverage Automation for Testing and Deployment

Strategy:

- Automate testing, deployment, and monitoring processes to increase efficiency and reduce human error.

- Use tools like Jenkins for continuous integration and deployment pipelines.

Benefits:

- Accelerates development cycles.
- Ensures consistent and reliable deployments.
- Frees up resources for more strategic tasks.

5. Foster a Culture of Learning and Innovation

Strategy:

- Encourage team members to stay updated with the latest advancements in AI and multi-agent systems.
- Promote experimentation and the exploration of new ideas and technologies.

Benefits:

- Drives innovation and keeps the system at the cutting edge.
- Enhances team skills and knowledge.
- Encourages proactive problem-solving and creative solutions.

6. Utilize Data-Driven Optimization

Strategy:

- Analyze system and agent performance data to identify trends and opportunities for optimization.
- Use data analytics and machine learning to predict future system behaviors and needs.

Benefits:

- Enables informed decision-making based on empirical evidence.
- Enhances system efficiency and performance.
- Supports proactive maintenance and optimization efforts.

Illustrative Table: Continuous Improvement Strategies

Strategy	Description	Benefits
Regular Performance Audits	Periodic assessments of system and agent performance	Identifies bottlenecks, ensures goal alignment
Implement Feedback Loops	Collect and utilize feedback from various sources	Enhances adaptability, improves satisfaction
Adopt Agile Practices	Use iterative and flexible development methodologies	Increases flexibility, promotes collaboration
Leverage Automation	Automate testing and deployment processes	Reduces errors, accelerates development cycles
Foster Learning and Innovation	Encourage continuous learning and experimentation	Drives innovation, enhances team skills
Utilize Data-Driven Optimization	Analyze and optimize based on performance data	Enables informed decisions, improves efficiency

19.5 Exercise: Troubleshooting Scenarios

Practical exercises help solidify your understanding of troubleshooting in multi-agent AI systems. Below are several scenarios that present common issues, along with guided questions to help you identify solutions.

Scenario 1: Communication Breakdown

Description: In a multi-agent system managing a smart home, the temperature control agent fails to communicate with the lighting agent. As a result, the lighting system does not adjust brightness based on room occupancy, leading to energy inefficiency.

Questions:

1. **Identify the Potential Causes:**
   - What could cause the communication failure between the temperature control agent and the lighting agent?

- How would you verify if the issue is with the communication protocol or the agents themselves?

2. **Propose Solutions:**
   - How would you implement a retry mechanism to handle temporary communication failures?
   - What steps would you take to ensure that the communication channels are reliable and secure?

3. **Prevent Future Issues:**
   - What monitoring tools or logging practices would you implement to detect and address similar communication issues promptly?
   - How can you design the system to handle communication failures gracefully without disrupting overall functionality?

Expected Solutions:

- **Potential Causes:** Network connectivity issues, protocol mismatches, agent crashes, or message format errors.
- **Solutions:** Implement retry mechanisms, verify protocol compatibility, ensure agents are running correctly, and validate message formats.
- **Prevention:** Use monitoring tools like Prometheus for real-time communication tracking, maintain detailed logs, and design fallback behaviors for communication failures.

Scenario 2: Deadlock in Resource Allocation

Description: In a warehouse management system, two agents—Robot A and Robot B—are each holding a resource needed by the other to complete their tasks. As a result, both agents are stuck, unable to proceed.

Questions:

1. **Identify the Deadlock Situation:**
   - How can you recognize that a deadlock has occurred in the system?
   - What are the indicators that both agents are waiting indefinitely?

2. **Analyze the Causes:**

- What design flaws or synchronization issues might have led to the deadlock?
- How does the current resource acquisition strategy contribute to the deadlock?

3. **Implement Solutions:**
   - How would you redesign the resource acquisition process to prevent such deadlocks?
   - What mechanisms can you introduce to detect and resolve deadlocks when they occur?

4. **Enhance System Robustness:**
   - What strategies can you employ to ensure that agents can recover from deadlocks without manual intervention?
   - How can you design agents to back off and retry resource acquisition in a controlled manner?

Expected Solutions:

- **Deadlock Recognition:** Both agents are stuck waiting for resources held by each other without making progress.
- **Causes:** Circular wait conditions due to inconsistent resource acquisition order or lack of timeouts.
- **Solutions:** Implement a global resource ordering strategy, use timeouts with back-off retries, and incorporate deadlock detection algorithms.
- **Robustness:** Design agents to release resources after timeout periods and attempt re-acquisition, ensuring that the system can recover autonomously.

Scenario 3: Inconsistent Agent Behavior Leading to System Errors

Description: In a financial trading system, some agents occasionally place incorrect trades due to inconsistent behavior caused by bugs in their decision-making algorithms. These errors lead to financial losses and system instability.

Questions:

1. **Diagnose the Inconsistencies:**

- o How would you identify and log instances of inconsistent agent behavior?
  - o What tools or methods can you use to trace the source of the bugs in the agents' algorithms?
2. **Implement Solutions:**
   - o What steps would you take to fix the bugs causing inconsistent behaviors?
   - o How can you ensure that the agents' decision-making processes are reliable and accurate?
3. **Prevent Recurrence:**
   - o What testing strategies would you implement to catch similar bugs before deployment?
   - o How can you enhance monitoring to detect and respond to inconsistent behaviors in real-time?

Expected Solutions:

- **Diagnosis:** Use logging frameworks to capture detailed agent actions, analyze logs for anomalies, and employ debugging tools to trace algorithm execution.
- **Solutions:** Fix identified bugs in the code, enhance algorithm validation, and implement thorough unit and integration tests.
- **Prevention:** Adopt test-driven development (TDD), implement continuous integration pipelines with automated testing, and use real-time monitoring tools to detect inconsistencies promptly.

Scenario 4: Scalability Issues During Peak Load

Description: A customer support system powered by multi-agent AI experiences significant slowdowns and increased response times during peak usage hours, impacting user satisfaction.

Questions:

1. **Identify Scalability Bottlenecks:**
   - o What aspects of the system are causing performance degradation under peak loads?
   - o How would you monitor and measure system performance to pinpoint these bottlenecks?
2. **Propose Scaling Solutions:**

- o How can you adjust the system architecture to handle increased loads efficiently?
- o What technologies or strategies can you employ to scale the number of agents dynamically based on demand?

3. **Optimize Resource Utilization:**
   - o How can you optimize agent resource usage to maintain performance without excessive scaling?
   - o What role do load balancers and distributed architectures play in addressing scalability issues?

Expected Solutions:

- **Bottlenecks Identification:** Monitor CPU, memory usage, network latency, and response times using tools like Grafana and Prometheus.
- **Scaling Solutions:** Implement auto-scaling with Kubernetes Horizontal Pod Autoscaler, distribute agents across multiple servers, and use load balancers to distribute incoming requests evenly.
- **Resource Optimization:** Optimize agent algorithms for efficiency, implement caching mechanisms, and use resource-efficient technologies to reduce the need for excessive scaling.

Scenario 5: Security Vulnerabilities in Agent Communication

Description: During a security audit, vulnerabilities are discovered in the communication protocols between agents, potentially allowing unauthorized access and data breaches.

Questions:

1. **Assess Security Risks:**
   - o What types of security vulnerabilities could exist in agent communication protocols?
   - o How would you evaluate the severity and potential impact of these vulnerabilities?
2. **Implement Security Enhancements:**
   - o What measures can you take to secure communication channels between agents?
   - o How can you authenticate and authorize agents to prevent unauthorized access?
3. **Maintain Ongoing Security:**

o   What practices can you adopt to regularly assess and update the security of your multi-agent system?
o   How can you ensure that new vulnerabilities are promptly identified and addressed?

Expected Solutions:

- **Security Risks Assessment:** Identify vulnerabilities such as lack of encryption, weak authentication mechanisms, and susceptibility to man-in-the-middle attacks.
- **Security Enhancements:** Implement encryption (e.g., TLS) for all communication channels, use robust authentication methods (e.g., OAuth), and enforce authorization policies to restrict agent access based on roles.
- **Ongoing Security Practices:** Conduct regular security audits, employ automated security scanning tools, stay updated with security patches, and establish a protocol for promptly addressing discovered vulnerabilities.

19.4 Tips from Industry Experts

Learning from industry experts can provide valuable insights and strategies to enhance the development and management of multi-agent AI systems. Below are key tips shared by seasoned professionals in the field.

1. Design for Failure

Expert Insight: *"Assume that failures will happen and design your system to handle them gracefully. Building resilience into your multi-agent system ensures continuity even when individual agents fail."*
— **Dr. Rebecca Thompson**, AI Systems Resilience Specialist

Application:

- Implement fault-tolerant architectures where agents can recover from failures without disrupting the entire system.
- Use redundancy and backup agents to take over tasks if primary agents fail.

- Design agents to detect failures and initiate recovery protocols autonomously.

2. Emphasize Clear Agent Roles and Responsibilities

Expert Insight: *"Each agent should have a well-defined role and responsibility. Clear boundaries prevent overlaps and conflicts, ensuring smooth coordination and efficiency."*
— **Mr. David Lee**, Lead AI Developer at FutureTech

Application:

- Define specific tasks and objectives for each agent.
- Avoid overlapping functionalities among agents to reduce complexity.
- Document agent roles clearly to facilitate team understanding and system maintenance.

3. Invest in Comprehensive Monitoring

Expert Insight: *"Monitoring is the backbone of any multi-agent system. Comprehensive monitoring allows you to track agent performance, detect issues early, and optimize system operations effectively."*
— **Ms. Angela Perez**, Systems Monitoring Expert at DataGuard

Application:

- Use monitoring tools to track key metrics such as agent response times, task completion rates, and error rates.
- Implement dashboards for real-time visualization of system performance.
- Set up alerts for critical issues to enable prompt intervention.

4. Prioritize Scalability and Flexibility

Expert Insight: *"Build your system to scale seamlessly and adapt to changing requirements. Flexibility in design allows your multi-agent system to grow and evolve without significant reengineering."*
— **Prof. James Wilson**, AI and Systems Engineering Professor

Application:

- Use scalable technologies like cloud computing, containerization, and microservices.
- Design agents to be stateless where possible, facilitating easier scaling and load balancing.
- Allow for dynamic addition or removal of agents based on system needs.

5. Foster Collaborative Development Teams

Expert Insight: *"A collaborative team environment enhances creativity and problem-solving. Encourage open communication and knowledge sharing among team members to drive innovation in your multi-agent systems."*
— **Dr. Maria Gonzalez**, AI Team Lead at InnovateAI

Application:

- Promote regular team meetings and brainstorming sessions.
- Use collaborative tools like version control systems, shared documentation, and project management platforms.
- Encourage continuous learning and skill development within the team.

6. Ensure Ethical AI Deployment

Expert Insight: *"Ethics should be at the core of your AI system design and deployment. Ensure that your multi-agent systems operate fairly, transparently, and responsibly, respecting user privacy and societal norms."*
— **Dr. Anil Kapoor**, Ethics in AI Researcher

Application:

- Implement data privacy measures and comply with relevant regulations (e.g., GDPR).
- Design agents to avoid biases and ensure fair decision-making.
- Establish accountability frameworks to track and address agent actions.

19.5 Continuous Improvement Strategies

Continuous improvement is vital for maintaining the effectiveness and relevance of multi-agent AI systems. By adopting systematic strategies, you can ensure that your systems evolve to meet changing demands and incorporate the latest advancements in AI technology.

1. Iterative Development and Feedback Loops

Strategy:

- Adopt an iterative development approach, releasing system updates in small, manageable increments.
- Incorporate feedback from users and stakeholders at each iteration to guide system enhancements.

Benefits:

- Allows for quick identification and resolution of issues.
- Ensures that system developments align with user needs and expectations.
- Facilitates agile responses to changing requirements.

2. Performance Benchmarking and Optimization

Strategy:

- Regularly benchmark system and agent performance against predefined metrics.
- Identify performance bottlenecks and optimize algorithms and resource usage accordingly.

Benefits:

- Maintains high system performance and responsiveness.
- Enhances resource efficiency, reducing operational costs.
- Provides data-driven insights for continuous optimization.

3. Knowledge Sharing and Training

Strategy:

- Encourage ongoing training and professional development for team members.
- Share knowledge through documentation, workshops, and collaborative projects.

Benefits:

- Keeps the team updated with the latest AI advancements and best practices.
- Enhances team expertise and problem-solving capabilities.
- Promotes a culture of continuous learning and improvement.

4. Incorporate Advanced AI Techniques

Strategy:

- Explore and integrate advanced AI techniques such as reinforcement learning, deep learning, and natural language processing to enhance agent capabilities.
- Stay informed about emerging AI research and technologies that can benefit your multi-agent systems.

Benefits:

- Improves agent intelligence and adaptability.
- Enables the system to handle more complex and dynamic tasks.
- Keeps your AI systems competitive and innovative.

5. Regular Security Audits and Updates

Strategy:

- Conduct regular security audits to identify and address vulnerabilities.
- Update security protocols and agent software to protect against new threats.

Benefits:

- Ensures the integrity and confidentiality of system data.
- Protects against cyber threats and unauthorized access.
- Maintains user trust and compliance with security standards.

6. Utilize Simulation and Modeling

Strategy:

- Use simulation and modeling tools to test system behaviors under various scenarios.
- Predict and evaluate the impact of potential changes before implementing them in the live system.

Benefits:

- Reduces the risk of deploying changes that could negatively impact system performance.
- Provides a safe environment to experiment with new features and configurations.
- Enhances understanding of system dynamics and agent interactions.

Illustrative Table: Continuous Improvement Strategies

Strategy	Description	Benefits
Iterative Development	Release updates in small increments with feedback	Quick issue resolution, aligns with user needs
Performance Benchmarking	Regularly measure and optimize system performance	Maintains high performance, reduces costs
Knowledge Sharing	Encourage training and documentation	Enhances team expertise, promotes learning
Advanced AI Techniques	Integrate cutting-edge AI methods	Improves agent capabilities, handles complexity
Security Audits	Conduct regular security assessments	Protects data, maintains trust

Strategy	Description	Benefits
Simulation and Modeling	Test system behaviors in simulated environments	Reduces deployment risks, informs changes

19.6 Exercise: Troubleshooting Scenarios

Engaging in practical exercises helps reinforce your understanding of troubleshooting and applying best practices in multi-agent AI systems. Below are several scenarios designed to challenge your problem-solving skills and apply the concepts discussed in this chapter.

Exercise 1: Resolving Communication Failures

Scenario: You are managing a multi-agent system in a smart city environment where traffic control agents communicate with emergency response agents. Recently, traffic control agents have been unable to send critical alerts to emergency response agents during peak traffic hours, causing delays in emergency responses.

Tasks:

1. **Diagnose the Issue:**
   o What steps would you take to identify the root cause of the communication failure?
   o What tools or logs would you examine to gather relevant information?
2. **Implement Solutions:**
   o How would you modify the communication protocols to handle high traffic volumes?
   o What redundancy measures can you introduce to ensure message delivery during peak times?
3. **Prevent Future Failures:**
   o What monitoring and alerting mechanisms would you set up to detect similar issues proactively?
   o How can you test the robustness of the communication system under simulated peak loads?

Expected Actions:

- **Diagnosis:** Check network bandwidth usage, inspect communication logs for errors, and monitor agent statuses during peak hours.
- **Solutions:** Upgrade communication infrastructure to handle higher volumes, implement message queuing systems like RabbitMQ or Kafka, and add redundant communication paths.
- **Prevention:** Use monitoring tools to track message delivery success rates, set up alerts for communication failures, and perform stress testing to ensure system resilience under peak loads.

Exercise 2: Handling Deadlocks in Resource Allocation

Scenario: In a manufacturing plant, two robot agents are assigned to assemble products. Robot A is holding Component X and waiting for Component Y, while Robot B is holding Component Y and waiting for Component X, resulting in a deadlock.

Tasks:

1. **Identify the Deadlock:**
   - How can you detect that a deadlock has occurred between Robot A and Robot B?
   - What are the signs indicating that the system is stuck in a deadlock?
2. **Analyze the Causes:**
   - What design flaws in the resource acquisition process could have led to this deadlock?
   - How does the current resource ordering contribute to the problem?
3. **Implement Deadlock Resolution:**
   - What strategies would you apply to resolve the existing deadlock without disrupting other system operations?
   - How can you redesign the resource acquisition process to prevent similar deadlocks in the future?
4. **Test the Solution:**
   - How would you simulate the deadlock scenario to ensure that your resolution strategy is effective?
   - What metrics would you monitor to confirm that deadlocks are resolved and prevented?

Expected Actions:

- **Deadlock Detection:** Implement monitoring to detect when agents are waiting indefinitely for resources.
- **Causes Analysis:** Recognize that agents are acquiring resources in conflicting orders, leading to a circular wait.
- **Resolution Strategies:** Use timeouts to release held resources after a certain period, implement a global resource ordering, or introduce a deadlock detection and recovery mechanism.
- **Prevention:** Ensure that all agents acquire resources in a predefined global order, eliminating circular waits.
- **Testing:** Create simulations where agents attempt to acquire resources in conflicting orders and verify that the system resolves deadlocks using the implemented strategies.

Exercise 3: Optimizing Agent Performance Under High Load

Scenario: A customer service chatbot system experiences slow response times and increased error rates during promotional campaigns when user interactions surge.

Tasks:

1. **Identify Performance Bottlenecks:**
   - What tools would you use to monitor the system's performance during high load periods?
   - How would you determine which components are causing slowdowns and errors?
2. **Implement Scaling Solutions:**
   - How can you adjust the number of chatbot agents dynamically to handle the increased load?
   - What infrastructure changes would you consider to support scalable performance?
3. **Optimize Agent Efficiency:**
   - What algorithmic optimizations can you apply to improve chatbot response times?
   - How can you enhance resource utilization to maintain high performance without excessive scaling?
4. **Evaluate the Improvements:**

- o After implementing scaling and optimizations, how would you assess the effectiveness of your changes?
- o What metrics would you track to ensure sustained performance during future high-load scenarios?

Expected Actions:

- **Bottleneck Identification:** Use monitoring tools like New Relic or Datadog to track CPU usage, memory consumption, and response times.
- **Scaling Solutions:** Implement auto-scaling policies using Kubernetes Horizontal Pod Autoscaler or cloud-based auto-scaling services to increase the number of chatbot instances during peak times.
- **Agent Optimization:** Optimize chatbot algorithms for faster processing, implement caching for frequent queries, and reduce computational overhead where possible.
- **Evaluation:** Compare performance metrics before and after changes, ensuring that response times have decreased and error rates have diminished during high-load periods.

Exercise 4: Securing Agent Communications

Scenario: During a security review, it was found that the communication between surveillance agents in a smart building lacks encryption, posing a risk of data interception and unauthorized access.

Tasks:

1. **Assess Security Vulnerabilities:**
   - o What specific vulnerabilities exist in the current communication setup?
   - o How could these vulnerabilities be exploited by malicious actors?
2. **Implement Security Enhancements:**
   - o What encryption methods would you apply to secure agent communications?
   - o How would you manage encryption keys to ensure secure and efficient communication?
3. **Ensure Compliance and Best Practices:**

o What industry standards and regulations should you adhere to when securing agent communications?
o How can you document and enforce security policies within your multi-agent system?

4. **Test Security Measures:**
   o How would you verify that the implemented encryption effectively protects against data interception?
   o What testing tools or methods would you use to assess the security of agent communications?

Expected Actions:

- **Vulnerabilities Assessment:** Identify lack of encryption, potential for man-in-the-middle attacks, and unauthorized access risks.
- **Security Enhancements:** Implement TLS/SSL encryption for all communication channels, use secure key management systems like AWS KMS or HashiCorp Vault.
- **Compliance and Best Practices:** Adhere to standards like ISO/IEC 27001, ensure compliance with regulations such as GDPR, and maintain detailed security documentation.
- **Testing Security Measures:** Conduct penetration testing using tools like Wireshark to ensure data is encrypted and cannot be intercepted, and verify that unauthorized agents cannot access communication channels.

19.6 Reflection Questions

Reflecting on troubleshooting scenarios and best practices enhances your ability to manage and improve multi-agent AI systems effectively. Consider the following questions to deepen your understanding and prepare for real-world challenges.

1. How do communication failures impact the overall performance and reliability of a multi-agent system?

Considerations:

- The role of inter-agent communication in coordinating actions and sharing information.

- The potential cascading effects of failed communications on system tasks and objectives.
- Strategies to mitigate communication failures and enhance system resilience.

2. What are the key factors to consider when designing synchronization mechanisms in multi-agent systems?

Considerations:

- The balance between concurrency and consistency.
- The complexity of synchronization algorithms and their scalability.
- The impact of synchronization on system performance and responsiveness.

3. In what ways can deadlocks be both a symptom and a cause of deeper system issues in multi-agent AI systems?

Considerations:

- How deadlocks can indicate flaws in resource management or agent coordination.
- The long-term effects of unresolved deadlocks on system stability and performance.
- Approaches to detect, resolve, and prevent deadlocks effectively.

4. Why is scalability crucial for multi-agent AI systems, and how can improper scaling strategies hinder system growth?

Considerations:

- The importance of handling increasing workloads and agent numbers without degrading performance.
- The risks associated with over-scaling or under-scaling, such as resource wastage or system bottlenecks.
- Best practices for implementing scalable architectures and dynamic resource allocation.

5. How can continuous monitoring and logging practices contribute to the proactive management of multi-agent AI systems?

Considerations:

- The role of monitoring in detecting performance issues, errors, and security threats.
- The importance of comprehensive logging for troubleshooting and system analysis.
- Tools and methodologies for effective monitoring and log management.

Chapter 20: Future Trends in Multi-agent AI

Multi-agent AI systems are evolving rapidly, driving innovations in various industries such as healthcare, finance, logistics, and autonomous systems. As these systems continue to mature, new trends and technologies will shape the landscape of AI automation, influencing everything from how AI systems are deployed to how agents interact with each other and the world. In this chapter, we will explore the key future trends in **multi-agent AI systems**, identify potential disruptions and innovations, and discuss how individuals and organizations can prepare for the upcoming era of AI-driven automation.

20.1 Predicting the Next Decade in AI Systems

The next decade promises significant advancements in AI, especially in the domain of **multi-agent systems**. As AI technologies mature and become more integrated into everyday life, the role of multi-agent systems will expand, enabling smarter, more adaptable, and autonomous solutions. Below are the key predictions for the future of multi-agent AI systems:

1. Increasing Autonomy and Adaptability

AI systems will become increasingly autonomous, meaning that multi-agent systems will need to make decisions without human intervention, based on the data and context they gather. These agents will adapt to changing environments, learning from experience and making decisions in real-time.

Example: Self-driving cars, powered by multi-agent systems, will need to adapt to dynamic road conditions and interact with other vehicles and pedestrians while making real-time decisions to ensure safety.

2. Enhanced Collaboration Between Agents

The next decade will see agents collaborating more effectively and efficiently. Multi-agent systems will be designed to work together to achieve common goals, using shared knowledge, resources, and strategies. **Swarm**

intelligence, which models the behavior of social insects like ants or bees, will be applied to enhance agent coordination and task completion.

Example: In supply chain management, multiple agents (e.g., warehouses, transportation systems, inventory agents) will work together in real-time to optimize logistics and inventory, adapting to disruptions like weather or sudden demand changes.

3. Ethical and Responsible AI Deployment

As multi-agent systems become more involved in decision-making processes, there will be increased focus on ensuring that these systems operate within ethical boundaries. Issues related to **bias**, **transparency**, and **accountability** will need to be addressed.

Example: In healthcare, AI agents will need to ensure that decisions regarding patient care are made in a manner that is both **fair** and **non-discriminatory**, adhering to privacy and regulatory standards.

4. Expansion into Complex Domains

AI will continue to penetrate complex and highly regulated sectors such as law, finance, and healthcare. Multi-agent systems will be able to handle increasingly sophisticated tasks, such as medical diagnostics, legal analysis, and financial portfolio management.

Example: AI agents in healthcare will not only assist with diagnosing diseases but will also collaborate with other agents to develop personalized treatment plans based on real-time patient data, research, and medical history.

20.2 Potential Disruptions and Innovations

As AI technology continues to evolve, it will undoubtedly disrupt various sectors, presenting both opportunities and challenges. Here are some potential disruptions and innovations in multi-agent AI systems:

1. Decentralized AI Networks

Decentralized AI, powered by blockchain and distributed ledger technologies, is expected to revolutionize the way multi-agent systems operate. By eliminating central control, decentralized systems enable agents to work autonomously while maintaining trust and security in their interactions.

Example: In a decentralized supply chain network, agents across different organizations could collaborate without the need for a central authority, using blockchain to validate transactions and ensure transparency and trust.

2. AI-Driven Automation Across Industries

The use of multi-agent AI systems in automation will lead to a paradigm shift across industries. **Robotic process automation (RPA)** and **autonomous systems** will be enhanced by multi-agent coordination, allowing entire workflows to be automated across departments and organizations.

Example: In manufacturing, AI agents will control robots, manage supply chains, and monitor equipment, all while working together to ensure seamless production and efficiency. These systems will not only manage individual machines but optimize entire factories through intelligent coordination.

3. Integration with Edge Computing and IoT

The increasing integration of multi-agent AI systems with **Edge Computing** and the **Internet of Things (IoT)** will enable real-time decision-making at the edge, where data is collected and processed close to the source, rather than relying on centralized data centers.

Example: In smart cities, AI agents will interact with IoT devices like traffic lights, waste management systems, and public transportation to dynamically optimize city operations, such as traffic flow or waste collection, without waiting for central systems to process and react.

4. Human-AI Collaboration and Assistants

Future multi-agent systems will foster deeper collaboration between humans and AI. Agents will evolve to assist humans in more meaningful ways, from personal assistants to collaborative decision-making agents that work alongside human teams to achieve shared goals.

Example: In the workplace, AI assistants will collaborate with human teams to manage schedules, perform research, or even assist in brainstorming sessions, learning from past interactions to become more effective over time.

5. Autonomous Decision-Making in Safety-Critical Environments

In safety-critical environments, such as aviation, healthcare, and autonomous driving, multi-agent systems will need to make decisions in high-stakes situations with minimal human intervention. The reliability of these systems will be paramount.

Example: In autonomous vehicles, agents will collaborate to navigate complex roadways and make safety-critical decisions, such as emergency braking or rerouting, while ensuring compliance with safety regulations.

20.3 Preparing for the Future of AI Automation

As we look toward the future of multi-agent AI, it is essential to prepare for the changes that AI-driven automation will bring. Below are strategies for both individuals and organizations to stay ahead of the curve:

1. Continuous Learning and Skill Development

AI and multi-agent systems are evolving rapidly, and professionals must stay up-to-date with the latest trends, tools, and techniques. Engaging in continuous learning and acquiring expertise in areas like machine learning, reinforcement learning, and blockchain will be crucial for staying competitive in the field.

Recommendations:

- Take online courses on platforms like Coursera, Udemy, or edX that cover topics such as AI, machine learning, and multi-agent systems.
- Attend industry conferences and workshops to network with professionals and learn about emerging technologies.
- Participate in hackathons or projects that involve AI and multi-agent systems to gain hands-on experience.

2. Building Interdisciplinary Knowledge

The future of multi-agent AI systems will require professionals to possess interdisciplinary knowledge. A strong foundation in computer science, along with an understanding of areas such as ethics, law, and economics, will be essential for designing systems that can operate responsibly in real-world environments.

Recommendations:

- Develop knowledge of regulatory frameworks governing AI and data privacy laws, such as GDPR.
- Understand the ethical implications of AI decision-making, particularly in sensitive areas like healthcare and criminal justice.
- Study interdisciplinary topics such as economics to understand how AI can impact industries and markets.

3. Embrace Collaboration with AI Systems

The ability to collaborate effectively with AI agents will be a key skill for the future. Professionals will need to understand how to interact with, guide, and integrate AI systems into their workflows and decision-making processes.

Recommendations:

- Develop soft skills such as communication and collaboration to work effectively with AI systems.
- Learn how to leverage AI systems as tools that can augment human capabilities, rather than replace them.
- Explore emerging tools and platforms that facilitate human-AI collaboration, such as AI-powered workflow automation systems and collaborative decision-making platforms.

4. Stay Informed About Technological Advancements

Technologies such as **Edge Computing**, **5G**, and **Quantum Computing** will have a profound impact on multi-agent AI systems. Staying informed about these advancements will help you anticipate future trends and adapt your approach to AI development.

Recommendations:

- Follow tech blogs, journals, and publications that focus on AI and emerging technologies.
- Participate in discussions on platforms like LinkedIn or Reddit to stay informed about industry news and breakthroughs.
- Engage with research papers and case studies to understand the latest developments in multi-agent AI systems.

20.4 Integrating Emerging Technologies

The integration of emerging technologies with multi-agent systems will unlock new possibilities and improve system efficiency, scalability, and intelligence. Below are some of the key technologies that will shape the future of AI:

1. Blockchain and Decentralized AI

Blockchain technology is poised to play a significant role in the future of multi-agent AI by enabling secure, decentralized collaboration among agents. Blockchain can provide trustless environments for agents to collaborate and share resources, making them more resilient and transparent.

Example: Decentralized supply chains powered by blockchain can allow agents from different organizations to share data and resources in a secure and verifiable manner, improving efficiency and reducing fraud.

2. Edge Computing and AI at the Edge

Edge computing will enable AI systems to process data locally, closer to the source, reducing latency and improving real-time decision-making. This will be particularly useful for applications such as autonomous vehicles, smart cities, and industrial IoT systems.

Example: Autonomous drones will use edge computing to process sensor data in real-time, making decisions about navigation, obstacle avoidance, and task execution without relying on cloud-based processing.

3. Quantum Computing for Complex Simulations

Quantum computing holds the potential to revolutionize multi-agent systems by enabling the processing of complex simulations and optimizations that were previously impossible with classical computers. This will allow for faster and more accurate decision-making in multi-agent environments.

Example: Quantum algorithms can be used to optimize the behavior of agents in large-scale, resource-constrained environments, such as energy grids or traffic systems, where traditional computation methods struggle to find optimal solutions.

4. Advanced Natural Language Processing (NLP)

Advancements in **NLP** will allow agents to interact more effectively with humans and other agents. Multi-agent systems will be able to process and understand human language, enabling them to assist with tasks like customer support, content creation, and conversational AI.

Example: Virtual assistants will use advanced NLP to understand and respond to customer queries, collaborate with other agents to resolve issues, and adapt their behavior based on user preferences and feedback.

20.5 Reflection Questions

To deepen your understanding of the future of multi-agent AI and how to prepare for upcoming trends, consider the following reflection questions:

1. How do you envision multi-agent AI systems transforming industries like healthcare, finance, and logistics in the next decade?

- Think about the current challenges faced in these industries and how multi-agent AI systems can help optimize processes, enhance decision-making, and improve outcomes.

2. What role do you think blockchain will play in the development of decentralized multi-agent systems, and how can it enhance trust and transparency in AI-driven environments?

- Reflect on how **distributed ledger technologies** can enable secure collaboration and data sharing among agents, particularly in sectors like supply chain management and finance.

3. How can professionals ensure that AI systems are developed and deployed in an ethically responsible manner, particularly as multi-agent systems become more autonomous?

- Consider the ethical challenges posed by autonomous AI agents and how transparency, accountability, and fairness can be ensured in the decision-making processes.

4. What steps can you take today to prepare for a career in multi-agent AI, considering the rapid technological advancements and the increasing demand for AI-driven solutions?

- Reflect on the skills and knowledge areas you need to focus on, such as AI algorithms, machine learning, blockchain, and interdisciplinary knowledge.

5. How can the integration of edge computing and 5G technologies improve the performance of multi-agent systems, especially in real-time applications like autonomous vehicles or smart cities?

- Think about how processing data closer to the source can reduce latency and enable more efficient, real-time decision-making in complex multi-agent environments.

Chapter 21: Building a Career in Multi-agent AI

The field of **multi-agent AI** is rapidly evolving, creating exciting opportunities for professionals who wish to contribute to AI advancements and innovation. Whether you're just beginning your career in AI or are already an experienced professional looking to specialize in multi-agent systems, understanding the required skills, career opportunities, networking strategies, and ways to stay updated with industry trends is crucial for long-term success. This chapter will guide you through the essential aspects of building a career in multi-agent AI, helping you navigate the path to success.

21.1 Skills and Qualifications Needed

To build a successful career in **multi-agent AI**, it's essential to acquire both technical and soft skills, as well as domain-specific knowledge. Below are the key skills and qualifications that will set you apart in this specialized field:

1. Technical Skills

a. Programming Languages:
Proficiency in programming languages like **Python**, **Java**, **C++**, and **MATLAB** is essential for developing and implementing AI models. Python, in particular, is the most commonly used language in the AI space due to its extensive libraries for machine learning (e.g., TensorFlow, PyTorch), and multi-agent systems (e.g., **Mesa**).

b. AI Algorithms and Techniques:
Deep knowledge of various AI algorithms is crucial. These include:

- **Reinforcement Learning (RL):** Used in multi-agent environments where agents must learn optimal policies through interactions with their environment.
- **Machine Learning:** Understanding supervised, unsupervised, and deep learning algorithms is critical for training agents.

- **Game Theory:** Essential for understanding and modeling strategic decision-making in multi-agent environments.
- **Planning and Coordination Algorithms:** These are essential to designing agents that can effectively coordinate and collaborate to achieve shared goals.

c. Multi-agent Systems (MAS) Frameworks:
Familiarity with frameworks and tools like **JADE (Java Agent DEvelopment Framework)**, **OpenAI Gym** for simulations, and **Mesa** for Python-based multi-agent systems is important for simulating and developing multi-agent AI applications.

d. Software Development Best Practices:

- **Version Control (e.g., Git)**: Ensures collaboration and code management.
- **Unit Testing & Debugging:** Ensures that AI algorithms and agent behaviors are reliable and robust.
- **Performance Optimization:** Ensuring that your multi-agent systems scale efficiently and perform well under load.

e. Cloud and Distributed Systems:
Many multi-agent systems are deployed in cloud environments or on distributed infrastructures. Familiarity with platforms like **AWS**, **Azure**, or **Google Cloud** is essential for designing scalable and fault-tolerant multi-agent systems. Tools for containerization (e.g., **Docker**, **Kubernetes**) are also key to managing and deploying AI systems at scale.

---

2. Soft Skills

a. Problem-Solving and Critical Thinking:
In multi-agent AI, you'll be designing systems that require thinking about how agents interact, coordinate, and solve problems collaboratively. Strong analytical skills are needed to understand complex problems and devise effective solutions.

b. Communication Skills:
As a professional in multi-agent AI, you will often need to explain complex AI models and strategies to stakeholders or team members who may not have

technical expertise. Strong communication skills—both written and verbal—are essential for this.

c. Collaboration and Teamwork:
Multi-agent AI systems are typically developed by teams of specialists, including AI researchers, software engineers, data scientists, and product managers. Being able to work effectively as part of a team is crucial.

d. Creativity and Innovation:
Multi-agent AI is a relatively new and evolving field. Creativity is necessary for designing novel algorithms, approaches, and systems that can solve new and challenging problems effectively.

---

3. Qualifications

While practical skills are critical, academic qualifications can also provide a strong foundation for a career in multi-agent AI. These include:

a. Bachelor's Degree (Fundamental Requirement):
A degree in **computer science**, **engineering**, **mathematics**, or a related field is typically the minimum requirement. Coursework should cover topics such as algorithms, data structures, AI, and machine learning.

b. Master's Degree or PhD (Specialization):
Advanced degrees in AI, machine learning, robotics, or a related discipline will provide specialized knowledge and a competitive edge. A **PhD** is particularly valuable if you're interested in conducting research or developing cutting-edge AI technologies.

c. Online Courses and Certifications:
Several online platforms offer specialized courses and certifications in multi-agent AI, machine learning, and reinforcement learning. These can help fill gaps in knowledge and allow you to stay updated with the latest developments.

Example:

- **Coursera** offers specialized courses like "Deep Learning Specialization" by Andrew Ng.

- **Udacity** provides a **Self-Driving Car Nanodegree** with a focus on multi-agent collaboration.

21.2 Career Paths and Opportunities

The demand for multi-agent AI expertise is growing across industries. Below are some of the key career paths and opportunities for professionals in this field:

1. AI Researcher/Scientist

As an **AI researcher** or **scientist**, your role would be to advance the underlying technologies that power multi-agent systems. This could involve researching new algorithms, improving existing methods, or exploring new applications for AI.

Key Responsibilities:

- Conducting original research on algorithms for multi-agent coordination, reinforcement learning, and agent-based modeling.
- Writing research papers and contributing to the academic community.
- Collaborating with universities, tech companies, and research labs.

Ideal Background:

- Advanced degree (PhD or MSc) in AI, machine learning, or a related field.
- Published papers or research on multi-agent AI topics.

2. AI Engineer/Developer

As an **AI engineer**, you will focus on implementing and deploying multi-agent systems in real-world applications. You will develop code, test algorithms, and integrate AI models into existing software environments.

Key Responsibilities:

- Developing software solutions based on multi-agent AI principles.

- Working with teams to integrate agents into broader applications, such as robotics, autonomous vehicles, or IoT.
- Optimizing code for performance, scalability, and robustness.

Ideal Background:

- Degree in computer science or software engineering.
- Proficiency in programming languages like Python, Java, or C++.
- Experience with AI frameworks (e.g., TensorFlow, PyTorch, OpenAI Gym).

3. Data Scientist/Data Engineer

Data scientists and engineers working in multi-agent AI will focus on preparing and analyzing the data that agents use to make decisions. Your role would involve preprocessing data, developing models, and tuning algorithms to improve agent performance.

Key Responsibilities:

- Preprocessing and cleaning large datasets to train multi-agent systems.
- Applying machine learning and statistical techniques to improve decision-making processes.
- Collaborating with AI engineers to implement data-driven AI models.

Ideal Background:

- Degree in data science, machine learning, or related fields.
- Experience with large-scale data analysis and machine learning frameworks.
- Expertise in tools like SQL, Hadoop, and Python-based libraries (e.g., Pandas, NumPy).

4. AI Solutions Architect

An **AI solutions architect** is responsible for designing and architecting AI-driven systems, including multi-agent AI systems. You'll work on designing scalable architectures that enable efficient deployment of multi-agent systems in production environments.

Key Responsibilities:

- Designing system architectures that integrate multi-agent AI.
- Collaborating with clients to tailor AI solutions to specific business needs.
- Ensuring systems are scalable, maintainable, and robust.

Ideal Background:

- Background in systems engineering, software development, or AI.
- Strong understanding of distributed systems, cloud computing, and containerization (e.g., Docker, Kubernetes).
- Experience with AI/ML development and deployment.

5. Product Manager for AI Technologies

Product managers in the AI field oversee the development and deployment of AI-powered products, such as intelligent agents or autonomous systems. You'll focus on understanding customer needs, defining product requirements, and working with engineering teams to deliver solutions.

Key Responsibilities:

- Defining product vision and strategy for AI-powered products.
- Working closely with engineers to ensure product development aligns with customer needs.
- Ensuring successful product launch and adoption by end-users.

Ideal Background:

- Experience in product management with a focus on AI or software products.
- Understanding of the AI landscape, multi-agent systems, and customer use cases.

21.3 Networking and Professional Development

Networking is crucial in the rapidly evolving field of multi-agent AI. Establishing professional relationships, learning from others, and staying informed about industry trends can open doors to new opportunities.

1. Attend Industry Conferences and Meetups

Conferences such as **NeurIPS (Conference on Neural Information Processing Systems)**, **ICML (International Conference on Machine Learning)**, and **AAMAS (International Conference on Autonomous Agents and Multi-Agent Systems)** are ideal places to meet like-minded professionals, researchers, and industry leaders.

Networking Tips:

- Attend both in-person and virtual events.
- Participate in panel discussions, workshops, and technical sessions to showcase your knowledge.
- Network with professionals on platforms like **LinkedIn** and **Twitter** during events.

2. Join Professional Organizations and Communities

Becoming a member of professional organizations such as **IEEE (Institute of Electrical and Electronics Engineers)**, **ACM (Association for Computing Machinery)**, or **AAAI (Association for the Advancement of Artificial Intelligence)** can help you stay connected with the AI community and access the latest resources.

Professional Organizations Provide:

- Access to journals, research papers, and newsletters.
- Opportunities to participate in special interest groups or local chapters.
- Job boards and career development resources.

3. Contribute to Open-Source Projects

Contributing to open-source projects in multi-agent AI can help you gain real-world experience, build a reputation in the community, and learn from other professionals.

Platforms for Open-Source Contribution:

- **GitHub** and **GitLab**: Contribute to repositories related to multi-agent AI frameworks.
- **OpenAI**, **DeepMind**, and other AI research organizations often welcome contributions to their open-source projects.

Benefits of Open-Source Contribution:

- Build a portfolio of work.
- Collaborate with experts in the field.
- Gain hands-on experience with real-world projects.

4. Mentorship and Peer Learning

Finding a mentor can significantly accelerate your career growth in multi-agent AI. A mentor can provide guidance on skill development, career paths, and navigating the challenges of the industry.

Mentorship Opportunities:

- Join AI-focused communities and seek mentorship programs.
- Engage in peer learning through online forums, study groups, or tech meetups.

21.4 Staying Updated with Industry Trends

The field of AI and multi-agent systems is dynamic, with constant advancements in algorithms, tools, and applications. Staying informed is essential for ensuring that you remain competitive and knowledgeable.

1. Follow Industry News and Research

Stay updated by regularly reading blogs, academic papers, and articles related to multi-agent systems and AI. Platforms like **arXiv**, **Google Scholar**, and **Medium** are great sources for the latest research and industry developments.

Key Topics to Follow:

- Reinforcement learning in multi-agent environments.
- Swarm intelligence and coordination algorithms.
- Applications of AI in robotics, autonomous systems, and healthcare.

2. Enroll in Online Learning Platforms

Platforms like **Coursera**, **edX**, and **Udacity** regularly offer courses on the latest AI technologies, including multi-agent systems. These platforms are valuable for keeping your knowledge up-to-date and learning new techniques in the field.

3. Experiment with Emerging Tools and Frameworks

Experimenting with emerging technologies such as **TensorFlow Agents**, **PyTorch** for reinforcement learning, and new multi-agent simulation frameworks will help you stay ahead of the curve.

21.5 Quiz

To help consolidate your understanding of the key concepts in building a career in multi-agent AI, here's a short quiz:

1. Which programming language is most commonly used for developing multi-agent AI systems and why?

2. What are the key differences between a career as an AI engineer and a data scientist in the multi-agent AI field?

3. Name two important skills for collaborating with multi-agent systems and explain why they are critical.

4. How can blockchain technology enhance multi-agent AI systems in real-world applications?

5. Describe two professional organizations you can join to stay informed and connected within the multi-agent AI community.

Chapter 22: Resources and Further Learning

Building a career in **multi-agent AI** or simply enhancing your understanding of this field requires continuous learning. The landscape of AI is rapidly evolving, and staying up to date with the latest tools, research, and techniques is critical for success. In this chapter, we provide a comprehensive list of resources that can help you further your knowledge, hone your skills, and stay connected with the broader AI community.

22.1 Comprehensive List of Tools and Libraries

To effectively develop multi-agent systems and AI applications, you'll need a set of tools and libraries that enable efficient modeling, simulation, and deployment. Below is a curated list of some of the most popular and useful tools and libraries for **multi-agent AI** development:

1. Multi-agent Simulation Frameworks

- **Mesa (Python):**
  Mesa is a Python framework for agent-based modeling and simulation. It is widely used in multi-agent systems to create models that simulate agent behaviors in a dynamic environment.

  Key Features:

  - Easily customizable agents with individual states and behaviors.
  - Support for running simulations in real-time or batch mode.
  - Built-in visualization tools for agent interactions and system states.

  Example: Mesa can be used to model traffic systems where each agent represents a vehicle, and the simulation tracks how vehicles interact with each other and traffic lights.

Installation:

```
pip install mesa
```

- **Repast (Java):**
  Repast is a suite of tools and libraries for agent-based modeling, primarily used for large-scale simulations. It's ideal for social science research, complex systems, and decision-making applications.

  Key Features:

  - Scalable for large agent populations.
  - Provides a range of predefined models for various domains (e.g., urban planning, healthcare).
  - Supports parallel and distributed computing for performance optimization.
- **NetLogo (Cross-platform):**
  NetLogo is another popular agent-based modeling platform, widely used for educational purposes as well as research.

  Key Features:

  - Intuitive drag-and-drop interface.
  - Large library of pre-built models for various applications.
  - Good for visualizing agent interactions in an interactive environment.

2. Machine Learning Libraries

- **TensorFlow / PyTorch:**
  Both **TensorFlow** and **PyTorch** are popular deep learning libraries that can be integrated with multi-agent systems, especially when agents require sophisticated decision-making processes powered by neural networks.

  Key Features:

  - TensorFlow provides excellent deployment capabilities for multi-agent systems at scale, especially when using **TensorFlow Agents** for reinforcement learning.
  - PyTorch is favored for research and provides an easy-to-use interface for implementing reinforcement learning algorithms.

Installation (PyTorch):

```
pip install torch torchvision
```

- **Stable Baselines3 (Python):**
  A set of reliable implementations of reinforcement learning algorithms built on top of PyTorch. It's often used for training agents in complex environments, including multi-agent setups.

  Key Features:

  - Implements algorithms like PPO, DQN, A2C, and more.
  - Easy-to-use interface for quick experimentation.
  - Works seamlessly with Gym, a toolkit for developing reinforcement learning environments.

  Installation:

  ```
  pip install stable-baselines3[extra]
  ```

3. Frameworks for Autonomous Agents

- **OpenAI Gym:**
  OpenAI Gym is a toolkit for developing and comparing reinforcement learning algorithms. It provides a variety of environments for testing multi-agent systems.

  Key Features:

  - Pre-built environments like **CartPole**, **Atari**, and custom scenarios for AI agent interaction.
  - Supports integration with other machine learning libraries (TensorFlow, PyTorch).

  Installation:

  ```
  pip install gym
  ```

- **Ray (Python):**
  Ray is a framework for distributed computing that supports scalable reinforcement learning algorithms and multi-agent systems. Ray's **RLlib** allows you to train multi-agent systems at scale.

269

Key Features:

- o Supports distributed execution and scaling.
- o Easy to integrate with other tools like PyTorch or TensorFlow.
- o Provides pre-built algorithms for reinforcement learning.

Installation:

```
pip install ray[rllib]
```

4. Multi-agent Coordination Libraries

- **AAMAS (Java):**
  The **AAMAS** framework supports the design and implementation of multi-agent systems using Java. It's particularly useful for developing decentralized agents that need to coordinate autonomously.

  Key Features:

  - o Strong support for communication protocols between agents.
  - o Implements a variety of agent decision-making algorithms.

22.2 Recommended Reading and Research Papers

Continuous learning through reading is a powerful way to stay updated on the latest advancements in multi-agent AI. Below is a list of books, papers, and research sources that will help you deepen your understanding of multi-agent systems, reinforcement learning, and related AI fields:

1. Books

- **"Artificial Intelligence: A Modern Approach" by Stuart Russell and Peter Norvig**
  This classic book offers an introduction to AI, including multi-agent systems, game theory, and decision-making.
- **"Multi-Agent Systems: Algorithmic, Game-Theoretic, and Logical Foundations" by Michael Wooldridge**

A comprehensive guide to multi-agent systems, covering algorithmic foundations, theoretical aspects, and applications in real-world scenarios.

- **"Reinforcement Learning: An Introduction" by Richard S. Sutton and Andrew G. Barto**
  This book covers the foundational concepts of reinforcement learning, a key aspect of multi-agent systems, including techniques used by agents to learn optimal behavior.
- **"The Handbook of Multi-Agent Systems" by Gerhard Weiss**
  A compilation of research on multi-agent systems, covering everything from theoretical underpinnings to practical applications.

2. Research Papers

- **"Cooperative Multi-agent Reinforcement Learning: A Review" by H. Leung et al.**
  This paper discusses various approaches to reinforcement learning for multi-agent systems, highlighting challenges and open problems.
- **"A Survey of Multi-Agent Systems" by S. L. P. K. Das and R. S. Sutton**
  A comprehensive review of the theory and application of multi-agent systems, including coordination, cooperation, and negotiation.
- **"The Multi-Agent Systems of the Future: Opportunities and Challenges" by V. V. Vazirani**
  This paper looks at the future trends in multi-agent systems and their potential applications in emerging technologies.

3. Journals and Conference Proceedings

- **Journal of Artificial Intelligence Research (JAIR):**
  A leading journal for AI research, publishing papers on topics such as multi-agent systems, reinforcement learning, and game theory.
- **Autonomous Agents and Multi-Agent Systems (AAMAS):**
  A highly regarded journal and conference that focuses on research in multi-agent systems, including theory, modeling, and applications.
- **International Conference on Autonomous Agents and Multi-Agent Systems (AAMAS):**
  The primary venue for research in multi-agent systems, with cutting-edge papers presented annually.

22.3 Online Courses and Certifications

Learning from reputable online platforms is an excellent way to build your expertise in multi-agent systems and AI. Below are some top-rated courses and certifications:

1. Coursera

- **"AI For Everyone" by Andrew Ng**
  This introductory course helps learners understand the broad implications of AI and how multi-agent systems fit into modern AI applications.
- **"Deep Learning Specialization" by Andrew Ng**
  This series of courses dives deeper into AI, covering reinforcement learning and deep learning, both of which are critical to multi-agent systems.
- **"Reinforcement Learning Specialization" by the University of Alberta**
  This is an in-depth series of courses focusing on reinforcement learning, an essential component for multi-agent system design.

2. edX

- **"Principles of Machine Learning" by Microsoft:**
  A good entry-level course for understanding machine learning algorithms that are foundational to multi-agent learning systems.
- **"Artificial Intelligence (AI)" by Columbia University:**
  This course provides an advanced understanding of AI algorithms and includes topics like multi-agent systems and game theory.

3. Udacity

- **"Artificial Intelligence Nanodegree"**
  Udacity offers a full nanodegree program that includes AI, machine learning, and multi-agent systems as part of the curriculum.
- **"Self-Driving Car Engineer Nanodegree"**
  Multi-agent systems are an essential component of autonomous vehicles, and this program helps you understand how agents can collaborate within such systems.

22.4 Communities and Professional Organizations

Networking with others in the AI field is an important way to learn from experts, share ideas, and stay up to date. Below are several communities and professional organizations that you should consider joining:

1. IEEE Computational Intelligence Society

- **Overview:**
  IEEE is a leading professional organization for engineers and researchers in the field of AI and computational intelligence. The Computational Intelligence Society focuses on topics like multi-agent systems, evolutionary computation, and machine learning.
- **Benefits:**
  - Access to technical publications and conferences.
  - Networking opportunities with industry professionals.
  - Membership discounts for events and workshops.

2. Association for the Advancement of Artificial Intelligence (AAAI)

- **Overview:**
  AAAI is one of the foremost AI organizations, offering research papers, conferences, and community events focused on advancing AI technologies.
- **Benefits:**
  - Access to AI-related research, articles, and journals.
  - Membership includes access to exclusive events and networking opportunities.

3. OpenAI Community

- **Overview:**
  OpenAI is a key player in the AI research community. By joining their forums and contributing to discussions, you can learn from the best in the field and stay up-to-date on their groundbreaking research.
- **Benefits:**
  - Access to OpenAI research papers, models, and tools.

- o Opportunities to participate in AI-related discussions and projects.

22.5 Interactive Resources: Accessing Online Repositories and Tutorials

Interactive resources are an excellent way to enhance your learning by engaging in hands-on projects, experimenting with AI models, and participating in tutorials. Below are platforms where you can access such resources:

1. GitHub

- **Overview:**
  GitHub hosts countless repositories where developers share code for AI models, multi-agent simulations, and reinforcement learning agents.
- **Example:**
  - o **OpenAI Baselines:** Pre-built reinforcement learning algorithms that you can experiment with and extend for multi-agent environments.
- **Link:** GitHub

2. Kaggle

- **Overview:**
  Kaggle is a popular platform for data science competitions, but it also has a wealth of tutorials, datasets, and code notebooks focused on machine learning and AI. You can use it to practice multi-agent AI tasks and learn from others' solutions.
- **Link:** Kaggle

3. Google Colab

- **Overview:**
  Google Colab allows you to run Jupyter notebooks in the cloud with free access to GPUs, making it an ideal tool for experimenting with multi-agent AI simulations and reinforcement learning projects.

- **Example:**
  - ○ Run reinforcement learning algorithms for multi-agent systems and visualize the training process in real-time.
- **Link:** Google Colab

Appendix A: Glossary of Terms

In the field of **multi-agent AI** and artificial intelligence (AI) systems, there are many key terms and concepts that professionals must understand to work effectively. This glossary provides clear definitions of the most important terms and terminology used throughout the book, ensuring that readers have a solid foundation in the language and concepts that drive multi-agent systems.

A

Agent

An **agent** is an entity in a system that can perceive its environment, reason about it, and take actions to achieve specific goals. Agents are autonomous in the sense that they can operate without continuous human intervention. In multi-agent systems, agents interact with each other to achieve shared or individual objectives.

Example: In a multi-agent traffic management system, each car could be an agent that decides when to accelerate, stop, or change lanes based on its environment and interactions with other vehicles.

Agent-based Modeling (ABM)

Agent-based modeling is a computational modeling approach in which agents interact within a defined environment, following a set of rules or behaviors. These models are widely used to simulate complex systems such as ecosystems, traffic patterns, and social dynamics.

Example: ABM is used to model the spread of diseases, where each individual is an agent that follows behavior rules, such as avoiding sick individuals or seeking medical help.

B

Blockchain

Blockchain is a decentralized and distributed digital ledger technology that records transactions across multiple computers in a secure and transparent manner. In the context of multi-agent systems, blockchain can provide a trusted platform for agents to collaborate without needing a central authority.

Example: In a decentralized supply chain, agents (such as warehouses and logistics providers) use blockchain to securely share transaction data without relying on a central server.

Bias

In AI, **bias** refers to a systematic deviation from fairness or accuracy, often arising from the data or models used. Bias can lead to unfair outcomes, such as favoring one group over another, and is particularly important when designing ethical multi-agent systems.

Example: A facial recognition agent might be biased if trained primarily on images of light-skinned individuals, resulting in lower accuracy for people with darker skin tones.

C

Collaboration

Collaboration refers to the ability of multiple agents to work together toward a common goal. In multi-agent systems, collaboration is essential for achieving optimal outcomes, especially in complex environments that require coordinated effort.

Example: In a multi-agent system for disaster response, agents representing different rescue teams must collaborate to effectively search for survivors, allocate resources, and manage communications.

Combinatorial Optimization

Combinatorial optimization is the process of finding the best solution from a finite set of possible solutions, especially in problems where the goal is to optimize a function or resource allocation. It is often used in multi-agent systems to solve problems like scheduling, resource allocation, and pathfinding.

Example: In a transportation system, combinatorial optimization might be used to find the most efficient route for a fleet of delivery trucks, considering constraints like time and distance.

D

Decentralized Decision-Making

Decentralized decision-making is a system design where multiple agents make decisions based on local information, without a central decision-maker. This allows for more robust and scalable systems, as agents can respond to changes in the environment without waiting for central instructions.

Example: In a multi-agent system for a smart city, traffic light agents could make decisions about when to change lights based on local traffic data, rather than waiting for a central system to make those decisions.

Deep Learning

Deep learning is a subset of machine learning that uses neural networks with multiple layers to model complex patterns in data. In multi-agent systems, deep learning is often used to enable agents to make decisions based on large datasets and to adapt to changing environments.

Example: A multi-agent AI system in a self-driving car uses deep learning to recognize road signs, pedestrians, and other vehicles, allowing the agents to make safe driving decisions.

E

Ethics in AI

Ethics in AI refers to the set of moral principles and considerations involved in the development and deployment of AI systems. For multi-agent systems, ethical concerns include fairness, transparency, accountability, and privacy, especially when agents interact with humans or make high-stakes decisions.

Example: A healthcare AI system must ensure that its recommendations are fair and equitable, without bias toward certain demographic groups, such as age, gender, or ethnicity.

F

Federated Learning

Federated learning is a machine learning technique where multiple agents (often located on different devices) collaboratively train a model while keeping the data decentralized. This technique ensures that sensitive data remains private while still enabling the training of high-performance models.

Example: Multiple mobile phones can collaboratively train a speech recognition model without sharing user data, keeping all the data on the local device.

Feedback Loop

A **feedback loop** occurs when the outputs of a system are fed back into the system as inputs. In multi-agent systems, feedback loops are essential for agents to adapt and improve their performance based on previous interactions or environmental changes.

Example: In reinforcement learning, an agent receives feedback from the environment (rewards or penalties) that influences its future actions, creating a feedback loop for continuous improvement.

G

Game Theory

Game theory is a mathematical framework for modeling the interactions between agents, where each agent's decision affects the outcomes of others. It is commonly used in multi-agent systems to model and analyze competitive or cooperative behaviors.

Example: In a multi-agent system for online auctions, game theory can be used to predict and analyze the strategies of bidders.

H

Heuristic

A **heuristic** is a rule of thumb or approach used to solve a problem more quickly or efficiently when optimal solutions are not feasible. In multi-agent systems, heuristics are often used when agents must make decisions under uncertainty or incomplete information.

Example: In a route-planning agent, a heuristic might be used to estimate the shortest path based on distance, even if a more precise solution is computationally expensive.

I

Intelligent Agent

An **intelligent agent** is an agent capable of perceiving its environment, reasoning, learning from experience, and taking actions to achieve specific goals. Intelligent agents form the foundation of multi-agent systems, allowing for complex behavior and decision-making.

Example: In a gaming environment, each character controlled by AI can be considered an intelligent agent, responding dynamically to player actions.

Interface

In the context of multi-agent systems, an **interface** refers to the mechanisms that allow agents to communicate with each other and with the outside environment. These interfaces are essential for coordination, collaboration, and information sharing among agents.

Example: In a multi-agent logistics system, an interface allows different agents (e.g., shipping, warehousing, and inventory agents) to exchange information about package locations, delivery times, and inventory levels.

J

JADE (Java Agent Development Framework)

JADE is a software framework for developing multi-agent systems in Java. It provides a platform for creating and managing agents, facilitating communication and coordination among them in a distributed environment.

Example: JADE is used to create agents in scenarios such as e-commerce systems, where agents can negotiate and trade products on behalf of users.

K

Kinematics

Kinematics refers to the study of motion, without considering the forces that cause it. In multi-agent systems, kinematics is often used in applications involving robots, where agents need to plan their movements to avoid collisions and optimize paths.

Example: In a multi-agent robotic system, agents use kinematic models to calculate and adjust their paths to avoid obstacles in a warehouse environment.

L

Learning Agent

A **learning agent** is an AI agent that improves its performance over time based on feedback from its environment. This learning can be supervised, unsupervised, or through reinforcement learning techniques.

Example: In a video game, a learning agent can adjust its strategy based on feedback from previous rounds, learning to outperform its opponents by improving its decision-making process.

M

Monte Carlo Simulation

Monte Carlo simulation is a statistical technique used to model the probability of different outcomes in processes that involve random variables. In multi-agent systems, Monte Carlo simulations can be used to predict the behavior of agents under uncertain conditions.

Example: In a financial market simulation, Monte Carlo methods can help predict how agents might behave in response to fluctuations in stock prices.

N

Neural Networks

Neural networks are computational models inspired by the human brain, used to identify patterns in data. In multi-agent systems, neural networks are often used to enable agents to learn complex behaviors through experience.

Example: In a multi-agent autonomous vehicle system, neural networks can be used to enable agents (vehicles) to recognize pedestrians, other vehicles, and road signs, improving navigation.

O

Optimization

Optimization refers to the process of finding the best solution from a set of possible options, subject to specific constraints. In multi-agent systems, optimization algorithms help agents make decisions that maximize or minimize an objective function.

Example: In a supply chain system, optimization algorithms can help agents decide on the best routes to minimize delivery time or cost.

P

Parallel Processing

Parallel processing involves executing multiple processes simultaneously, improving the efficiency and speed of computations. In multi-agent systems, parallel processing is often used to manage the large number of agents and interactions that occur in complex environments.

Example: In a simulation involving thousands of agents, parallel processing allows multiple agents to perform calculations at the same time, significantly speeding up the simulation process.

Q

Q-Learning

Q-learning is a type of reinforcement learning algorithm where an agent learns the value of taking specific actions in a particular state. It is commonly used in multi-agent systems to enable agents to learn optimal strategies based on trial and error.

Example: In a game, Q-learning can help agents learn the best moves to make in order to win, based on feedback from previous moves.

R

Reinforcement Learning (RL)

Reinforcement learning is a type of machine learning where agents learn by interacting with an environment and receiving rewards or penalties based on their actions. It is one of the most common methods for training multi-agent systems to perform tasks.

Example: In robotics, reinforcement learning allows agents (robots) to learn how to manipulate objects by trial and error, receiving positive reinforcement for successful actions.

S

Swarm Intelligence

Swarm intelligence refers to the collective behavior of decentralized, self-organized systems. It is inspired by the behavior of social insects like ants and bees, and is often applied in multi-agent systems for tasks like optimization and search.

Example: In a multi-agent system for search and rescue, agents may work together in a swarm-like fashion to search an area more efficiently than if they were operating individually.

T

Task Allocation

Task allocation is the process of assigning tasks to agents in a way that optimizes performance. In multi-agent systems, task allocation is critical for ensuring that the system operates efficiently and that each agent performs its role effectively.

Example: In a warehouse system, task allocation ensures that different agents (robots) are assigned to pick items, transport them, and package them without overlap or delays.

U

Utility Theory

Utility theory is a branch of decision theory that deals with making choices based on the expected satisfaction or value of different options. In multi-agent systems, utility functions are used to guide agents' decisions toward outcomes that are beneficial for them or the system as a whole.

Example: In an auction system, agents use utility functions to determine the maximum value they are willing to bid for an item based on their preferences.

V

Virtual Agents

Virtual agents are software programs or models that simulate the behavior of real agents. These agents can operate autonomously in virtual environments, performing tasks like customer support or automated decision-making.

Example: A virtual customer service agent might interact with users on a website, answering questions and providing information based on predefined scripts or learned behaviors.

W

Web Services

Web services are standardized ways for software applications to communicate with each other over the internet. Multi-agent systems often use web services to exchange information and collaborate on tasks.

Example: In an e-commerce multi-agent system, agents representing sellers, buyers, and payment processors use web services to exchange product information, process transactions, and deliver goods.

X

XAI (Explainable AI)

Explainable AI refers to methods and techniques in AI that make the decision-making process of models transparent and understandable to humans. In multi-agent systems, XAI helps stakeholders understand why agents make specific decisions.

Example: In healthcare, XAI can be used to explain why an AI system recommends certain treatments for patients, ensuring trust and accountability in decision-making.

Y

Yarn

Yarn is a package manager for JavaScript applications, used for managing dependencies and scripts. While not directly related to multi-agent systems, developers may use Yarn to manage AI libraries and dependencies in web-based agent applications.

Z

Zero-shot Learning

Zero-shot learning is a machine learning technique where a model is able to make predictions or decisions about tasks it has not been explicitly trained for. This is particularly useful in multi-agent systems where agents may face unfamiliar situations or environments.

Example: A robot in a multi-agent manufacturing system could use zero-shot learning to perform a new task based on a similar task it has learned previously.

This **Glossary of Terms** provides the foundational knowledge for understanding the language and concepts associated with **multi-agent AI systems**.

Appendix B: Technical Specifications

This appendix provides detailed technical information and specifications for the essential tools, libraries, and frameworks used in the development of multi-agent AI systems. Understanding the specifications of these tools and frameworks is crucial for making informed decisions when selecting the right tools for your projects. Below, we cover the technical details of the most widely-used tools in the multi-agent AI ecosystem, including simulation frameworks, machine learning libraries, and agent-based modeling platforms.

1. Mesa (Python) - Multi-agent Simulation Framework

Mesa is a versatile Python framework designed for developing agent-based models and simulations. It is commonly used for creating complex multi-agent environments where agents interact with one another and with their environment.

Technical Specifications

- **Language:** Python
- **Installation:**
  Mesa is easy to install using Python's package manager, pip:
- `pip install mesa`
- **Dependencies:**
  Mesa requires Python 3.6 or later, and the following libraries:
  - **NumPy:** For numerical operations.
  - **Matplotlib:** For data visualization and agent tracking.
  - **Pandas:** For data handling and analysis.
- **Key Features:**
  - **Agent-Based Modeling:** Mesa allows users to define agents with unique states, behaviors, and goals.
  - **Environment Simulation:** The framework supports grid-based and continuous space environments for agent interactions.

- o **Visualization:** Built-in tools to visualize the simulation progress, including agent movement and state transitions.
- o **Real-time or Batch Simulations:** Simulations can be run in real-time for interactive scenarios or in batch mode for statistical analysis.

Example Code: Below is a simple example of how to set up a basic agent and run a simulation using Mesa:

```python
from mesa import Agent, Model
from mesa.time import RandomActivation
from mesa.space import MultiGrid
from mesa.datacollection import DataCollector

class MyAgent(Agent):
    """ An agent that moves randomly on the grid """
    def __init__(self, unique_id, model):
        super().__init__(unique_id, model)
        self.x = self.random.randint(0, model.grid.width-1)
        self.y = self.random.randint(0, model.grid.height-1)

    def step(self):
        # Move the agent to a random adjacent grid cell
        possible_steps =
self.model.grid.get_neighbors(self.pos, moore=True,
include_center=False)
        new_position = self.random.choice(possible_steps)
        self.model.grid.move_agent(self, new_position)

class MyModel(Model):
    """ A simple model with agents that move on a grid """
    def __init__(self, width, height):
        self.num_agents = 10
        self.grid = MultiGrid(width, height, True)
        self.schedule = RandomActivation(self)
        self.datacollector =
DataCollector(agent_reporters={"Position": "pos"})

        # Create agents
        for i in range(self.num_agents):
            a = MyAgent(i, self)
            self.schedule.add(a)
            x = self.random.randint(0, self.grid.width-1)
            y = self.random.randint(0, self.grid.height-1)
            self.grid.place_agent(a, (x, y))

    def step(self):
```

```
self.datacollector.collect(self)
self.schedule.step()
```

2. TensorFlow / PyTorch - Machine Learning Libraries

Both **TensorFlow** and **PyTorch** are powerful machine learning libraries used to train AI models, including deep learning models and reinforcement learning agents. They are widely used for developing multi-agent AI systems, particularly for tasks such as decision-making, perception, and planning.

TensorFlow Specifications

Language: Python (with bindings for other languages like C++, Java, JavaScript)

Installation:

```
pip install tensorflow
```

Dependencies:

Python 3.6 or later

Numpy, six, protobuf, keras-preprocessing, etc.

Key Features:

Keras API: High-level API for building and training deep learning models easily.

TensorFlow Agents: A library for reinforcement learning, useful for training agents in multi-agent environments.

Ecosystem Support: Wide support for deployment, with options to deploy on mobile devices, embedded systems, and distributed computing environments (e.g., TensorFlow Serving).

Example Code: Here is a simple TensorFlow example that demonstrates how to create and train a neural network for classification:

```python
import tensorflow as tf
from tensorflow.keras.models import Sequential
from tensorflow.keras.layers import Dense
from tensorflow.keras.datasets import mnist

# Load the MNIST dataset
(x_train, y_train), (x_test, y_test) = mnist.load_data()

# Normalize the data
x_train, x_test = x_train / 255.0, x_test / 255.0

# Build the model
model = Sequential([
    tf.keras.layers.Flatten(input_shape=(28, 28)),
    tf.keras.layers.Dense(128, activation='relu'),
    tf.keras.layers.Dropout(0.2),
    tf.keras.layers.Dense(10)
])

# Compile the model
model.compile(optimizer='adam',

loss=tf.keras.losses.SparseCategoricalCrossentropy(from_lo
gits=True),
              metrics=['accuracy'])

# Train the model
model.fit(x_train, y_train, epochs=5)

# Evaluate the model
model.evaluate(x_test, y_test, verbose=2)
```

PyTorch Specifications

Language: Python (with bindings for C++)

Installation:

```
pip install torch torchvision
```

Dependencies:

Python 3.6 or later

NumPy, SciPy, matplotlib, and more.

Key Features:

- o **Dynamic Computation Graphs:** PyTorch uses dynamic computation graphs (eager execution), making it easier to debug and experiment with new ideas.
- o **Autograd:** PyTorch includes an automatic differentiation library, simplifying backpropagation in neural networks.
- o **Torch RL:** PyTorch also supports **reinforcement learning** through libraries like **TorchRL**, which can be used to train multi-agent systems.
- o **Scalability:** While great for research, PyTorch is also suited for large-scale deployment, supported by integration with distributed training frameworks like **Horovod**.

Example Code: Here's a simple PyTorch example for a basic neural network to classify MNIST digits:

```
import torch
import torch.nn as nn
import torch.optim as optim
from torchvision import datasets, transforms

# Define the neural network model
class SimpleNN(nn.Module):
    def __init__(self):
        super(SimpleNN, self).__init__()
        self.fc1 = nn.Linear(28*28, 128)
        self.fc2 = nn.Linear(128, 10)

    def forward(self, x):
        x = torch.flatten(x, 1)
        x = torch.relu(self.fc1(x))
        x = self.fc2(x)
        return x

# Load the MNIST dataset
transform = transforms.Compose([transforms.ToTensor(),
transforms.Normalize((0.5,), (0.5,))])
train_dataset = datasets.MNIST('.', train=True,
download=True, transform=transform)
train_loader = torch.utils.data.DataLoader(train_dataset,
batch_size=64, shuffle=True)

# Initialize model, loss function, and optimizer
model = SimpleNN()
```

```
criterion = nn.CrossEntropyLoss()
optimizer = optim.Adam(model.parameters(), lr=0.001)

# Train the model
for epoch in range(5):
    model.train()
    running_loss = 0.0
    for images, labels in train_loader:
        optimizer.zero_grad()
        outputs = model(images)
        loss = criterion(outputs, labels)
        loss.backward()
        optimizer.step()
        running_loss += loss.item()
    print(f'Epoch {epoch+1}, Loss:
{running_loss/len(train_loader)}')
```

3. OpenAI Gym - Reinforcement Learning Toolkit

OpenAI Gym is a toolkit for developing and comparing reinforcement learning algorithms. It provides various environments for training agents and is often used in conjunction with multi-agent systems to test and deploy reinforcement learning models.

Technical Specifications

Language: Python

Installation:

```
pip install gym
```

Dependencies:

Python 3.6 or later

NumPy, matplotlib, etc.

Key Features:

Pre-built Environments: OpenAI Gym includes classic control tasks, Atari games, robotics, and custom environments for testing RL algorithms.

Environment Interface: It provides a standard API for interacting with environments, making it easy to implement, test, and compare algorithms.

Multi-agent Support: Gym allows multiple agents to interact within the same environment, useful for testing multi-agent collaboration or competition.

Example Code: Here's an example that shows how to use OpenAI Gym for a simple CartPole environment, which is commonly used in reinforcement learning tutorials:

```
import gym

# Create the environment
env = gym.make('CartPole-v1')

# Initialize the environment
env.reset()

for _ in range(1000):
    env.render()  # Display the environment
    action = env.action_space.sample()  # Random action
    state, reward, done, info = env.step(action)  # Take
the action and observe the result
    if done:
        break

env.close()
```

4. Ray - Distributed AI Framework

Ray is a framework for distributed computing that is particularly suited for training machine learning models and running reinforcement learning tasks at scale. It provides support for multi-agent systems, including parallel and distributed processing.

Technical Specifications

Language: Python (with C++ for core)

Installation:

```
pip install ray[rllib]
```

Dependencies:

Python 3.6 or later

TensorFlow or PyTorch (depending on the preferred backend for reinforcement learning)

Key Features:

Scalable Reinforcement Learning: Ray includes **RLlib**, a library for scaling reinforcement learning algorithms to large distributed systems.

Distributed Computing: Ray enables running tasks on a distributed cluster, allowing for multi-agent training on large datasets.

Parallel Execution: It is optimized for parallel execution, which is crucial for training multi-agent models.

Example Code: Below is a basic Ray example for running a simple reinforcement learning task:

```python
import ray
from ray import tune
from ray.rllib.agents.ppo import PPOTrainer

ray.init()

config = {
    "env": "CartPole-v1",  # Environment name
    "framework": "tf",  # Use TensorFlow for training
}

# Train the model using Proximal Policy Optimization (PPO)
trainer = PPOTrainer(config=config)
```

```python
for i in range(10):
    result = trainer.train()
    print(f"Iteration {i}:
{result['episode_reward_mean']}")
```

Appendix C: Sample Code and Repositories

This appendix provides access to sample code, GitHub repositories, and online resources that can help you better understand how to implement multi-agent AI systems. These resources contain pre-built models, frameworks, and examples that can serve as starting points for your projects, or as learning tools to understand key concepts and techniques in multi-agent systems.

---

1. GitHub Repositories for Multi-agent AI Systems

1.1 Mesa - Agent-based Modeling Framework

Mesa is a popular Python framework for agent-based modeling (ABM). It allows users to create simulations with agents that interact within an environment. The Mesa repository includes a variety of sample code that demonstrates how to build and simulate multi-agent systems.

Repository Link:
https://github.com/projectmesa/mesa

Key Features:

Simulate agent-based models using grids, networks, and continuous spaces.

Built-in tools for visualization and data collection.

Examples include traffic simulation, predator-prey models, and more.

Example Code: Below is an example of creating a simple agent-based model using Mesa, where agents move randomly on a grid:

```
from mesa import Agent, Model
```

```python
from mesa.time import RandomActivation
from mesa.space import MultiGrid
from mesa.datacollection import DataCollector

class RandomMoveAgent(Agent):
    """ An agent that moves randomly on the grid """
    def __init__(self, unique_id, model):
        super().__init__(unique_id, model)
        self.x = self.random.randint(0, model.grid.width-
1)
        self.y = self.random.randint(0, model.grid.height-
1)

    def step(self):
        # Move the agent randomly on the grid
        possible_steps =
self.model.grid.get_neighbors(self.pos, moore=True,
include_center=False)
        new_position = self.random.choice(possible_steps)
        self.model.grid.move_agent(self, new_position)

class RandomMoveModel(Model):
    """ A simple model where agents move randomly """
    def __init__(self, width, height):
        self.num_agents = 10
        self.grid = MultiGrid(width, height, True)
        self.schedule = RandomActivation(self)
        self.datacollector =
DataCollector(agent_reporters={"Position": "pos"})

        # Create agents and place them on the grid
        for i in range(self.num_agents):
            a = RandomMoveAgent(i, self)
            self.schedule.add(a)
            x = self.random.randint(0, self.grid.width-1)
            y = self.random.randint(0, self.grid.height-1)
            self.grid.place_agent(a, (x, y))

    def step(self):
        self.datacollector.collect(self)
        self.schedule.step()
```

1.2 Ray - Distributed AI Framework

Ray is an open-source framework for building and deploying distributed applications. It provides tools for scaling multi-agent AI systems, reinforcement learning (RL), and machine learning.

- **Repository Link:**
  https://github.com/ray-project/ray
- **Key Features:**
  - Distributed execution for parallel agent training.
  - Built-in libraries like **RLlib** for scaling reinforcement learning tasks.
  - Easy integration with other machine learning frameworks like TensorFlow and PyTorch.

Example Code: Here's how to set up a reinforcement learning agent with Ray:

```python
import ray
from ray.rllib.agents.ppo import PPOTrainer
from ray.tune import run

ray.init()

# Define the configuration for reinforcement learning
using PPO
config = {
    "env": "CartPole-v1",
    "framework": "tf",
    "num_workers": 4  # Scale to 4 workers for parallelism
}

# Run the training
trainer = PPOTrainer(config=config)
for i in range(100):
    result = trainer.train()
    print(f"Iteration {i}:
{result['episode_reward_mean']}")
```

1.3 OpenAI Gym - Reinforcement Learning Environments

OpenAI Gym is a toolkit for developing and comparing reinforcement learning algorithms. It provides a variety of environments where multi-agent AI systems can be trained and tested.

Repository Link:
https://github.com/openai/gym

Key Features:

Includes environments for games, robotics, and control problems.

Standard API for reinforcement learning tasks.

Support for multi-agent environments and custom scenarios.

Example Code: Here's how to set up a basic CartPole environment using OpenAI Gym:

```
import gym

# Create the CartPole environment
env = gym.make('CartPole-v1')

# Reset the environment
env.reset()

for _ in range(1000):
    env.render()  # Display the environment's graphical
output
    action = env.action_space.sample()  # Random action
selection
    state, reward, done, info = env.step(action)  # Take
action and observe results
    if done:
        break

env.close()
```

---

2. Online Resources

2.1 TensorFlow Agents

TensorFlow Agents is an open-source library for reinforcement learning in TensorFlow. It is designed to make it easy to develop, train, and deploy RL algorithms for multi-agent environments.

- **Repository Link:**
  https://github.com/tensorflow/agents
- **Key Features:**
  o Modular RL algorithms.
  o Easily integrates with TensorFlow and TensorFlow's ecosystem.
  o Support for multi-agent reinforcement learning.

Example Code: Here's a sample for training an agent in TensorFlow:

```
import tensorflow as tf
import tensorflow_agents as tfa
from tf_agents.environments import suite_gym
from tf_agents.agents.dqn import dqn_agent
from tf_agents.networks import q_network

# Load an environment
env = suite_gym.load('CartPole-v0')

# Define Q-network and agent
q_net = q_network.QNetwork(env.observation_spec(),
env.action_spec())
optimizer =
tf.compat.v1.train.AdamOptimizer(learning_rate=1e-3)
agent = dqn_agent.DqnAgent(env.time_step_spec(),
env.action_spec(), q_network=q_net, optimizer=optimizer)
agent.initialize()

# Training code (simplified)
for _ in range(1000):
    time_step = env.reset()
    action = agent.policy.time_step_to_action(time_step)
    time_step = env.step(action)
```

2.2 RLlib (Ray) - Distributed Reinforcement Learning Library

RLlib is a scalable reinforcement learning library built on top of **Ray**, designed to train large-scale AI systems and multi-agent environments. It supports deep reinforcement learning (DRL) algorithms such as **PPO**, **A3C**, and **DDPG**.

Repository Link:
https://github.com/ray-project/ray/tree/master/rllib

Key Features:

Support for multiple RL algorithms.

Scalable across multiple nodes in a distributed system.

Compatible with both TensorFlow and PyTorch.

Example Code: This simple example trains a reinforcement learning agent using **Proximal Policy Optimization (PPO)** with **RLlib**:

```python
import ray
from ray.rllib.agents.ppo import PPOTrainer
from ray.tune import run

ray.init()

# Configure and train PPO model
config = {
    "env": "CartPole-v1",
    "num_workers": 2  # Use 2 workers for parallel training
}

# Run training
trainer = PPOTrainer(config=config)
for i in range(10):
    result = trainer.train()
    print(f"Episode Reward Mean: {result['episode_reward_mean']}")
```

3. Interactive Resources

3.1 Kaggle - Data Science and Machine Learning Competitions

Kaggle is a popular platform for data science competitions and a great resource for learning machine learning techniques, including multi-agent AI. Kaggle hosts a variety of problems that involve AI, data modeling, and optimization.

- **Website:**
  https://www.kaggle.com
- **Key Features:**
  - Competitions that provide real-world problems and datasets.
  - A wealth of public datasets for experimenting with multi-agent AI algorithms.
  - Kaggle Kernels allow you to run code and share it with the community.
- **Example:** Kaggle hosts numerous multi-agent related competitions, such as those focused on autonomous vehicle navigation or optimization in logistics.

3.2 Google Colab - Interactive Jupyter Notebooks

Google Colab provides a cloud-based Jupyter notebook environment that allows for the easy development and execution of machine learning and AI projects. It supports GPU acceleration, making it ideal for training deep learning models, including multi-agent systems.

- **Website:**
  https://colab.research.google.com
- **Key Features:**
  - Free access to GPUs and TPUs.
  - Integration with Google Drive for saving notebooks and data.
  - Support for running complex multi-agent AI models in an interactive and collaborative environment.

Appendix D: Template Documents

This appendix provides essential **template documents** that will help streamline the development process for multi-agent AI projects. These templates are designed to aid in project planning, ensure proper documentation standards, and maintain ethical integrity throughout the development cycle of AI systems. By following these templates, you can establish a structured workflow and ensure that your multi-agent systems are built in a reliable, transparent, and responsible manner.

---

1. Project Planning Templates

1.1 Multi-agent AI Project Plan Template

A comprehensive project plan helps organize the development of multi-agent AI systems, from initial concept to deployment. Below is a detailed template that can guide your project planning process.

Template: Multi-agent AI Project Plan

Section	Description
Project Overview	Provide a brief description of the project, including its goals, scope, and deliverables. Include any background information necessary for understanding the project context.
Objectives	List the specific objectives the multi-agent system is designed to achieve. This could include tasks such as decision-making, optimization, and coordination.
Stakeholders	Identify the key stakeholders in the project, such as AI engineers, researchers, end-users, and regulatory bodies.
Team Structure	List the roles and responsibilities of each team member, including project managers, AI specialists, software engineers, etc.
Resources	List the required resources, including hardware, software, libraries, and any other dependencies needed to build and deploy the multi-agent system.

Section	Description
Timeline	Define key milestones and timelines for each phase of the project, from research and design to implementation, testing, and deployment.
Budget	Outline the budget for the project, detailing costs for development, resources, and any additional expenditures.
Risk Management	Identify potential risks (technical, ethical, regulatory) and describe mitigation strategies.
Evaluation Metrics	Define how success will be measured, such as system performance, user acceptance, or regulatory compliance.
Deliverables	Outline the final deliverables, including the multi-agent system itself, documentation, and any related assets like code repositories or simulation results.

Example:

```
### Project Overview
The project aims to develop a multi-agent AI system to
optimize logistics and supply chain management in real-time,
focusing on efficiency and minimizing delays.

### Objectives
1. Develop autonomous agents that can communicate and
coordinate with each other.
2. Implement a decision-making system that adjusts
dynamically to fluctuating conditions.
3. Optimize the flow of goods from warehouses to consumers.

### Stakeholders
- AI Engineers: Responsible for the development of algorithms
and agent logic.
- Product Managers: Oversee project scope and ensure
alignment with business goals.
- End Users: Logistics managers who will use the system to
monitor and control the supply chain.
```

1.2 Gantt Chart for Project Planning

A **Gantt chart** is a visual tool for planning and tracking project timelines. It helps ensure tasks are completed on schedule, and stakeholders can see progress at a glance. The chart includes all the key stages of the multi-agent AI development process.

Template: Gantt Chart

Task	Start Date	End Date	Dependencies
Define Project Scope and Objectives	2025-02-01	2025-02-07	None
Research on Multi-agent Algorithms	2025-02-08	2025-02-21	Define Project Scope
Develop Agent Models	2025-02-22	2025-03-10	Research on Algorithms
Simulation and Testing	2025-03-11	2025-03-25	Develop Agent Models
Deployment and Monitoring	2025-03-26	2025-04-10	Simulation and Testing

Example:

```
Task: Develop Agent Models
Start Date: 2025-02-22
End Date: 2025-03-10
Dependencies: Research on Algorithms
```

2. Documentation Standards

Proper documentation is crucial for maintaining a transparent development process and ensuring that your multi-agent AI system is understandable, reproducible, and easy to maintain. Below is a template for creating **AI system documentation**, covering key areas such as system architecture, agent design, and code comments.

2.1 System Architecture Documentation Template

Template: System Architecture

Section	Description
Overview	Provide a high-level summary of the system, including its purpose and scope.

Section	Description
System Components	List and describe each component of the system, such as agents, communication protocols, and external interfaces.
Agent Behavior and Logic	Describe the behavior of each agent, including decision-making processes, algorithms used, and learning strategies.
Communication and Coordination	Explain how agents communicate and coordinate with each other. This can include communication protocols and methods for achieving synchronization.
Data Flow and Management	Outline how data is collected, processed, and exchanged between agents and other system components.
System Architecture Diagram	Include a diagram that visualizes the architecture of the system, showing components and their interactions.
Technology Stack	List all tools, libraries, and frameworks used in the development of the system.
Scalability and Optimization	Provide details on how the system scales to handle larger numbers of agents or more complex tasks.

Example:

```
### Overview
This multi-agent AI system aims to optimize traffic flow by
controlling traffic lights in a city. It uses real-time data
from sensors and adjusts traffic signals to minimize
congestion.

### Agent Behavior and Logic
Each traffic light agent observes traffic patterns at its
intersection and adjusts its timing to ensure efficient
traffic flow. The agents communicate with one another to
coordinate signal changes.

### Communication and Coordination
Agents use a message-passing protocol to inform neighboring
agents of traffic conditions. This allows for synchronized
signal changes across multiple intersections.
```

2.2 Code Documentation Standards

Effective code documentation ensures that the system is maintainable and understandable for other developers. This includes **inline comments**, **docstrings**, and **README files** that explain the functionality, inputs, and outputs of the system components.

Template: Code Documentation Standards

Inline Comments:
Comments should explain the purpose of complex code blocks or decisions that may not be immediately obvious to other developers. Inline comments should be concise and placed directly above or beside the code they describe.

```
# Initialize agent with a random position
self.x = self.random.randint(0, self.grid.width - 1)
```

Docstrings for Functions and Classes: Every function and class should include a docstring that describes its purpose, parameters, and return values.

```
class TrafficLightAgent:
    """
    A traffic light agent that controls the timing of
traffic signals.

    Parameters:
        grid (Grid): The environment grid that holds
traffic light agents.
        intersection_id (int): Unique identifier for the
intersection.
    """
    def __init__(self, grid, intersection_id):
        """
        Initializes the traffic light agent with a grid
and intersection ID.

        Args:
            grid (Grid): The environment grid.
            intersection_id (int): The ID of the
intersection.
        """
        self.grid = grid
        self.intersection_id = intersection_id
```

README File Template:

The `README.md` file should provide an overview of the system, its requirements, and how to run it.

```
# Multi-agent Traffic System

## Overview
This system simulates a multi-agent traffic control
system that adjusts traffic lights based on real-time
data to reduce congestion.

## Installation
1. Clone the repository:
```

git clone https://github.com/username/traffic-agent-system.git

```
2. Install dependencies:
```

pip install -r requirements.txt

```
## Running the System
To start the simulation, run:
```

python run_simulation.py

```
## Contributing
Contributions are welcome. Please fork the repository
and submit a pull request for any enhancements or bug
fixes.
```

3. Ethical Guidelines Templates

Ethical considerations are fundamental when developing AI systems, particularly in multi-agent systems where agents interact with humans or other agents. These guidelines ensure that AI technologies are developed responsibly, without causing harm or unethical consequences.

3.1 Ethical Guidelines for Multi-agent AI Systems

Template: Ethical Guidelines for AI Systems

Guideline	Description
Fairness and Bias Mitigation	Ensure that AI agents operate without bias and make decisions that are fair and equitable for all users.
Transparency	Maintain transparency in the decision-making processes of agents, allowing stakeholders to understand how decisions are made.
Accountability	Establish clear lines of accountability for actions taken by AI agents, particularly when these actions affect humans or sensitive systems.
Privacy and Data Protection	Ensure that agents respect user privacy, secure sensitive data, and comply with relevant regulations (e.g., GDPR).
Non-maleficence	Ensure that the AI system does not cause harm to people, communities, or the environment.
Human-in-the-loop (HITL) Systems	In critical situations, provide mechanisms for humans to intervene in decision-making processes to avoid errors or harm.
Sustainability	Design AI agents that promote environmental sustainability, avoiding energy consumption or resource depletion when possible.

Example:

```
### Ethical Guidelines for Traffic Light Agents

1. **Fairness and Bias Mitigation:**
   Traffic light agents must ensure that all vehicles,
including those belonging to minority groups, are treated
fairly, without bias towards certain routes or intersections.

2. **Transparency:**
   The decision-making processes of each agent will be logged
and made available for review, ensuring transparency in how
traffic light timings are adjusted.

3. **Privacy:**
```

The agents will only use anonymized traffic data, ensuring that no personal information about drivers or passengers is collected.

Index

An index is a crucial component of any book, particularly one that serves as a comprehensive guide. It helps readers quickly find the specific topics, concepts, or keywords they are looking for within the book. For a technical book like this one, which covers multi-agent AI systems and related fields, a well-organized index makes it easier for the reader to locate key ideas, frameworks, and examples discussed in the chapters.

Here's an example of how an index might look:

A

B

C

X

Y

Z

www.ingramcontent.com/pod-product-compliance
Lightning Source LLC
La Vergne TN
LVHW081516050326
832903LV00025B/1515